Margins and Mainstreams

Margins and Mainstreams

Asians in American History and Culture

GARY Y. OKIHIRO

University of Washington Press

SEATTLE & LONDON

University of Washington Press
PO Box 50096
Seattle, WA 98145-5096, USA
www.washington.edu/uwpress

Library of Congress Cataloging-in-Publication Data
Okihiro, Gary Y., 1945–
Margins and mainstreams:
Asians in American history and culture / Gary Y. Okihiro.
p.   cm.
Includes bibliographical references (p.) and index.
ISBN 978-0-295-97339-5 (paper: alk. paper)
1. Asian Americans—History. I. Title.
E184.06038   1994   93-44382
973'.0495—DC20   CIP

To My Students, My Mentors

Contents

Preface

I N the spring of 1992, I delivered six lectures under the overall title "Margins and Mainstreams: Asians in American History and Culture" at Amherst College during my tenure there as the John J. McCloy '16 Professor of American Institutions and International Relations. With slight modification, this book consists of those lectures as I gave them. The writing, accordingly, bears the syncopation—the beat and stresses—of an oral reading.

Swirling around me, as I contemplated the theme for the lecture series, was fervent and oftentimes heated debate about the idea of a mainstream, about the core of American history and culture, about intellectual "ghettoization" and ethnic "balkanization." Pluralism and diversity, many argued, only served to divide and fracture the nation. The debate over the nature and primacy of Western civilization and its canon of "great books" on college campuses, they warned, was just the leading edge of a coming chill that threatened the "disuniting" of America. Implicit within the Eurocentric argument was the appeal, intellectual and otherwise, to those on the margins to join and be absorbed by the mainstream.

Margins and Mainstreams contends that the core values and ideals of the nation emanate not from the mainstream but from the margins—from among Asian and African Americans, Latinos and American Indians, women, and gays and lesbians. In their struggles for equality, these groups have helped preserve and advance the principles and ideals of democracy and have thereby made America a freer place for all. Herein lies the true significance of Asians in American history and culture. That is the subject of this book's conclusion, chapter 6, titled "Margin as Mainstream."

Chapter 1 examines the question of the when and where of Asians' entry into the European and American historical consciousness. By beginning with Greek representations of Asia as early as the fifth century B.C.E., I do not mean that Asian American history starts with European constructions of their Other; I understand that to be a profoundly Eurocentric and historically skewed viewpoint. Rather, I am simply exploring the margins of European and American historical consciousness and how Asians have long occupied, and continue to be located by Europeans and Americans within, those fringes. The chapter shows that Asians did not first come to America; Europeans went to Asia. And the engendered and systematic ideology that accompanied European imperialists—Orientalism—informed the colonization of Asians in Asia and America.

The argument is provocative but hardly original. Other scholars have described and interpreted the eastward and westward expansion of Europeans, and it is a well-known fact that the scope of America's manifest destiny transformed the Far East into its Far West. The argument, further, is simplistic. Ideologies do not stand apart from their time and place; they are rooted within prevailing social relations, which we know change over time, and representations are struggled over and contested by those who are the objects of hegemony. We cannot, therefore, speak of a uniform and timeless Orientalism transmitted from the fifth-century B.C.E Greeks to late-twentieth-century C.E. European Americans. I understand those limitations to my argument.

What I attempt, nonetheless, is to widen considerably the canvas of Asian American history, which hitherto was deemed to have begun in the mid-nineteenth century and in California. Further, I write against a widely held and persistent view that Asians were like European immigrants, as opposed to Africans or Latinos, in that they chose to leave their homelands and sojourn in America for the opportunities of the West. The when and where of Asian American history, I insist, are of an ancient vintage and of a global scale, and they situate Asians with Africans and Latinos along the margins.

Chapter 2 attempts to locate Asians within America's racial formation and poses the false problematic: is yellow black or white? Asians have been marginalized to the periphery of race relations in America because of its conceptualization as a black and white issue—with Asians, Latinos, and American Indians falling between the cracks of that divide. Thus, to many, Asians are either "just like blacks" or "almost whites." I test that proposition and show the closer affinity of Asian Americans with African, as opposed to European, Americans, through evidence drawn mainly from the American South, in contrast to the dominant historical discourse, which focuses on the Pacific Coast.

The lecture was written and delivered months before the April and May 1992 violence in Los Angeles in the aftermath of the first Rodney G. King verdict. In what must surely be seen as a watershed event, Asian Americans and their property were among the special targets of some African American (and Latino and white) "rioters" and "looters," but we have long known about the growing conflict between Asian and African Americans on college campuses and within urban communities from the East to the West coasts. What we have ignored or forgotten are the commonalities, the bases for solidarity between African and Asian Americans, and that was one of my principal motives in writing this chapter. Africans and Asians have both been relegated to the margins of American racial politics as "nonwhites," but European Americans have also differentiated Asians from Africans, mainly by prohibiting Asians from becoming naturalized and thereby denying them the rights of life, liberty, and property. Thus, yellow is neither black nor white, and Asians, situated between blacks and whites, receive special opportunities but also face unique disabilities.

Sociologists posit Asians as middlemen minorities and as crucial components of a split labor market, and historians depict Asians as sojourners and strangers. I follow and question those leads, but I also understand that America's two-tiered racial order forces Asians and all people of color, including those who are bi-racial, to choose between black and white. And with the present pervasiveness of the notion of the "model minority," Asians have all too often identified and been identified with Europeans while confronting invisible ceilings and visible anti-Asian violence from both ends of the supposed racial spectrum. I accordingly argue, like many of my generation involved in the struggle for ethnic studies and for a Third World identity, that insofar as Asians oc-cupy the racial margins of "nonwhite" with blacks, yellow is a shade of black, and black, of yellow.

In chapter 3, I continue a theme I first delineate in chapter 1: gender and the margins of gender. Women, I hold, have been rele-gated to the fringes of Asian American studies by men, who thereby institute and maintain a system of repression and privi-lege. Employing some of the insights of feminist writings, I try to refigure a woman-centered Asian American history, made espe-cially difficult by the demographics of nineteenth-century Asian America, which was predominantly male. I argue for a transpa-cific site for Asian American history, similar to the global con-struct of international labor migration and the world-system, and I highlight the links between the lives of the migrant men in Amer-ica and those of women in Asia. And because of the current stress on America to the near-exclusion of Asia within Asian American studies, I focus on women historical actors in Asia.

Besides the stretching of spatial borders, the recentering of women within Asian American history requires a new periodiza-tion that articulates on the pivot of gender, as opposed to race or class, relations. Thus, for example, instead of seeing the middle to late nineteenth century as the period of the bachelor society, we might understand those decades to be the era of feminism's rise, accompanying the struggle for decolonization in Asia and Amer-ica. Of course, feminism should not be conflated with national-ism, and gender relations in America cannot be considered in isolation from race and class relations, which differed signifi-cantly from social relations in Asia. We know social relations to be much more textured and complex than a simple focus upon women. Further, we know gender to be a social construct that is malleable and contested, and women operate on multiple levels, as individuals, within families, and within society. I consider in chapter 3 some of the consequences of destabilizing the margins of gender and of recentering women in Asian American history.

Chapter 4 explores the margins of class. History, as written, is generally the province of "great men," reflecting both a gender and a class bias. In this chapter, I stress the thoughts and deeds of so-called ordinary women and men, who have been relegated to the backdrop of history but who constitute the majority of Asian America. I recognize the gross inadequacy of my discussion of class in this chapter; I do not attempt to map out the relations of power within the Asian American social formation, nor do I offer a definition of class. Instead, my "family album history" pieces together disparate vignettes of human experience organized around the themes of arrivals and departures. Although devoid of a theoretical construct, the chapter, I trust, offers a good read and turns our attention to the margins of class.

In chapter 5, I range the terrain of culture and cultural politics. The ideas of the "yellow peril" and "model minority" have perhaps been the most enduring of all the images of Asians and Asian Americans. Whereas the notion of the yellow peril implies a threat to the nation's body politic, the stereotype of the model minority affirms the status quo. The former is filled with negative images, and the latter, with positive ones. Critics of the model minority stereotype assert that it divides minority groups, pitting one against the other, and prevents truly needy Asians from receiving assistance. But both proponents and critics of the concept of model minority generally agree that it stands in opposition to the earlier notion of the yellow peril.

I argue, in this chapter, that both notions are anti-Asian and form a closed loop that ameliorates and reinforces both. Thus, the model minority blunts the threat of the yellow peril, but the former, if taken too far, becomes the yellow peril. I also note that the two stereotypes are engendered categories, a product of the when and where of Asians' entry into the European historical consciousness, and can be both passive and active, weak and strong, nurturing and threatening. The "masculine" yellow peril is imbued with "womanly" threats, and the "feminine" model minority, with "manly" perils. In fact, the dual natures of both ideas, like biracial/bicultural people, present a special problem because they destabilize the borders that delineate power and disempowerment. The perils of the body (the yellow peril) and mind (the model minority) are rooted within a cultural politics of assimilation and exclusion, but they also arise out of economic and political contestation. The chapter, thus, roams not only the margins of culture but also the margins of the social formation.

This book is as much inspired by my "admiration" for neoconservative success in subverting and simplifying complex issues as by my dismay with the failure of Asian American studies to break out of our established hierarchies and ways of thinking. The Reagan–Bush era, it seems to me, provided a lesson in the packaging and marketing of ideas, if not presidencies, wherein affirmative action became "affirmative discrimination," goals became "quotas," liberal education became "illiberal education," and the roles of perpetrator and victim in the matter of Clarence Thomas and Anita Hill underwent dramatic reversal. My modest attempt to move the pivot away from the mainstream and toward the margin borrows from that New Right gamebook.

But *Margins and Mainstreams* also seeks to destabilize some of the standard assumptions and categories within Asian American studies, including the sites of time and place, race and ethnicity, gender and sexuality. Often those positions are layered on top of one another such that together they form a discrete image that can only be reconstituted by refiguring the layers one at a time. Thus, the dominant figures of Asian American history are Chinese and Japanese immigrants, heterosexual men who labored in California from the mid-nineteenth century. When we think about the beginnings of Asian American history, we invariably call up that layered portrait of ethnicity, gender, sexuality, time, and place.

In these essays, I call into question the exceptionalist streak of Asian American studies by positing a global dimension to Asian

American history from the Orientalism of the ancient Greeks to European imperialism and the world-system, from America to Asia, from the Pacific to the Indian and Atlantic oceans, from California to the Caribbean and American South. The Asian American immigrant, like his sojourner stereotype, should be relegated to the dustbin of Eurocentrisms. Perhaps less successfully but just as important, I have consciously tried to reorder the gender and ethnic hierarchies so dominant within the field by recentering women and South and Southeast Asians in my historical narrative.

Finally, Asian American studies must reject the simplistic yellow and white racial dyad, like its deficient black and white cousin, that has influenced our periodization, choice of major historical themes, and interpretation of immigration and contact, conflict, and adaptation. Herein I sketch a more complex, inclusive social universe with multiple racial pivots, involving relations among nonwhites as well as between whites and nonwhites. Yet in my attempt to reconfigure the strands of Asian American history, I know that I have merely pointed in a direction without having yet embarked on the journey. In truth, I have only just begun to disassemble and reconstitute the ideas that have shaped my understanding of Asian, American, and world history.

In my exuberance, my rethinking has led me to new simplifications and verities. I have essentialized and conflated diverse and complicated times and places, ideas and cultures, institutions and classes. I fully realize that Asians oppress, exploit, and hate one another, that Asians and Africans hold mutual racialisms, that Europeans struggle against exploitation, racism, and sexism. I repudiate "victim studies" and recognize that there are multiple sites of power and powerlessness, repression and resistance. The white man is neither the sole nor an unbridled locus of privilege.

"I'm the bad guy?" asks an incredulous Michael Douglas in the 1993 movie *Falling Down*. The question seems to echo the sentiments of white men awash in the sea of multicultural America. "Say it loud: they're white and they're cowed. But are they victims of multiculturalism, or are they just sports?" muses writer David

Gates in *Newsweek*'s March 29, 1993, issue in his discussion of the film's meaning and the controversy it generated. Significantly, Douglas's transformation from Bill Foster, a pliant ex–missile plant worker, to the take-no-guff "D-Fens" takes place in a Korean-owned convenience store during a confrontation over language and prices. Wresting the Korean owner's baseball bat away from him, Foster smashes the store's merchandise and declares: "We're rolling back prices to 1965. What do you think of that?" The good times of pre-1965 America, recalls a remasculinized Foster to the cowering, feminized Korean shopkeeper, were soured by the 1965 Immigration Act, which opened the nation to an infusion of Latinos and Asians.

Dead (or living) white men are not unequivocal villains. Women and people of color are not unqualified heroes. There is ample cause to distribute praise and blame among all of us. But complexity should never obscure or obliterate the fact that the relations of power are defined and circumscribed by race, gender, class, and sexuality. In this work, I have tried to be unambiguously clear about my positions, and I invite debate and dialogue over my imperfect offering. I will have succeeded if these unadorned ideas, naked as a newborn babe, stimulate a chattering among us.

I have never had more fun, or learned so much, than in writing this book. I must thank Amherst College and the McCloy professorship for this opportunity to reflect upon a field of study that has given me over twenty years of agony and fulfillment. In particular, Allen Guttmann and Gordon Levin were instrumental in Amherst College's invitation to me, and were such gracious hosts, bearing through all six lectures and presiding over sumptuous dinners. I cannot fail to mention the supreme irony of the auspices under which these lectures were commissioned, the John J. McCloy Distinguished Visiting Professorship, named for the college's noted son, distinguished public servant, and prominent advocate of Japanese American detention during World War II. I feel a special sense of responsibility to those who suffered the consequences of his (and others') deed.

I also stand in debt to the kindness of my colleagues, who must be distanced from this flawed work, but who must be acknowledged and thanked for their valued criticism and suggestions. My Cornell history colleagues have brought me much sunshine amid Ithaca's usual gloom. Thomas Borstelmann and Barry Strauss helped me rethink much of chapter 1, Mary Beth Norton offered cogent comments on chapter 3, and Richard Polenberg gave me valuable assistance with chapter 6. Two Cornell undergraduate students, Moon-Ho Jung and Jane J.Y. Kim, have influenced my views in chapter 5, for which I am grateful. I benefited from audiences at Colgate University, the University of Michigan, and the University of Wisconsin, Madison, having delivered to them various versions of chapter 2, and from Rogers Smith and a gathering at Yale, who heard a shortened version of chapter 5. My colleagues in Asian American studies have long been my reality check, especially after having left California several years ago for my present perch "high above Cayuga's waters." John M. Liu and Michael Omi read and commented on the entire manuscript, Sucheng Chan reviewed chapter 3, Shirley Hune and Sucheta Mazumdar gave me some general advice, and Stephen H. Sumida helped me with my use (and abuse) of Asian American literature. The book would have been far shakier without the steadying hands of my students, colleagues, and friends.

When Amherst College's acting president Ralph Beals offered me the McCloy professorship in January 1991, he asked that I address the subject of Asian Americans in six lectures. Had he asked me to deliver seven, this book would consist of seven chapters. But having limited me to six presentations on a subject matter that involves 2.9 percent (7.3 million) of America's people, representing over twenty-four ethnic groups, I thought long and hard on how I would do justice to that complex and expansive topic. I decided upon the overall, unifying theme of margins and mainstreams and tried to articulate, from the positions of historical consciousness, race, gender, class, and culture, a six-part synthesis of the Asian American experience. *Margins and Mainstreams* is the result of that attempt, but as notes, it is only a beginning.

Margins and Mainstreams

1

When and Where I Enter

A SOLITARY figure defies a tank, insofar as a solitary figure can defy a tank. A "goddess of liberty" in the image of the Statue of Liberty arises from the midst of a vast throng gathered in Beijing's Tiananmen Square. The November 1, 1991, issue of *Asiaweek* carries the caption "Welcoming Asians" under a picture of the Statue of Liberty in New York Harbor awash in the light of fireworks.[1] Contained within those images—vivid and memorable—is what Swedish social scientist Gunnar Myrdal called the American creed. Democracy, equality, and liberty form the core of that creed, and the "mighty woman with a torch" has come to symbolize those ideals to, in the words of the poet Emma Lazarus, the tired, the poor, the huddled masses "yearning to breathe free."

On another island, on the other coast, stands not a statue but a wooden barrack. Solitary figures hunch over to carve poems on the walls.[2]

> The sea-scape resembles lichen twisting and
>   turning for a thousand li.
> There is no shore to land and it is difficult to
>   walk.

1 I have taken the title of this chapter from a narrative history of African American women by Paula Giddings, *When and Where I Enter: The Impact of Black Women on Race and Sex in America* (New York: William Morrow, 1984).

2 Poems published in Him Mark Lai, Genny Lim, and Judy Yung, *Island: Poetry and History of Chinese Immigrants on Angel Island, 1910–1940* (Seattle: University of Washington Press, 1991), pp. 34, 52.

With a gentle breeze I arrived at the city thinking
  all would be so.
At ease, how was one to know he was to live in a
  wooden building?

In the quiet of night, I heard, faintly, the whistling
  of wind.
The forms and shadows saddened me; upon
  seeing the landscape, I composed a poem.
The floating clouds, the fog, darken the sky.
The moon shines faintly as the insects chirp.
Grief and bitterness entwined are heaven sent.
The sad person sits alone, leaning by a window.

Angel Island, not Ellis Island, was the main port of entry for Chinese migrants "yearning to breathe free" from 1910 to 1940.[3] There, separated by cold currents from the golden shore, the migrants were carefully screened by U.S. Immigration officials and held for days, weeks, and months to determine their fitness for America. The 1882 Chinese Exclusion Act had prohibited entry to Chinese workers, indicative of a race- *and* class-based politics, because according to the act, "in the opinion of the Government of the United States, the coming of Chinese laborers to this country endangers the good order of certain localities within the territory thereof."[4]

In New York City, a year after passage of the Chinese Exclusion

3 A third island, Sullivan's Island, was the point of entry for many African slaves during the eighteenth century. "Sullivan's Island," wrote historian Peter H. Wood, "the sandy spit on the northeast edge of Charlestown harbor where incoming slaves were briefly quarantined, might well be viewed as the Ellis Island of black Americans" (*Black Majority: Negroes in Colonial South Carolina from 1670 through the Stono Rebellion* [New York: Alfred A. Knopf, 1975], p. xiv).

4 The text of the 1882 Chinese Exclusion Act is quoted in Cheng-Tsu Wu, ed., *"Chink!" A Documentary History of Anti-Chinese Prejudice in America* (New York: World Publishing, 1972), pp. 70–75.

Act, Emma Lazarus wrote the poem that now graces the base of the Statue of Liberty. But the statue had not been envisioned as a symbol of welcome to the world's "wretched refuse" by its maker, French sculptor Frederic Auguste Batholdi, and at its unveiling in 1886, President Grover Cleveland proclaimed that the statue's light would radiate outward into "the darkness of ignorance and man's oppression until Liberty enlightens the world."[5] In other words, the statue commemorated republican stability, and according to the October 29, 1886, *New York World*, it stood forever as a warning against lawlessness and anarchy and as a pledge of friendship with nations that "dare strike for freedom." That meaning was changed by European immigrants, who saw the statue as welcoming them, and by Americanizers, who, during the 1920s and 1930s, after the 1924 Immigration Act restricting mass immigration, sought a symbol to instill within the children of immigrants patriotism and a love for country.[6]

The tale of those two islands, separated by the vast interior and lapped by different waters, comprises a metaphor of America and the Asian American experience. America was not always a nation of immigrants, nor was America unfailingly a land of democracy, equality, and liberty. The romantic sentiment of the American identity, "this new man," expressed by French immigrant J. Hector St. John de Crèvecoeur was probably not the dominant view, nor did it apply to all of America's people. Writing in 1782, Crèvecoeur exclaimed: "What then is the American, this new man? . . . I could point out to you a family whose grandfather was an Englishman, whose wife was Dutch, whose son married a French woman, and whose present four sons have now four wives of different nations. *He* is an American, who leaving behind him all his ancient prejudices and manners, receives new ones from the new mode of life he has embraced, the new government he obeys, and

5 John Higham, *Send These to Me: Jews and Other Immigrants in Urban America* (New York: Atheneum, 1975), pp. 71–72, 74, 75.
6 Ibid., pp. 75, 77, 79.

the new rank he holds. He becomes an American by being received in the broad lap of our great *Alma Mater*. Here individuals of all nations are melted into a new race of men."[7]

Instead, the prevailing view was a narrower construction that distinguished "settler," or original colonist, from "immigrant," and that required a single origin and common culture. Americans, John Jay wrote in the *Federalist* papers, were "one united people—a people descended from the same ancestors, speaking the same language, professing the same religion, attached to the same principles of government, very similar in their manners and customs."[8] That eighteenth-century discrimination between settler and immigrant proved inadequate for the building of a new republic during the nineteenth century. The quest for a unifying national identity, conceived along the lines of Crèvecoeur's notion whereby "individuals of all nations are melted into a new race of men," an idea later called the "melting pot," paralleled the building of networks of roads, railroads, and communications links that unified and bound the nation.[9]

Although Asians helped to construct those iron links that connected East to West, they, along with other peoples of color, were excluded from the industrial, masculine, destroying melting pot. Ellis Island was not their port of entry; its statue was not their goddess of liberty. Instead, the square-jawed, androgynous visage of the "Mother of Exiles" turned outward to instruct, to warn, and to repel those who would endanger the good order of America's shores, both at home and abroad. The indigenous inhabitants of Africa, Asia, and the Americas were not members of the community but were more akin to the wilderness, which required penetration and domestication. Three years after the Constitution was ratified, the first Congress met and restricted admission

---

7 J. Hector St. John de Crèvecoeur, *Letters from an American Farmer* (New York: Fox, Duffield & Co., 1904), pp. 54–55.

8 Higham, *Send These to Me*, p. 3.

9 Ibid., p. 199.

into the American community to "free white persons" through the Naturalization Act of 1790. Although the act was modified to include "persons of African nativity or descent" in 1870 and Chinese nationals in 1943, the racial criterion for citizenship was eliminated completely only in 1952, 162 years after the original delineation of the Republic's members, or, according to the Naturalization Act, the "worthy part of mankind."

In 1886, African American educator Anna Julia Cooper told a group of African American ministers: "Only the BLACK WOMAN can say 'when and where I enter . . . then and there the whole *Negro race enters with me.*'"[10] Cooper's confident declaration held profound meaning. African American men bore the stigma of race, but African American women bore the stigmata of race and gender. Her liberation, her access to the full promise of America, embraced the admission of the entire race. The matter of "when and where," accordingly, is an engendered, enabling moment. The matter of "when and where," in addition, is a generative, transformative moment. The matter of "when and where," finally, is an extravagant, expansive moment. That entry into the American community, however enfeebled by barriers to full membership, parallels the earlier entry into historical consciousness, and the "when and where" of both moments are engendered/enabling, generative/transformative, extravagant/expansive.

Asians entered into the European American historical consciousness long before the mid-nineteenth-century Chinese migration to "Gold Mountain" and, I believe, even before Yankee traders and American diplomats and missionaries traveled to China in the late eighteenth century. The "when and where" of the Asian American experience can be found within the European imagination and construction of Asians and Asia and within their expansion eastward and westward to Asia for conquest and trade.

Writing in the fifth or fourth century B.C.E., Hippocrates, Greek physician and "father of medicine," offered a "scientific"

10 Giddings, *When and Where I Enter*, pp. 81–82.

view of Asia and its people.[11] Asia, Hippocrates held, differed "in every respect" and "very widely" from Europe. He attributed those contrasts to the environment, which shaped the peoples' bodily conformations and their characters. Asia's mild, uniform climate supported lush vegetation and plentiful harvests, but under those conditions "courage, endurance, industry and high spirit could not arise" and "pleasure must be supreme." Asians reflected the seasons in their natures, exhibiting a "monotonous sameness" and "stagnation," and their form of government, led by kings who ruled as "despots," enfeebled Asians even more. Among Asians, Hippocrates reported, were "Longheads" and "Phasians." The latter had yellowish complexions "as though they suffered from jaundice." Because of the differing environments in which they lived, Hippocrates concluded that Europeans had a wider variety of physical types and were more courageous and energetic than Asians, "for uniformity engenders slackness, while variation fosters endurance in both body and soul; rest and slackness are food for cowardice, endurance and exertion for bravery."[12]

Aristotle mirrored Hippocrates' views of Asia during the fourth century B.C.E. In his *Politics*, Aristotle observed that northern Europeans were "full of spirit, but wanting in intelligence and skill," whereas Asians were "intelligent and inventive," but lacked spirit and were therefore "always in a state of subjection and slavery." The Greeks, in contrast, lived between those two groups and thus were both "high-spirited and also intelligent." Further, argued Aristotle, barbarians were by nature "more servile in character" than Greeks, and he reported that some Asians practiced canni-

11 For Hippocrates, Asia meant Asia Minor, or the area between the Mediterranean and Black seas. Depending upon who was writing and when, Asia meant variously Asia Minor (or Anatolia), the Levant, Southwest Asia, Central Asia, or India. Generally, during the fifth and fourth centuries B.C.E. the Greeks called the Persians "Asians."

12 *Hippocrates*, trans. W. H. S. Jones (Cambridge: Harvard University Press, 1923), 1:105–33.

balism.[13] The fourth-century B.C.E. conflict between Persia and Greece, between barbarism and civilization, between inferior and superior, tested the "great chain of being" idea propounded by Plato and Aristotle. Alexander the Great's thrust into India, to "the ends of the world," was a one-sided affair, according to the Roman historian Arrian, a chronicler of the expedition. Using contemporary accounts but writing some four hundred years after Alexander's death in 323 B.C.E., Arrian contrasted Alexander's ingenuity and dauntless spirit—"he could not endure to think of putting an end to the war so long as he could find enemies"—with the cowardice of the barbarian hordes, who fled pellmell at the sight of the conqueror.[14] In a speech to his officers, as recorded by Arrian, Alexander reminded them that they were "ever conquerors" and their enemies were "always beaten," that the Greeks were "a free people" and the Asians, "a nation of slaves." He praised the strength and valor of the Greeks, who were "inured to warlike toils," and he declared that their enemies had been "enervated by long ease and effeminacy" and called them "the wanton, the luxurious, and effeminate Asiatics."[15]

Such accounts of Asia, based upon the belief in a generative relationship between the environment and race and culture, enabled an exotic, alienating construction of Asians, whether witnessed or

---

13 *The Politics of Aristotle*, trans. Benjamin Jowett (Oxford: Clarendon Press, 1885), pp. 96, 218, 248. "Barbarians," it should be noted, could refer to Europeans, such as Thracians and Illyrians, as well as to Asians.

14 *Arrian's History of the Expedition of Alexander the Great, and Conquest of Persia*, trans. John Rooke (London: W. McDowall, 1813), pp. 112, 117, 123, 146.

15 Ibid., p. 42. Arrian was an Asian from Nicomedia in northern Turkey and wrote in Greek, despite serving as a Roman governor. See also Alexander's contrast of intelligent Greeks with Persian and Indian hordes in the influential work of late Greek literature *The Greek Alexander Romance*, trans. Richard Stoneman (London: Penguin Books, 1991), pp. 105, 128, 181; and a similar representation of Persians by Romans during the third century C.E. in Michael H. Dodgeon and Samuel N.C. Lieu, comps. and eds., *The Roman Eastern Frontier and the Persian Wars (AD 226–363): A Documentary History* (London: Routledge, 1991), pp. 19, 26.

simply imagined. Literary critics Edward W. Said and Mary B. Campbell have characterized that European conception of Asia and Asians—"the Other"—as "almost a European invention," according to Said, a place of "romance, exotic beings, haunting memories and landscapes, remarkable experiences," and for Campbell, that conception was "the ground for dynamic struggles between the powers of language and the facts of life."[16] Accordingly, the Greek historian Ctesias, writing probably in the fifth century B.C.E., reveled in the accounts of "dog-faced creatures" and "creatures without heads" that supposedly inhabited Africa, and he peopled his Asia with those same monstrous beasts. Likewise, the author of the early medieval account *Wonders of the East* described Asian women "who have boars' tusks and hair down to their heels and oxen's tails growing out of their loins. These women are thirteen feet tall, and their bodies have the whiteness of marble, and they have camels' feet and donkeys' teeth." Alexander the Great, hero of *Wonders of the East*, kills those giant, tusked, and tailed women "because of their obscenity" and thereby eliminates strangeness and makes the world sane and safe again. Asia in *Wonders of the East*, writes Campbell, "stands in opposition to the world we know and the laws that govern it," and thus was beyond and outside the realm of order and sensibility.[17]

That otherworldliness, that flight from reality, pervades the earliest Christian European text to define Europe in opposition to Asia, the *Peregrinatio ad terram sanctam* by Egeria, probably written during the late fourth century C.E. Although her account of her journey to the Holy Land contained "moments of awe, reverence, wonder or gratitude," it described an exotic Asia that served to highlight the positive, the real, the substantial Europe. *De locis sanctis*, written during the late seventh century C.E. by

16 Edward W. Said, *Orientalism* (New York: Random House, 1978), p. 1; and Mary B. Campbell, *The Witness and the Other World: Exotic European Travel Writing, 400–1600* (Ithaca: Cornell University Press, 1988), p. 3.

17 Campbell, *Witness*, pp. 51, 63–65, 68–69, 84. See also *Greek Alexander Romance*, p. 124.

Adamnan, abbot at Iona's monastery, recounted a similar Asia from the travels of Bishop Arculf to the Holy Land. Asia, according to *De locis sanctis*, was a strange, even demonic place, where people exhibited grotesque inversions and perversions of human nature, and where a prerational, stagnant configuration existed, "a world stripped of spirit and past."[18]

Asia, according to Campbell and Said, was Europe's Other.[19] Asia was the location of Europe's oldest, greatest, and richest colonies, the source of its civilization and languages, its cultural contestant, and the wellspring of one of its most persistent images of the Other. At the same time, cautions Said, the assumptions of Orientalism were not merely abstractions and figments of the European imagination but composed a system of thought that supported a "Western style for dominating, restructuring, and having authority over" Asia. Within Orientalism's lexicon, Asians were inferior to and deformations of Europeans, and Orientalism's purpose was to stir an inert people, raise them to their former greatness, shape them and give them an identity, and subdue and domesticate them. That colonization, wrote Said, was an engendered subordination, by which European men aroused, penetrated, and possessed a passive, dark, and vacuous "Eastern bride," imposing movement and giving definition to the "inscrutable Orient," full of secrecy and sexual promise.[20] The feminization of Asia was well under way before the colonization of Asia by Europe in the sixteenth century, as evident in the accounts of Hippocrates, Herodotus,[21] Aristotle, Arrian, Egeria, and Adamnan.

18 Campbell, *Witness*, pp. 7–8, 21, 26, 44–45.

19 Ibid., p. 3; and Said, *Orientalism*, p. 1. See also Christopher Miller, *Blank Darkness: Africanist Discourse in French* (Chicago: University of Chicago Press, 1985), who contends that Africa was Europe's Other.

20 Said, *Orientalism*, pp. 1, 59, 62, 72, 74, 86, 207–8, 211, 222. For a cautionary critique of Said, see Lisa Lowe, *Critical Terrains: French and British Orientalisms* (Ithaca: Cornell University Press, 1991).

21 The contest between Greece and Asia was a major theme in ancient Greek literature, as seen in the writings of Homer, Aeschylus, Euripides, Xenophon, and many others. The work of Herodotus, written in the fifth century

Arrian's account of Alexander's effortless victory over "effeminate" Asian men, for example, parallels his discussion of Greek
men's easy conquest of erotic Asian women. Indian women, wrote
the Roman historian, "who will suffer themselves to be deflow-
ered for no other gift, will easily condescend, when an elephant is
promised as the purchase," thinking it "an honour to have their
beauty valued at so high a rate."[22] The conqueror took for himself
several Asian wives, he "bestowed the daughters of the most il-
lustrious" Persians on his friends, and more than 10,000 of his soldiers married Asian women. Further, commented Arrian, despite
being "in the very heat of youth," Alexander curbed his sexual desires and thereby displayed the triumph of mind over body, ratio-
nality over sensuality, Greek over Asian. "The daughter of
Oxyartes was named Roxana, a virgin, but very marriageable,
and, by the general consent of writers, the most beautiful of all the
Asiatic women, Darius's wife excepted," wrote Arrian. "Alexander was struck with surprise at the sight of her beauty; nevertheless, being fully resolved not to offer violence to a captive, he
forbore to gratify his desires till he took her, afterwards, to wife
. . . and herein showed himself no less a pattern of true conti-
nency, than he had before done of heroic fortitude." "As to those
pleasures which regarded the body," wrote Arrian in eulogizing
Alexander, "he shewed himself indifferent; as to the desires of the
mind, insatiable."[23]

The Greek representation of Asia yielded not only soft men and
erotic women but also hard, cruel men and virile, martial women.
Fifth-century B.C.E. polarities of Greek/barbarian, male/female,
and human/animal helped to define the citizens of the *polis*—
Greek men—as the negation of their Other—barbarian, female,
animal—who were linked by analogy such that barbarian was

B.C.E., is perhaps the best known example of this genre. I simply present a se-
lection of the evidence.

22 *Arrian's History*, p. 220.

23 Ibid., pp. 112–13, 181, 205. Arrian was a Stoic philosopher, accounting for his stress on mind over body.

like female was like animal.[24] Athenian patriarchy held that men were the norm, were superior, and brought order, whereas women were abnormal, inferior, and brought chaos. Marriage domesticated women, civilizing their wild, untamed sexuality and disciplining them for admittance into the city. Amazons reversed the gender relations of the *polis* and stood in opposition to its androcentrism by being members of a society of women who refused to marry and become mothers to sons and who assumed the preeminent male characteristics of aggressiveness, leadership, and strength. Although the myth of Amazons originated before the Persian wars, the Greeks considered Asia to be the Amazons' homeland, and they equated Persians with Amazons, in that both Persians and Amazons were barbarians and, according to Isocrates in 380 B.C.E., Amazons "hated the whole Greek race" and sought "to gain mastery over all." Athenians, explained Isocrates, defended themselves against Amazon expansion, defeated them, and destroyed them "just as if they had waged war against all mankind."[25] Besides posing a political threat, Asia served as an object lesson of how, when men ceased to act as men, order and normalcy vanished, resulting in the topsy-turvy world of the Amazons.[26]

The Mongol invasions of the thirteenth century not only breached Alexander's wall but also made palpable a hitherto-distant, alien people and culture. "Swarming like locusts over the face of the earth," Friar William of Rubruck wrote in 1255, the

24 Page duBois, *Centaurs and Amazons: Women and the Pre-history of the Great Chain of Being* (Ann Arbor: University of Michigan Press, 1982), pp. 4–5.

25 Quoted in W. Blake Tyrrell, *Amazons: A Study in Athenian Mythmaking* (Baltimore: Johns Hopkins University Press, 1984), pp. 15–16. For another view of Amazons and their relation to Greek patriarchy, see duBois, *Centaurs and Amazons*, pp. 4–5, 34, 70.

26 On the ambiguities of Greek attributions of male and female and the rhetoric of discourse and reality of practice, see John J. Winkler, *The Constraints of Desire: The Anthropology of Sex and Gender in Ancient Greece* (New York: Routledge, 1990).

Mongols "have brought terrible devastation to the eastern parts [of Europe], laying waste with fire and carnage . . . it seemed that God did not wish them to come out; nevertheless it is written in sacred history that they shall come out toward the end of the world, and shall make a great slaughter of men."[27] The Mongols, of whom the Tatars were the most prominent group, appeared as avenging angels from hell, "Tartarus," and hence the corruption of their name to "Tartars."[28] Although in awe of the Mongols' military prowess and strength, Friar William saw little to admire in their filth and barbarism: "the poor provide for themselves by trading sheep and skins; and the slaves fill their bellies with dirty water and are content with this. They also catch mice, of which many kinds abound there; mice with long tails they do not eat but give to their birds; they eat doormice and all kinds of mice with short tails."[29]

The late-thirteenth-century account of Asia by the Venetian Marco Polo contains both feminine and masculine attributions, chaste women and diabolical men, and grotesque and wondrous objects and people, including unicorns, Amazons, dog-headed creatures, mountain streams flowing with diamonds, and deserts full of ghouls. His narrative is a distillation of the brew that had preceded him. John Masefield, in his introduction to the 1908 edition of Polo's *Travels*, wrote that "his picture of the East is the picture which we all make in our minds when we repeat to ourselves those two strange words, 'the East,' and give ourselves up to the image which that symbol evokes."[30] A prominent part of that image was the exotic and the erotic, highlighted in Polo's ample accounts of prostitutes, sex, and women, leading Henry Hart to speculate: "One may surmise that the numerous references to

27 Campbell, *Witness*, pp. 88–89.

28 David Morgan, *The Mongols* (London: Basil Blackwell, 1986), pp. 56–57.

29 Campbell, *Witness*, p. 114.

30 *The Travels of Marco Polo the Venetian* (London: J. M. Dent, 1908), p. xi.

women—the intimate descriptions of their persons, their various aptitudes in sex relations and many other details not usually related even by hardy travelers of that or a later day . . . were largely, if not entirely, called forth by the frank curiosity and continual questionings of the stay-at-home Westerners for whom his tale was told and written." Polo wrote of the Chinese that "their ladies and wives are also most delicate and angelique things, and raised gently, and with great delicacy, and they clothe themselves with so many ornaments and of silk and of jewels, that the value of them cannot be estimated."[31]

In Europe, *The Travels of Sir John Mandeville* was the most influential book about Asia from 1356, when it was first published, to the eighteenth century. "Mandeville" was a pseudonym for perhaps a number of authors, who claimed to have traveled from England to the Holy Land, Egypt, Arabia, and even to the court of the Great Khan in Cathay. Like Polo, Mandeville described the marvels and monsters of the East, from the bounties of gold, silver, precious stones, cloves, nutmeg, and ginger to the horrors of one-eyed and headless beasts, giants, pygmies, and cannibals. In a single passage, Mandeville poses an apparently curious juxtaposition of sexuality and war, but upon reflection, the feminine (sexuality) and masculine (war) so constructed are really two sides of the same coin: the dominance of men over women and territory, achieved through heterosexual sex and war, and, by extension, under imperialism, European men's superiority over Asian women and men and their control of reproduction and the state. On the island of "Calonak" near Java, wrote Mandeville, the king "hath as many wives as he will. For he maketh search all the country to get him the fairest maidens that may be found, and maketh them to be brought before him. And he taketh one one night, and another another night, and so forth continually suing; so that he hath a thousand wives or more. And he lieth never but one night

31 Henry H. Hart, *Marco Polo: Venetian Adventurer* (Norman: University of Oklahoma Press, 1967), pp. 117, 135.

with one of them, and another night with another; but if that one happen to be more lusty to his pleasance than another. And therefore the king getteth full many children, some-time an hundred, some-time a two-hundred, and some-time more." Without a paragraph break, Mandeville continued: "And he hath also into a 14,000 elephants or more that he maketh for to be brought up amongst his villains by all his towns. For in case that he had any war against any other king about him, then [he] maketh certain men of arms for to go up into the castles of tree made for the war, that craftily be set upon the elephants' backs, for to fight against their enemies."[32]

Christopher Columbus was a great admirer of "Mandeville" and, along with English explorers Martin Frobisher and Walter Raleigh and Flemish cartographer Gerhardus Mercator, read and believed Mandeville's account of Asia and his idea of a circumnavigable and universally inhabited world.[33] The fabulous East, the earthly paradise "discovered" and described by Columbus, was to him and his contemporaries Asia—the "Indies"—and its peoples were Asians—the "Indians." They were just as surely Asian as the lands and peoples in Polo's and Mandeville's travelogues. As Columbus noted in the preface to his ship's daily log, the expedition's purpose was to go "to the regions of India, to see the Princes there and the peoples and the lands, and to learn of their disposition, and of everything, and the measures which could be taken for their conversion to our Holy Faith."[34] Columbus compared the new lands to the virtuous Garden before the Fall, where people were like children, innocent and unselfconscious in their nakedness, and where the feminized land invited conquest. His log entry for October 12, 1492, reported: "At dawn we saw naked

32 *The Travels of Sir John Mandeville* (London: Macmillan, 1900), pp. 127–28.

33 Campbell, *Witness*, pp. 10, 161; and *The Log of Christopher Columbus*, trans. Robert H. Fuson (Camden, Maine: International Marine Publishing, 1987), p. 25.

34 *Log of Christopher Columbus*, p. 51.

people, and I went ashore in the ship's boat, armed. . . . I unfurled the royal banner. . . . After a prayer of thanksgiving I ordered the captains of the Pinta and Niña . . . to bear faith and witness that I was taking possession of this island for the King and Queen."[35] Much of the land was bountiful and laden with fruit, and on his third voyage, Columbus described the mouth of the Orinoco River as shaped "like a woman's nipple," from whence issued the waters of paradise into the sea.[36]

Some islanders, reported Columbus, were friendly, domestic, tractable, and even cowardly, but others were warlike, monstrous, and evil, even cannibalistic (a word derived from the name "Carib" Indians). "I also understand that, a long distance from here," wrote Columbus on November 4, 1492, "there are men with one eye and others with dogs' snouts who eat men. On taking a man they behead him and drink his blood and cut off his genitals."[37] The timid Indians were eager to submit to Europeans, being "utterly convinced that I and all my people came from Heaven," according to Columbus, whereas the fearless ones required discipline. Both kinds of Indians, "feminine" and "masculine," were fair game for capture, or, in Columbus's euphemism, "I would like to take some of them with me."[38] That, in fact, was what the admiral did, as easily as plucking leaves from the lush, tropical vegetation, to serve as guides, servants, and specimens. Columbus's text and others like it helped to justify a "Christian imperialism" and were the means by which the invaders "communicated—and helped control—a suddenly larger world."[39]

35 Ibid., pp. 75–76.
36 Campbell, *Witness*, pp. 171, 247. Walter Raleigh also believed the Orinoco led to paradise (ibid., pp. 246–47).
37 *Log of Christopher Columbus*, p. 102.
38 Ibid., pp. 145, 173; and "Letter of Columbus," in *The Four Voyages of Columbus*, ed. and trans. Cecil Jane (New York: Dover Publications, 1988), p. 10.
39 Campbell, *Witness*, p. 166.

That world grew even larger in about 1510, when a few Europeans questioned Columbus's "India" and proposed the existence
of a new continent that stood between Europe and Asia, although
cartographers continued to append American discoveries to the
Asian coast until the late sixteenth century. Accompanying and
justifying their expanded physical world was an ideology, articulated in texts, of a growing racial and cultural distance between
Europeans and the peoples of Asia, Africa, and the Americas. The
first cracks had appeared, in the perceptions of Asians by Europeans, in the fifth-century B.C.E. works of Hippocrates, who had
posited "very wide" differences "in every respect" between Europeans and Asians. The fissures continued to widen thereafter to
the degree that Asia, Africa, and the Americas became antipodes
of Europe, the habitations of monstrous beasts and perversions of
nature itself. That world, it seemed, needed to be appropriated,
worked over, and tamed.

The process of colonization and the relationship between colonizer and colonized were incisively described by Albert Memmi,
the twentieth-century Tunisian philosopher and author. "The colonialist stresses those things which keep him separate, rather
than emphasizing that which might contribute to the foundation
of a joint community." That focus on difference is not of itself racist, but it takes on a particular meaning and function within a racist context. According to Memmi: "In those differences, the
colonized is always degraded and the colonialist finds justification
for rejecting his subject. . . . The colonialist removes the factor
[the colonized] from history, time, and therefore possible evolution. What is actually a sociological point becomes labeled as
being biological or, preferably, metaphysical. It is attached to the
colonized's basic nature."[40] Whether because of race or culture, of
biology or behavior, of physical appearance or social construct,
Asians appeared immutable, engendered, and inferior. These dif-

40 Albert Memmi, *The Colonizer and the Colonized* (Boston: Beacon
Press, 1967), p. 71.

ferences not only served to set Asians apart from the "joint community" but also helped to define the European identity as a
negation of its Other.

Reflecting on works published on the five-hundredth anniver-
sary of Columbus's "discovery," anthropologist Wilcomb E.
Washburn, noted interpreter of American Indian culture and director of the Office of American Studies at the Smithsonian Institution, reminded his readers that the initiative for discovery came
from the West and not the East, and thus "Asia was more sharply
etched on the European mind than on the Asian mind. . . . Both
America and Asia were relatively stagnant," he explained, "being
more wedded to their traditions than was the West, which found
the novelty of other climes and other cultures stimulating. While
the Western mind did not always move in directions that we
would now applaud, it moved—indeed, darted here and there—
as the Asian mind too often did not."[41]

Following Columbus's "great enterprise" and his "taking possession" of "Asia," the penetration of Asia proper began with the
Portuguese, who seized parts of India and Southeast Asia during
the early sixteenth century, established a colony at Macao in
1557, and controlled much of the trade with China and Japan.
Despite Portugal's presumed, sole possession of the hemisphere
east of the 1493 papal line of demarcation, Spain, the Nether-
lands, France, and Britain also participated in the trade with and
colonization of Asia. The conquest and colonization of the Americas was, of course, a product of that global expansion of Europeans, and the "when and where" of the Asian American
experience must be similarly situated. I do not claim, however,
that Orientalism's restructuring and domination of Asia simply
migrated with Europeans to America, nor am I arguing a necessary relationship between European and European American perceptions of Asians. My contention is that there is a remarkable

41 Wilcomb E. Washburn, "Columbus: On and off the Reservation," *National Review*, October 5, 1992, pp. 57–58.

familiarity to Orientalism's face on both shores of the Atlantic and that its resemblance extends to European constructions of American Indians and Africans.[42]

Historian Stuart Creighton Miller, in his 1969 book, *The Unwelcome Immigrant: The American Image of the Chinese, 1785–1882*, argued that although it was sensible to assume that American attitudes toward Asians were rooted in the European heritage, he could find no direct connection between those views. Neither the writings nor the libraries of America's leading figures during the colonial period showed an interest in or even curiosity about Asians. Miller characterized that lacuna as indicative of an "innocent, unstructured perception of China in the American mind" and, as proof, pointed to George Washington, who was surprised to learn in 1785 that the Chinese were nonwhites. Further, Miller noted that the English failed to share the Continent's enthusiasm for Chinese government and law and for Confucian philosophy made popular by Jesuit missionaries and by the iconoclasts of the Age of Reason. In fact, in Britain, Sinophobes such as Daniel Defoe, Samuel Johnson, Jonathan Swift, and Adam Smith launched a vitriolic attack against the Chinese. The American image of Asians, Miller concluded, took shape only after direct American trade with China began with the departure of the *Empress of China* from New York Harbor in 1784.[43]

Miller underestimates the malleability and mobility of racial attitudes and notions of the Other, characteristics that have been amply demonstrated by scholars. Europeans, as noted by historian Dwight W. Hoover, "did not approach new lands and new people devoid of preconceptions. Instead, they brought with them a whole set of ideas concerning both the natural and historical worlds."[44] Some of those preconceptions included the idea of a bi-

42 See chapter 5 for an elaboration of this theme.

43 Stuart Creighton Miller, *The Unwelcome Immigrant: The American Image of the Chinese, 1785–1882* (Berkeley and Los Angeles: University of California Press, 1969), pp. 11–14.

44 Dwight W. Hoover, *The Red and the Black* (Chicago: Rand McNally, 1976), p. 4.

ological chain of being that evolved from ape to wild man to man and the biblical notion of postdiluvian degeneration and diversity originating with the Tower of Babel.[45] Despite their manifest variety, ideas of race distinguished Europeans from their shadow—non-Europeans—and claimed superiority for the civilized, Christian portion of humankind.

William Shakespeare's *The Tempest*, first performed in 1611, was likely set in Bermuda but might just as well have been an allegory of race relations during the age of European overseas expansion and colonization, or perhaps even an account of the sugar plantation system that was installed along the European Mediterranean coast and on islands like Cyprus and Crete and that was driven mainly by Asian and African slave labor by the late fourteenth century.[46] Prospero, "a prince of power" and lover of books, is set adrift with his daughter, Miranda, and lands on an enchanted island which he takes from Caliban, whom he enslaves and banishes to the island's wasteland. Caliban (anagram of the word "cannibal") is everything Prospero is not; he is dark and physically deformed; he is "poisonous," "lying," "filth," "capable of all ill," and begotten of "the devil himself." He is both African and Indian, his mother was from Algiers and he is descended from Brazilians, Patagonians, and Bermudans but is also part fish, part beast. Caliban's mother, Prospero said, was a "damn'd witch," a "hag," who had given birth to Caliban like an animal—"she did litter here" her son, who was "not honour'd with a human shape." Despite being excluded from their company and despite Miranda's abhorrence of him, Caliban is indispensable to Prospero and Miranda, because he "does make our fire, fetch in our wood; and serves in offices that profit us." Prospero pities Cali-

45 I merely allude to the vast literature on the history of racism and racist thought and cite as particularly helpful Arthur O. Lovejoy, *The Great Chain of Being: A Study of the History of an Idea* (Cambridge: Harvard University Press, 1936); and George L. Mosse, *Toward the Final Solution: A History of European Racism* (New York: Howard Fertig, 1978).

46 Hoover, *Red and Black*, pp. 1–2; and David Brion Davis, *Slavery and Human Progress* (New York: Oxford University Press, 1984), pp. 52–57.

ban, tutors him, and takes "pains to make [him] speak"; Prospero gives meaning to Caliban's "gabble." Instruction, however, proves insufficient. The wild man is driven by savage lust and tries to kill Prospero and rape the virginal Miranda, but he is repulsed by Prospero's magic.[47]

Caliban, the "savage man of Inde," was African and Indian, but he was also Asian insofar as Indians came from Asia, as was contended by Samuel Purchas, scholar and chaplain to the archbishop of Canterbury, in his widely read book *Purchas his Pilgrimage*, published in 1613, and seconded by the astronomer Edward Brerewood in his 1614 book, *Enquiries touching the diversity of languages, and religions through the chiefe parts of the world*, and by Walter Raleigh in his 1614 *History of the World*. The fact that Indians were once Asians accounted for their barbarism, according to these English writers.[48] Thus, although a separate race, Indians were still Asians, both groups having descended from the biblical Shem; and Asians, Indians, and Africans all belonged to the darker races of men, the Calibans of the earth, who were ruled by beastly passions, sought to impregnate white women (to people "this isle with Calibans"), and, although given a language and trained in useful labor, still turned against their benefactors and had to be subdued.[49] Perhaps influenced by those European views, Thomas Jefferson hypothesized the kinship of Asians and America's Indians: "the resemblance between the Indians of America and the eastern inhabitants of Asia would in-

47 *The Complete Works of William Shakespeare* (New York: Walter J. Black, 1937), pp. 2–6; Ronald T. Takaki, *Iron Cages: Race and Culture in Nineteenth-Century America* (New York: Alfred A. Knopf, 1979), pp. 11–12; and Leslie A. Fielder, *The Return of the Vanishing American* (New York: Stein & Day, 1968), pp. 42–49. See O. Mannoni, *Prospero and Caliban: The Psychology of Colonization*, trans. Pamela Powesland (London: Methuen, 1956), for a more complex reading of the play, esp. pp. 105–6.

48 Hoover, *Red and Black*, pp. 35–37.

49 See Winthrop Jordan, *White over Black* (Chapel Hill: University of North Carolina Press, 1968), for British and American racial attitudes toward Indians and Africans from 1550 to 1812.

duce us to conjecture that the former are descendants of the latter, or the latter of the former."[50]

Although they arrived in the New World carrying the baggage of the Old World, Americans developed their own projections and invented their own mythologies, peering from their "clearing" into the "wilderness." George Washington may have been reflecting the light of European ideology bent by the prism of American experience when he declared that "being upon good terms with the Indians" was based upon economy and expediency, and instead of driving them "by force of arms out of their Country; which . . . is like driving the wild Beasts of ye forest . . . the gradual extension of our settlements will as certainly cause the savage, as the wolf, to retire; both being beasts of prey, tho' they differ in shape."[51] And Jefferson might have defended Indians as "a degraded yet basically noble brand of white man," but he was also defending the American environment and its quadrupeds, those "other animals of America," against French naturalist Georges Buffon's claim of American inferiority. Having failed to assimilate and civilize the savage and childish Indians, Jefferson argued for their extermination, made "necessary to secure ourselves against the future effects of their savage and ruthless warfare."[52] Jefferson, having reached that conclusion about Indians, linked America's determination to clear the forests with a New World version of British expansion and colonization and predicted that the "confirmed brutalization, if not extermination of this race in our America is . . . to form an additional chapter in the English history of [oppression of] the same colored man in Asia, and of the brethren of their own color in Ireland."[53]

50 Frederick M. Binder, *The Color Problem in Early National America as Viewed by John Adams, Jefferson and Jackson* (The Hague: Mouton, 1968), p. 83.

51 Quoted in Richard Drinnon, *Facing West: The Metaphysics of Indian-Hating and Empire-Building* (New York: New American Library, 1980), p. 65.

52 Ibid., pp. 80–81, 98; and Jordan, *White over Black*, pp. 475–81.

53 Drinnon, *Facing West*, p. 81.

When Yankee traders arrived in China during the late eighteenth century, they saw the Chinese through lenses that had already been ground with the grit of European views of Asia and Asians and the rub of historical and contemporary relations between European Americans and American Indians and Africans. The traders' diaries, journals, and letters were mostly free of racial prejudice, reports Miller, and the negative images of the Chinese that did appear concerned China's government and the officials with whom the traders dealt, whom they saw as despotic, corrupt, barbarous, begging, and cowardly. But traders' accounts also revealed extreme ethnocentrism. According to a trader, the Chinese were "the most vile, the most cowardly and submissive of slaves," and whites could bully even Chinese soldiers, whose "silly grunts and menaces mean nothing and are to be disregarded," wrote another.[54] A prominent theme was the bizarre and peculiar nature of the Chinese in their alleged taste for dogs, cats, and rats, in their music, which was a "mass of detestible discord," and in their theater, which was "ridiculous or disgracefully obscene." The records, wrote Miller, "portrayed him [the Chinese] as a ludicrous specimen of the human race and [were] not designed to evoke the admiration and respect for Chinese culture." The focus on the exotic, on "strange and curious objects," was complemented by a featuring of vice—gambling and prostitution—and practices showing the "moral debasement" of the people, including idolatry, polygamy, and infanticide. The Chinese, wrote a trader contemptuously, are "grossly superstitious . . . most depraved and vicious: gambling is universal . . . ; they use pernicious drugs, . . . are gross gluttons," and are "a people refined in cruelty, bloodthirsty, and inhuman."[55]

The journey begun in New England and continuing around South America's Cape Horn was just the start of America's masculine thrust westward toward Asia's open shores.[56] Like those

54 Miller, *Unwelcome Immigrant*, pp. 21, 25–27, 34.

55 Ibid., pp. 27–32, 35.

56 The phrase "masculine thrust toward Asia" is from the title of chapter 11 of Takaki's *Iron Cages*, p. 253.

Yankee China trade vessels, the Conestoga wagons and prairie schooners pushed their way through "vacant, virgin" land to the Pacific and in the process built a continental empire that stretched "from sea to shining sea." In 1879, Robert Louis Stevenson rode the iron rails that bound the nation together, and his account, "Across the Plains: Leaves from the Notebook of an Emigrant between New York and San Francisco," might be read as the great American epic. America was "a sort of promised land" for Americans, like Stevenson, who were immigrants from Europe and who found themselves among a diverse lot of fellow passengers, "a babel of bewildered men, women, and children." As the train carried them westward, Stevenson described, like Crèvecoeur, the beauties of the land, where "all times, races, and languages have brought their contribution." That equality, that melting pot, however, was broken at Chicago, at the frontier of civilization, where the travelers were placed on an "emigrant train" that consisted of segregated coaches: one for white men, another for white women and children, and yet another for Chinese. Stevenson reflected upon the hatreds that had prompted that racial, gender, and age segregation as the train "pushed through this unwatered wilderness and haunt of savage tribes." America, he wrote, was the meeting ground, where "hungry Europe and hungry China, each pouring from their gates in search of provender, had here come face to face," and where Europeans had come with preconceived hatreds of the Chinese that had moved them from one field of conflict to another. "They [Europeans] seemed never to have looked at them [Chinese], listened to them, or thought of them, but hated them *a priori*," observed Stevenson. "The Mongols were their enemies in that cruel and treacherous battle-field of money."[57]

Despite his contempt for those "stupid," albeit modified, Old World prejudices, prejudices given further license once having left civilization for the "unwatered wilderness" of the frontier, Steven-

57 Robert Louis Stevenson, *Across the Plains, with Other Memories and Essays* (New York: Charles Scribner's Sons, 1900), pp. 1, 11, 26–27, 48, 60, 62; and Drinnon, *Facing West*, pp. 219–21.

son was not entirely free of those same perceptions of the Chinese. His fellow Europeans, reported Stevenson, saw the Chinese as physically repulsive, such that the mere sight of them caused "a kind of choking in the throat." "Now, as a matter of fact," admitted the observant Scotsman, "the young Chinese man is so like a large class of European women, that on raising my head and suddenly catching sight of one at a considerable distance, I have for an instant been deceived by the resemblance"—although, he offered, "I do not say it is the most attractive class of our women." And while looking upon the Chinese with "wonder and respect," Stevenson saw them as creatures from "the other" world: "They [the Chinese] walk the earth with us, but it seems they must be of different clay." "They hear the clock strike the same hour, yet surely of a different epoch. They travel by steam conveyance, yet with such a baggage of old Asiatic thoughts and superstitions as might check the locomotive in its course. . . . Heaven knows if we had one common thought or fancy all that way, or whether our eyes, which yet were formed upon the same design, beheld the same world out of the railway windows."[58]

Stevenson's view of the Chinese as "different clay" might have been conditioned by his European origins, but Herman Melville, surely no stranger to the American metaphysics of race relations, cannot be similarly dismissed. His retelling of a story by James Hall, "Indian hating.—Some of the sources of this animosity.—Brief account of Col. Moredock," not only offered a stinging critique of inhumanity masked as morality, embodied in the "confidence-man" and Indian-hater John Moredock, but also foresaw, according to Richard Drinnon, that "when the metaphysics of Indian-hating hit salt water it more clearly became the metaphysics of empire-building." Although believed to be a barbarian, predicted Melville, "the backwoodsman would seem to America what Alexander was to Asia—captain in the vanguard of conquering civilization." Melville, Drinnon points out, correctly saw that the relentless westward advance of the Indian-

58 Stevenson, *Across the Plains*, pp. 62, 65–66.

hater would, after reaching the Pacific Ocean, continue on to Asia, and in Melville's words, his hatreds would ride "upon the advance as the Polynesian upon the comb of the surf."[59] And like Alexander, who had sought to conquer all of India, the "backwoodsman," the "barbarian," "could not endure to think of putting an end to the war so long as he could find enemies."

In truth, America's manifest destiny was "an additional chapter" in the Orientalist text of Europe's "dominating, restructuring, and having authority over" Asia. In July 1853, Commodore Matthew C. Perry pushed into Tokyo Bay carrying a letter from the U.S. president demanding the opening of trade relations. That "opening" of Japan was accomplished, like the "opening" of the American West, with the iron fist of industry and the might of military arms; Perry's "black ships" under full steam power and with matchless guns were complements of the iron horses and Kentucky rifles of the backwoodsmen, who were simultaneously taming the wilderness. Reflecting on the second period of America's manifest destiny, after the annexation of the Philippines and Hawaii in 1898 and after Secretary of State John Hay's pronouncement of an "Open Door" with China, Theodore Roosevelt declared: "Of course our whole national history has been one of expansion. . . . That the barbarians recede or are conquered, with the attendant fact that peace follows their retrogression or conquest, is due solely to the power of the mighty civilized races which have not lost the fighting instinct, and which by their expansion are gradually bringing peace into the red wastes where the barbarian peoples of the world hold sway."[60]

The filling of those "red wastes," those empty spaces, was, of course, the white man's burden. John Hay, a son of the frontier of sorts, sought "to draw close the bonds" that united "the two Anglo-Saxon peoples" of Britain and America in a common des-

59 Herman Melville, *The Confidence-Man: His Masquerade*, ed. Elizabeth S. Foster (New York: Hendricks House, 1954), pp. lxv–lxx, 164, 334–41; and Drinnon, *Facing West*, pp. 214–15.

60 Quoted in Drinnon, *Facing West*, p. 232.

tiny and mission: "All of us who think cannot but see that there is a sanction like that of religion which binds us to a sort of partnership in the beneficent work of the world. Whether we will it or not, we are associated in that work by the very nature of things, and no man and no group of men can prevent it. We are bound by a tie which we did not forge and which we cannot break; we are the joint ministers of the same sacred mission of liberty and progress, charged with duties which we cannot evade by the imposition of irresistible hands."[61] China's "Open Door" and America's "splendid little war" with Spain, observed Hay, were of that beneficent quality. "We have done the Chinks a great service," wrote Hay of his policy, "which they don't seem inclined to recognize," and he admonished the next generation of backwoodsmen, "as the children of Israel encamping by the sea were bidden, to Go Forward." Indeed, noted Hay, America had gone forward and had charted a "general plan of opening a field of enterprise in those distant regions where the Far West becomes the Far East."[62] In becoming a Pacific power, America had fulfilled a European people's destiny and, like Columbus, had gone ashore, unfurled the royal banner, offered a prayer of thanksgiving, and taken possession of the land. America's Far West had become the Far East, where Indian-fighters became "goo-goo" fighters in the Philippines and Indian savages became Filipino "niggers," and where a war of extermination was pursued with no less determination than the chastising of the Iroquois urged by George Washington in 1779, when he instructed Major General John Sullivan: "but you will not by any means, listen to any overture of peace before the total ruin of their settlement is effected. . . . Our future security will be in their inability to injure us . . . and in the terror with which the severity of the chastizement they receive will inspire them."[63]

Asians, it must be remembered, did not come to America;

61 Ibid., p. 267.
62 Ibid., pp. 277, 278.
63 Ibid., p. 331.

Americans went to Asia. Asians, it must be remembered, did not come to take the wealth of America; Americans went to take the wealth of Asia. Asians, it must be remembered, did not come to conquer and colonize America; Americans went to conquer and colonize Asia. And the matter of the "when and where" of Asian American history is located therein, in Europe's eastward and westward thrusts, engendered, transformative, expansive. But another context of the "when and where" is the historical moment in America, where Prospero ruled over the hideous, the imperative Caliban. Asia not only provided markets for goods and outposts for military and naval bases but also supplied pools of cheap labor for the development of America's "plantations" along its southern and western frontiers. In 1848, Aaron H. Palmer, a counselor to the U.S. Supreme Court, anticipated the nation's destiny in the American Southwest and Asia when he predicted that San Francisco would become "the great emporium of our commerce on the Pacific; and so soon as it is connected by a railroad with the Atlantic States, will become the most eligible point of departure for steamers to . . . China." To build that rail link and to bring the fertile valleys of California under cultivation, Palmer favored the importation of Chinese workers, explaining that "no people in all the East are so well adapted for clearing wild lands and raising every species of agricultural product . . . as the Chinese."[64]

It was within those American "plantations" that Asians joined Africans, Indians, and Latinos in labor, making Prospero's fire, fetching his wood, and serving in offices that profited him. It was within those "plantations" that Europeans tutored Asians, Africans, Indians, and Latinos and gave meaning to their gabble. And it was within those "plantations" that Asians, Africans, Indians, and Latinos rose up in rebellion against their bondage and struck for their freedom.

In 1885, a Chinese American described his reaction to being solicited for funds for erecting the Statue of Liberty. He felt honored to be counted among "citizens in the cause of liberty," he wrote,

64 Takaki, *Iron Cages*, p. 229.

"but the word liberty makes me think of the fact that this country is the land of liberty for men of all nations except the Chinese. I consider it an insult to us Chinese to call on us to contribute toward the building in this land a pedestal for a statue of liberty. That statue represents liberty holding a torch which lights the passage of those of all nations who come into this country. But are the Chinese allowed to come? As for the Chinese who are here, are they allowed to enjoy liberty as men of all other nationalities enjoy it?"[65] For China's prodemocracy students in 1989 and for Asians in America, the "goddess of liberty," featured so prominently by the American news media, situated squarely within the mainstream, and lifting up her torch above the masses in Tiananmen Square, was not their symbol of liberation. Instead, their true symbol, relegated to the background as the camera panned the crowd, situated inconspicuously along the margins, was the declaration emblazoned by the Chinese students on the banners they waved, the shirts they wore, and the fliers they distributed: the words were, "We Shall Overcome."

65 Renqiu Yu, *To Save China, To Save Ourselves: The Chinese Hand Laundry Alliance of New York* (Philadelphia: Temple University Press, 1992), pp. 199–200.

2

Is Yellow Black or White?

Everytime I wanna go get a fucking brew
I gotta go down to the store with a tool
Oriental ones (can you count) mother-fuckers
They make a nigger mad enough to cause a ruckus
Thinking every brother in the world's on the take
So they watch every damn move that I make
They hope I don't pull out a gat and try to rob
their funky little store, but bitch, I gotta job.
So don't follow me up and down your market
Or your little chop-suey ass will be a target
Of the nationwide boycott
Choose with the people
That's what the boy got
So pay respect to the Black fist
Or we'll burn down your store, right down to a crisp
And then we'll see you
'Cause you can't turn the ghetto into Black Korea.[1]

BETWEEN 1985 and 1990 in New York City, there were three major protests against Korean storeowners in African com-

---

1 "Black Korea," by Ice Cube, from the album *Death Certificate*, Priority Records. In a letter dated February 8, 1992, O'Shea Jackson (Ice Cube) explained that the album "was not intended to offend anyone or to incite violence of any kind" and promised that during his concerts he would "discourage violence against store owners or anyone else" (*Korea Times*, May 4, 1992).

munities, while in Los Angeles, as one boycott ended in the summer of 1991, another began, and within a six-month period, five Korean grocery stores were firebombed. In a Los Angeles courtroom, the television monitors showed fifteen-year-old Latasha Harlins punch Soon Ja Du and turn to leave the store, when Du lifts a gun and fires pointblank at Harlins's head, killing her. On December 15, 1991, Yong Tae Park died of bullet wounds received during a robbery on his liquor store the previous day; Park was the seventh Korean storeowner killed in Los Angeles by African male suspects that year. "Black Power. No Justice, No Peace! Boycott Korean Stores! The Battle for Brooklyn," the poster read. "Crack, the 'housing crisis,' and Korean merchants is a conspiracy to destabilize our community. . . . The Korean merchants are agents of the U.S. government in their conspiracy to destabilize the economy of our community. They are rewarded by the government and financed by big business."[2] In south central Los Angeles in April and May 1992, following the acquittal of police officers in the beating of African American Rodney G. King, Koreatown was besieged, eighteen-year-old Edward Song Lee died in a hail of bullets, nearly fifty Korean merchants were injured, and damage to about 2,000 Korean stores topped $400 million. Parts of Japantown were also hit, and losses to Japanese businesses exceeded $3 million. Is yellow black or white?

In laying the intellectual foundation for what we now call the model minority stereotype, social scientists William Caudill and George De Vos stated their hypothesis: "there seems to be a significant compatibility (but by no means identity) between the value systems found in the culture of Japan and the value systems found in American middle class culture." That compatibility, they cautioned, did not mean similarity but rather a sharing of certain values and adaptive mechanisms, such that "when they [Japanese and white middle-class Americans] meet under conditions favorable for acculturation . . . Japanese Americans, acting in terms of

2 Poster of the December 12th Movement, Brooklyn Chapter, 1990.

their Japanese values and personality, will behave in ways that are favorably evaluated by middle class Americans."[3] Although Caudill and De Vos tried to distinguish between identity and compatibility, similarity and sharing, subsequent variations on the theme depicted Asians as "just like whites." And so, is yellow black or white?

The question is multilayered. Is yellow black or white? is a question of Asian American identity. Is yellow black or white? is a question of Third World identity, or the relationships among people of color. Is yellow black or white? is a question of American identity, or the nature of America's racial formation.[4] Implicit within the question is a construct of American society that defines race relations as bipolar—between black and white—and that locates Asians (and American Indians and Latinos) somewhere along the divide between black and white. Asians, thus, are "near-whites" or "just like blacks."[5] The construct is historicized, within the progressive tradition of American history, to show the evolution of Asians from minority to majority status, or "from hardship and discrimination to become a model of self-respect and achievement in today's America."[6] "Scratch a Japanese-American," social scientist Harry Kitano was quoted as saying, "and you find a Wasp," and Asians have been bestowed the high-

3 William Caudill and George De Vos, "Achievement, Culture and Personality: The Case of the Japanese Americans," *American Anthropologist* 58 (1956): 1107.

4 For a definiton of racial formation, see Michael Omi and Howard Winant, *Racial Formation in the United States: From the 1960s to the 1980s* (New York: Routledge & Kegan Paul, 1986), pp. 57–86.

5 See, e.g., James W. Loewen, *The Mississippi Chinese: Between Black and White* (Cambridge: Harvard University Press, 1971).

6 *U.S. News & World Report*, December 26, 1966. See also Dan Caldwell, "The Negroization of the Chinese Stereotype in California," *Southern California Quarterly* 53 (June 1971): 123–31, on the convergence of the Chinese and African American physiognomy; and Dennis M. Ogawa, *From Japs to Japanese: The Evolution of Japanese-American Stereotypes* (Berkeley: McCutchan Publishing, 1971), on the progression of Japanese American stereotypes.

est accolade of having "outwhited the Whites."[7] The construct, importantly, is not mere ideology but is a social practice that assigns to Asian Americans, and indeed to all minorities, places within the social formation. Further, the designations, the roles, and the relationships function to institute and perpetuate a repression that begets and maintains privilege. Asian Americans have served the master class, whether as "near-blacks" in the past or as "near-whites" in the present or as "marginal men" in both the past and the present. Yellow is emphatically neither white nor black; but insofar as Asians and Africans share a subordinate position to the master class, yellow is a shade of black, and black, a shade of yellow.

We are a kindred people, African and Asian Americans. We share a history of migration, interaction and cultural sharing, and commerce and trade. We share a history of European colonization, decolonization, and independence under neocolonization and dependency. We share a history of oppression in the United States, successively serving as slave and cheap labor, as peoples excluded and absorbed, as victims of mob rule and Jim Crow. We share a history of struggle for freedom and the democratization of America, of demands for equality and human dignity, of insistence on making real the promise that all men and women are created equal. We are a kindred people, forged in the fire of white supremacy and struggle, but how can we recall that kinship when our memories have been massaged by white hands, and how can we remember the past when our storytellers have been whispering amid the din of Western civilization and Anglo-conformity?

We know each other well, Africans and Asians. Some of the first inhabitants of South and Southeast Asia were a people called "Negrito," who were gatherers and hunters and slash-and-burn cultivators. They may have been absorbed or expelled by the Veddoids, a later group of immigrants to the Indian subcontinent, but remnants survive today as the Semang of the Malay Peninsula,

---

7 "Success Story: Outwhiting the Whites," *Newsweek*, June 21, 1971.

the Mincopies of the Andaman Islands, and the Negritos of the Philippines. One branch of the Dravidians, who arrived in South Asia probably after 1000 B.C.E, were black people, who at first apparently intermarried with the lighter-skinned Indo-Aryan branch of Dravidians, but who were later denigrated in the caste system that evolved on the Gangetic plains.[8]

Trade, if not migration, between Africa and Asia predated the arrival of Portuguese ships in the Indian Ocean by at least a thousand years. African ambergris, tortoiseshell, rhinoceros horns, and especially ivory left African ports for Arabia, India, Indonesia, and China. The *Periplus of the Erythraean Sea*, a handbook compiled by a Greek-Egyptian sailor sometime during the first three centuries C.E., described Indonesian food crops, such as coconuts, and cultural items, such as sewn boats, along the East African coast perhaps as far south as Mozambique, and historians believe that Indonesians may have settled on Madagascar in the early centuries C.E., but after the time of the *Periplus*.[9] The Chinese Ch'eng-shih Tuan, in his *Yu-yang-tsa-tsu* written in the ninth century C.E., described East Africa, or the "land of Po-pa-li," where the women were "clean and well-behaved" and where the trade products were ivory and ambergris.[10]

From the eighth through twelfth centuries, the Hindu kingdom of Sri Vijaya, centered on Sumatra, was the dominant mercantile power in the Indian Ocean; it controlled the sea routes between India and China and likely traded directly with people along the East African coast. About the same time, the Chola kingdom in southeast India sent traders to East Africa, where their cowrie currency, system of weights, and trade beads became standard and

8 Hugh Tinker, *South Asia: A Short History* (Honolulu: University of Hawaii Press, 1990), pp. 1–5.

9 J. E. G. Sutton, *The East African Coast: An Historical and Archaeological Review* (Dar es Salaam: East African Publishing House, 1966), p. 8.

10 G. S. P. Freeman-Grenville, ed., *The East African Coast: Select Documents from the First to the Earlier Nineteenth Century* (London: Oxford University Press, 1962), p. 8.

widespread. By the thirteenth century, both Sri Vijaya and the Chola kingdom fell into decline, and the west Indian Ocean became an Islamic sphere. Still, the Ming dynasty, which gained control of China in 1368, sent a fleet to East Africa in 1417 and again in 1421, and Ming porcelain has been found in abundance among the ruins of mosques, tombs, houses, and palaces on the islands and on the mainland along the East African coast. Fei-Hsin, a junior officer on the 1417 expedition, described the townspeople of Mogadishu: "the men wear their hair in rolls which hang down all round and wrap cotton cloths round their waists" and the women "apply a yellow varnish to their shaven crowns and hang several strings of disks from their ears and wear silver rings round their necks."[11]

Besides the trade in goods, Africans and Asians engaged in a slave trade that was "probably a constant factor" in the Indian Ocean from the tenth to the thirteenth centuries.[12] Much of that trade was conducted by Africanized Muslims, who sent African slaves to the shores of the Persian Gulf, to India, and to China. In the year 1119, "most of the wealthy in Canton possessed negro slaves," and East African slave soldiers were used extensively by the Sassanian kings of Persia during the seventh century and by the Bahmanid kings of the Deccan in India during the fourteenth and fifteenth centuries.[13] Africans in Asia sometimes rose from the ranks of slaves to become military and political leaders, such as Malik Sarvar of Delhi, who became the sultan's deputy in 1389, was appointed governor of the eastern province, and eventually ruled as an independent king. Perhaps most influential was Malik Ambar, who was born in Ethiopia around 1550, sold into slavery in India, and rose to become a commander and ruler in the Deccan. Ferista, a contemporary Arab historian, called Ambar "the

11 Gervase Mathew, "The East African Coast until the Coming of the Portuguese," in *History of East Africa*, ed. Roland Oliver and Gervase Mathew (London: Oxford University Press, 1963), 1:116, 120–21.

12 Ibid., p. 106.

13 Ibid., pp. 101, 108, 121.

most enlightened financier of whom we read in Indian history," and he reported that "the justice and wisdom of the government of Mullik Ambar have become proverbial in the Deccan."[14] The East African slave trade remained small in volume until the nineteenth century, when European colonies in the Americas and the Indian Ocean opened a larger market for slaves.[15]

The creation of that global system of labor and the conjunction of Africans, Asians, and Europeans began long before the nineteenth century. African and Asian civilizations contributed much to the dawning of European civilization in the Greek city-states. The armies of the Islamic Almoravids ranged across the Sudan and North Africa to Carthage and the Iberian Peninsula, and the Mongol armies of Chingiz Khan penetrated the European heartland. The invaders brought not only devastation but also religion, culture, and science. That intimacy would later be denied by the Europeans, who, after crusades to expel the "infidels" from Christendom and after the rise of nationalism and mercantile capitalism, conceived an ideology that justified their expansion and appropriation of land, labor, and resources in Africa, Asia, and the Americas. That ideology, in the name of religion and science, posited the purity and superiority of European peoples and cultures, unsullied by the anti-Christian, uncivilized non-Europeans—the Other—and found expression in European colonization of the Third World.

Seeking first the kingdom of gold, Europeans set sail for Asia down the African coast and around the Cape of Good Hope to India and China, and later west across the Atlantic Ocean to India, where instead they stumbled into the landmass they named the Americas. Colonization followed trade just as surely as capital required labor. European plantations in the Americas devoured

14 Joseph E. Harris, *The African Presence in Asia: Consequences of the East African Slave Trade* (Evanston: Northwestern University Press, 1971), pp. 78–79, 91–98.

15 Ibid., pp. 7–10; and Edward A. Alpers, *The East African Slave Trade* (Dar es Salaam: East African Publishing House, 1967), pp. 4–5.

the native inhabitants and, unsated, demanded African laborers from across the Atlantic in the miserable system of human bondage that supplied an outlet for European manufactures and produced the agricultural products that enriched the metropole. The reciprocal of European development was Third World underdevelopment, and the web spun by European capitalism crisscrossed and captured the globe, creating a world-system in which capital and labor flowed as naturally as the ocean currents that circled the Atlantic and Pacific.

Some of the earliest Asians in the Americas came by way of the Spanish galleon trade between Manila and Acapulco in the early seventeenth century. Chinese and Filipino crew members and servants on those Spanish ships settled in Mexico, and Filipino "Manilamen" found their way to Louisiana, where, in 1763, they created the oldest continuous Asian American communities in North America.[16] The Filipinos named their fishing and shrimping settlements Manila Village, St. Malo, Leon Rojas, Bayou Cholas, and Bassa Bassa. But the main body of Asian migration to the Americas came after the termination of the African slave trade in the nineteenth century and the consequent need for a new source of labor for the plantations, mines, and public works in Central and South America, Africa, and the islands of the Pacific and Caribbean.

A forerunner of the nineteenth-century coolie trade and the successor of the earlier East African slave trade was the use of Asian and African slaves on board European ships in the Indian Ocean and a European carrying trade that took Asian slaves from Bengal, southern India and Sri Lanka, the Indonesian archipelago, the Philippines, and Japan to Dutch and Portuguese possessions in Asia and Africa. Beginning in the early sixteenth century, largely because of the debilitating effects of disease upon European sailors, Arab, South Asian, Malay, and African slaves frequently made up the majority of the crews on Portuguese vessels plying In-

16 Marina E. Espina, *Filipinos in Louisiana* (New Orleans: A. F. Laborde & Sons, 1988), p. 1.

dian Ocean waters.[17] Asian slaves were joined by Africans taken from Madagascar and East Africa and were brought to the Dutch settlement at the Cape of Good Hope after 1658. By 1795, there were 16,839 slaves in the colony, and in 1834, the year slavery was abolished at the Cape, there were approximately 34,000 slaves.[18] The slaves produced mixed offspring with the indigenous San and Khoikhoi and with whites, forming the group the Europeans called the Cape Coloured. South Asians arrived on the East Coast of eighteenth-century America as indentured workers and slaves. Brought to Massachusetts and Pennsylvania on board English and American trade vessels possibly during the 1780s and 1790s, South Asians with Anglicized names such as James Dunn, John Ballay, Joseph Green, George Jimor, and Thomas Robinson served indentures, were sold and bought as slaves, likely married African American women, and became members of the local African American communities.[19]

In 1833, slavery was formally abolished in the British Empire, but during the period of transition, slaves over six years of age served apprenticeships from four to six years as unpaid and later as paid labor. Apprenticeships ended in the British colonies in 1838, leading to the claim by sugar planters of a chronic labor shortage and a determination "to make us, as far as possible, independent of our negro population," according to John Gladstone, father of Robert and William Gladstone and one of the largest slaveholders and proprietors of estates in British Guiana.[20]

17 Arnold Rubin, *Black Nanban: Africans in Japan during the Sixteenth Century* (Bloomington: African Studies Program, Indiana University, 1974), pp. 1–2, 9.

18 R. L. Watson, *The Slave Question: Liberty and Property in South Africa* (Hanover: Wesleyan University Press, 1990), pp. 9–10; and Robert Ross, *Cape of Torments: Slavery and Resistance in South Africa* (London: Routledge & Kegan Paul, 1983), pp. 11, 13.

19 Joan M. Jensen, *Passage from India: Asian Indian Immigrants in North America* (New Haven: Yale University Press, 1988), pp. 12–13.

20 Alan H. Adamson, *Sugar without Slaves: The Political Economy of British Guiana, 1838–1904* (New Haven: Yale University Press, 1972), pp. 31, 41.

Slavery, as pointed out by historian Hugh Tinker, produced both "a system and attitude of mind" that enabled a new system of slavery—coolieism—that incorporated many of the same oppressive features of the old.[21]

White planters saw the "new slaves" as subhuman and mere units of production. In 1836, anticipating the end of African slave apprenticeships, John Gladstone inquired about purchasing a hundred coolies from Gillanders, Arbuthnot & Company, who had supplied thousands of South Asians to Mauritius. The firm assured Gladstone that the Dhangars, or "hill coolies" of India, were "always spoken of as more akin to the monkey than the man. They have no religion, no education, and in their present state no wants beyond eating, drinking and sleeping: and to procure which they are willing to labour."[22] In May 1838, the first contingent of what would become a veritable stream of indentured labor arrived in British Guiana. The 396 Asian Indians were contracted to work nine to ten hours a day (as compared with seven and a half hours daily under apprenticeships) for sixteen cents (compared with thirty-two cents for free workers). In addition to economic exploitation, the indentured laborers were subject to disease and harsh treatment, particularly during the "seasoning," or breaking-in, period, resulting in numerous runaways and high mortality rates. From May 1845 to December 1849, 11,437 Asian Indians were indentured on sugar estates in British Guiana. Of that total as of December 1849, only 6,417 still remained on the estates, whereas 643 were listed as sick, vagrants, paupers, or children, 2,218 had died on the estates in jails and hospitals or were found dead elsewhere, and 2,159 were unaccounted for, of

21 Hugh Tinker, *A New System of Slavery: The Export of Indian Labour Overseas, 1830–1920* (London: Oxford University Press, 1974), p. 19. For overviews of Asian Indian and Chinese migration and indentureship in the Caribbean, see K. O. Laurence, *Immigration into the West Indies in the 19th Century* (Mona, West Indies: Caribbean Universities Press, 1971); and William A. Green, *British Slave Emancipation: The Sugar Colonies and the Great Experiment, 1830–1865* (London: Oxford University Press, 1976), pp. 276–86, 289–93.

22 Tinker, *New System of Slavery*, p. 63.

whom more than half were probably dead. Even those who had served their period of contract were left to wander "about the roads and streets, or lie down, sicken and die" or were castigated as "vagrants" who were stereotyped as "eating every species of garbage . . . filthy in [their] habits, lazy and addicted to pilfering."[23] Little wonder that Asian Indian indentures composed and sang this song as they sailed for Trinidad:

> *What kind plate,*
> *What kind cup,*
> *With a ticket to cut*
> *in Trinidad,*
> *O people of India*
> *We are going to die there.*[24]

Chinese and Asian Indian "coolies" were sold and indentured to European and American ship captains in a barter called by the Chinese "the buying and selling of pigs." The Chinese coolies, or "pigs," were restrained in "pigpens"; one such barracoon on Amoy in 1852 was described in a British report: "the coolies were penned up in numbers from 10 to 12 in a wooden shed, like a slave barracoon, nearly naked, very filthy, and room only sufficient to lie; the space 120 by 24 feet with a bamboo floor near the roof; the number in all about 500."[25] On shore, the coolies

23 Adamson, *Sugar without Slaves*, p. 48. Asian Indian and Chinese indentured laborers inherited, in the minds of the white planters, the alleged vices of African slaves in Trinidad. See David Vincent Trotman, *Crime in Trinidad: Conflict and Control in a Plantation Society, 1838–1900* (Knoxville: University of Tennessee Press, 1986), pp. 69, 87–88.

24 Noor Kumar Mahabir, *The Still Cry: Personal Accounts of East Indians in Trinidad and Tobago during Indentureship (1845–1917)* (Tacarigua, Trinidad: Calaloux Publications, 1985), p. 41. For life on the sugar estates, see Adamson, *Sugar without Slaves*, pp. 104–59; and Judith Ann Weller, *The East Indian Indenture in Trinidad* (Rio Piedras, P.R.: Institute of Caribbean Studies, University of Puerto Rico, 1968).

25 Cited in Ching-Hwang Yen, *Coolies and Mandarins: China's Protection of Overseas Chinese during the Late Ch'ing Period (1851–1911)* (Singapore: Singapore University Press, 1985), p. 59.

were stripped naked and on their chests were painted the letters
C (California), P (Peru), or S (Sandwich Islands), denoting their
destinations. Once on board the ship, they were placed below
deck in the hold, where they were usually confined for the dura-
tion of the transpacific passage. Overcrowding and a short supply of food and water led to revolts, suicides, and murders.
Fearing a revolt, the crew of an American ship, the *Waverly*,
drove the Chinese coolies below deck and closed the hatch on
October 27, 1855: "on opening them some twelve or fourteen
hours afterwards it was found that nearly three hundred of the
unfortunate beings had perished by suffocation."[26] Chao-ch'un
Li and 165 other coolies petitioned the Cuba Commission about
ill-treatment and abuse: "When quitting Macao," they testified,
"we proceeded to sea, we were confined in the hold below; some
were even shut up in bamboo cages, or chained to iron posts, and
a few were indiscriminately selected and flogged as a means of
intimidating all others; whilst we cannot estimate the deaths
that, in all, took place, from sickness, blows, hunger, thirst, or
from suicide by leaping into the sea."[27] As many as a third of the
coolies died during the journey across the Pacific on board ships
bound for the Americas. During the years 1860 to 1863, for example, of the 7,884 Chinese coolies shipped to Peru, 2,400, or
30.4 percent, died en route.[28] The African slave and Asian coolie
were kinsmen and kinswomen in that world created by European
masters.

26 Shih-shan H. Tsai, "American Involvement in the Coolie Trade," *American Studies* 6, nos. 3 and 4 (December 1976): 54. For a more detailed account of U.S. involvement in the coolie trade and coolie resistance, see Robert
J. Schwendinger, *Ocean of Bitter Dreams: Maritime Relations between
China and the United States, 1850–1915* (Tucson: Westernlore Press, 1988),
pp. 18–62.

27 Yen, *Coolies and Mandarins*, pp. 61–62.

28 Persia C. Campbell, *Chinese Coolie Emigration to Countries within the
British Empire* (London: P. S. King & Son, 1923), p. 95; and Watt Stewart,
Chinese Bondage in Peru (Durham: Duke University Press, 1951), pp. 62, 66,
97. See also Yen, *Coolies and Mandarins*, p. 62.

Between 1848 and 1874, 124,813 Chinese coolies reached
Cuba from Macao, Amoy, Canton, Hong Kong, Swatow, Saigon,
and Manila. Within Cuba's plantation system, wrote historian
Franklin W. Knight, the Chinese became "coinheritors with the
Negroes of the lowliness of caste, the abuse, the ruthless exploitation. . . . Chinese labor in Cuba in the nineteenth century was
slavery in every social aspect except the name."[29] Coolies were
sold in the open market, following advertisements that appeared
in the local newspapers. Prospective buyers inspected the human
merchandise, lined up on a platform, before the bargaining began, and the Asians were "virtually sold to the planters."[30] Conditions on Cuba's plantations were desperate. Chien T'ang, Chao
Chang, A-chao Wen, and about three hundred of their compa-
triots in labor testified that they worked daily from between 2 and
4 a.m. until midnight, including Sundays, and others described
the harsh treatment they received at the hands of overseers and
masters. Confinement, shackling with chains, flogging, and cutting off fingers, ears, and limbs were methods employed to ensure
docility and productivity in the workplace. A-pa Ho reported that
for making a cigarette, "I was flogged with a rattan rod so severely
that my flesh was lacerated and the bones became visible." A-chen
Lu stated: "I have seen men beaten to death, the bodies being afterwards buried, and no report being made to the authorities";
A-sheng Hsieh told of Chen and Liang, who committed suicide after having been severely beaten. "The administrator accused them
of cutting grass slowly," testified Hsieh, "and directing four men
to hold them in a prostrate position, inflicted with a whip, a flog-

29 Franklin W. Knight, *Slave Society in Cuba during the Nineteenth Century* (Madison: University of Wisconsin Press, 1970), p. 119. African slavery
in Cuba, of course, was governed by slave codes that differed significantly
from the institutions that regulated the coolie system. On the complementar-
ity and distinctions between African slavery and Chinese indentured labor,
see Rebecca J. Scott, *Slave Emancipation in Cuba: The Transition to Free Labor, 1860–1899* (Princeton: Princeton University Press, 1985), pp. 29–35,
109–10.

30 Yen, *Coolies and Mandarins*, p. 63; and Knight, *Slave Society*, p. 116.

ging which almost killed them. The first afterwards hanged himself, and the second drowned himself."[31]

In the United States, white planters similarly saw Chinese laborers as the "coinheritors with the Negroes of the lowliness of caste, the abuse, the ruthless exploitation." Before the Civil War, southern planters saw African slaves as a counter to immigration to their region by, in the words of Edmund Ruffin, "the hordes of immigrants now flowing from Europe." After the war, the planters saw free blacks as a troublesome presence and sought to deport and colonize them outside the United States and to replace them with Europeans and Asians.[32] In 1869, Godfrey Barnsley, a Georgia planter and New Orleans factor, predicted that Mississippi Valley planters would recruit "large numbers of Chinese to take the place of negroes as they are said to be better laborers[,] more intelligent and can be had for $12 or $13 per month and rations." William M. Lawton, chair of the Committee on Chinese Immigrants for the South Carolina Agricultural and Mechanical Society, put it more bluntly: "I look upon the introduction of Chinese on our Rice lands, & especially on the unhealthy cotton lands as new and essential machines in the room of others that have been destroyed [or are] wearing out, year by year."[33] Africans and Asians, according to that point of view, were mere fodder for the fields and factories of the master class.

Africans and Asians, however, were not the same. After the Civil War, southern employers viewed African Americans not

---

31 Yen, *Coolies and Mandarins*, pp. 64, 66–68. For a comparison, see Jan Breman, *Taming the Coolie Beast: Plantation Society and the Colonial Order in Southeast Asia* (Delhi: Oxford University Press, 1989); and Wing Yung, *My Life in China and America* (New York: Henry Holt, 1909), p. 195, on Chinese coolies in Peru.

32 James L. Roark, *Masters without Slaves: Southern Planters in the Civil War and Reconstruction* (New York: W. W. Norton, 1977), p. 165. See also Rowland T. Berthoff, "Southern Attitudes toward Immigration, 1865–1914," *Journal of Southern History* 17, no. 3 (August 1951): 328–60; and George E. Pozzetta, "Foreigners in Florida: A Study of Immigration Promotion, 1865–1910," *Florida Historical Quarterly* 53, no. 2 (October 1974): 164–80.

33 Roark, *Masters without Slaves*, p. 167.

only as essential laborers but also as political liabilities insofar as they voted and voted Republican.[34] The problem, thus, was how to maintain white political supremacy while employing cheap and efficient "colored" workers, thereby ensuring white economic supremacy. William M. Burwell, in an essay published in the July 1869 issue of *De Bow's Review*, described the challenge: "We will state the problem for consideration. It is: To retain in the hands of the whites the control and direction of social and political action, without impairing the content of the labor capacity of the colored race." Asian migrant workers, it seemed to some southerners, provided the ideal solution to the problem in that they were productive laborers and noncitizens who could not vote. Further, Asian workers would be used to discipline African workers and depress wages. On June 30, 1869, the *Vicksburg Times*, a proponent of Asian migration, editorialized: "Emancipation has spoiled the negro, and carried him away from fields of agriculture." The *Times* went on to exult at the impending arrival of several hundred Chinese coolies: "Our colored friends who have left the farm for politics and plunder, should go down to the *Great Republic* today and look at the new laborer who is destined to crowd the negro from the American farm." Arkansas Reconstruction governor Powell Clayton observed: "Undoubtedly the underlying motive for this effort to bring in Chinese laborers was to punish the negro for having abandoned the control of his old master, and to regulate the conditions of his employment and the scale of wages to be paid him."[35]

African and Asian workers, nonetheless, were related insofar as they were both essential for the maintenance of white supremacy, they were both members of an oppressed class of "colored" laborers, and they were both tied historically to the global network of labor migration as slaves and coolies. As anthropologist Lucy M. Cohen has shown, the planters in the American South were members of a Caribbean plantation complex, and the plans they

34 Loewen, *Mississippi Chinese*, pp. 21–24.
35 Ibid., p. 23.

formulated for Chinese migration drew from their cultural bonds with West Indian societies.[36] For example, during the 1850s, Daniel Lee of the *Southern Cultivator* and J. D. B. De Bow of *De Bow's Review*, despite their preference for African slaves, informed their readers about the growing use of Asian coolie labor in the plantations of the West Indies, and after the Civil War in October 1865, John Little Smith, an eminent jurist, reported in several southern newspapers that, according to an American ship captain who had taken Chinese coolies to Cuba, the Chinese were the "best and cheapest labor in the world" and would make good plantation workers and unparalleled servants.[37]

Despite their interest in Asian coolies, southern planters were stymied by the 1862 act of Congress that had prohibited American involvement in the coolie trade. To skirt federal restrictions on the importation of Asian workers, the planters and labor contractors crafted a distinction between coolies, who were involuntary and bonded labor, and Asian migrants, who were voluntary and free labor. That distinction, they noted, enabled the comparatively easy entry of Chinese into California, and when a shipload of Chinese from Cuba was impounded in 1867 at the port of New Orleans, planter Bradish Johnson argued: "What if the government should forbid the employment of the thousands of Chinese who have worked on the railroads, on the mines, and agriculture of California? No reason had been found for their exclusion and they were valuable for that country. The cultivators of cane and cotton would not be made an exception."[38] Johnson won his point, and the case was discontinued. Meanwhile, planters held Chinese labor conventions, such as the 1869 Memphis conven-

---

36 Lucy M. Cohen, *Chinese in the Post–Civil War South: A People without a History* (Baton Rouge: Louisiana State University Press, 1984); idem, "Entry of Chinese to the Lower South from 1865 to 1879: Policy Dilemmas," *Southern Studies* 17, no. 1 (Spring 1978): 5–37; and idem, "Early Arrivals," *Southern Exposure*, July/August 1984, pp. 24–30.

37 Cohen, "Entry of Chinese," pp. 8–12.

38 Ibid., p. 20.

tion that drew delegates from Alabama, Arkansas, Georgia, Kentucky, Louisiana, Mississippi, Missouri, South Carolina, Tennessee, and California, representing agricultural, railroad, and other business interests, and formed immigration committees and companies, and labor agents continued to bring Chinese workers, under contract, to the South, procuring them from Cuba, California, and China. After 1877, when white supremacist Democrats had broken the grip of Reconstruction through fraud and violence, southern planters reverted to a preference for African American workers, and interest in Asians declined and vanished.[39]

Although advocates of Chinese labor in the South learned to distinguish slave from coolie, and coolie from migrant, the migration of Asians to America cannot be divorced from the African slave trade, or from the coolie trade that followed in its wake. Both trades were systems of bonded labor, and both trades formed the contexts and reasons for the entry of Asians into America. Contract labor was the means by which Chinese and Japanese migrated to the Hawaiian kingdom and the American South, whereas the credit-ticket system was the means by which many Chinese gained admittance into California. But a system that advanced credit to laborers and constrained those workers to a term of service until the debt was paid was a scant advance over the earlier forms of coolie and contract labor,[40] and, perhaps more importantly, all of the successive systems of labor—from slave to coolie to contract to credit-ticket—were varieties of migrant labor

39 Loewen, *Mississipi Chinese*, p. 26.
40 Cohen, *Chinese in the Post–Civil War South*, p. 44; and Gunther Barth, *Bitter Strength: A History of the Chinese in the United States, 1850–1870* (Cambridge: Harvard University Press, 1964), p. 67. See also Shih-shan Henry Tsai, *The Chinese Experience in America* (Bloomington: Indiana University Press, 1986), pp. 3–7; idem, "American Involvement"; Roger Daniels, *Asian America: Chinese and Japanese in the United States since 1850* (Seattle: University of Washington Press, 1988), pp. 13–15; and Sucheng Chan, *This Bitter-Sweet Soil: The Chinese in California Agriculture, 1860–1910* (Berkeley and Los Angeles: University of California Press, 1986), pp. 21, 26.

and functioned to sustain a global order of supremacy and sub-ordination.[41] The lines that directed Africans and Asians to America's shore converge at that point, and the impetus for that intersection came from the economic requirement and advantage of bonded labor buttressed by the belief in the centrality of whiteness and the marginality of its negation—nonwhiteness.

African Americans recognized early on the wide embrace of racism and equated racism directed at Asians with racism directed at Africans. Frederick Douglass pointedly declared that the southern planters' scheme to displace African with Asian labor was stimulated by the same economic and racist motives that supported the edifice of African slavery. The white oligarchy of the South, he stated, "believed in slavery and they believe in it still." During the late 1870s and early 1880s, when a Chinese exclusion bill was being debated in the Congress, Blanche K. Bruce of Mississippi, the lone African American senator, spoke out and voted against the discriminatory legislation, and the *Christian Recorder*, an African American newspaper in Boston, editorialized: "Only a few years ago the cry was, not 'The Chinese must go,' but 'The niggers must go' and it came from the same strata of society. There is not a man to-day who rails out against the yellow man from China but would equally rail out against the black man if opportunity only afforded."[42]

41 June Mei, "Socioeconomic Origins of Emigration: Guangdong to California, 1850 to 1882," in *Labor Immigration under Capitalism: Asian Workers in the United States before World War II*, ed. Lucie Cheng and Edna Bonacich (Berkeley and Los Angeles: University of California Press, 1984), p. 220; and Sucheng Chan, *Asian Americans: An Interpretive History* (Boston: Twayne Publishers, 1991), p. 4.

42 David J. Hellwig, "Black Reactions to Chinese Immigration and the Anti-Chinese Movement: 1850–1910," *Amerasia Journal* 6, no. 2 (1979): 27, 30, 31. See also Philip S. Foner, "Reverend George Washington Woodbey: Early Twentieth Century California Black Socialist," *Journal of Negro History* 6, no. 2 (April 1976): 149–50. In their 1943 struggle for repeal of the exclusion laws, Chinese Americans recognized a common cause with African Americans in their quest for equality. Renqiu Yu, "Little Heard Voices: The Chinese Hand Laundry Alliance and the *China Daily News'* Appeal for Repeal of the Chinese Exclusion Act in 1943," in *Chinese America: History and*

In his *Observations Concerning the Increase of Mankind*, published in 1751, Benjamin Franklin divided humankind along the color line of white and nonwhite. The number of "purely white people," he noted with regret, was greatly exceeded by the number of blacks and "Tawneys," who inhabited Africa, Asia, and the Americas. Whites had cleared America of its forests and thereby made it "reflect a brighter light"; therefore, argued Franklin, "why should we . . . darken its people? Why increase the sons of Africa, by planting them in America, where we have so fair an opportunity, by excluding all Blacks and Tawneys, of increasing the lovely White . . . ?"[43] According to historian Alexander Saxton, the same racism that sought to increase the "lovely White" and that justified the expulsion and extermination of American Indians and the enslavement of Africans was carried, like so much baggage, west across the American continent, where it was applied to Asians, the majority of whom resided along the Pacific coast.[44]

Franklin's binary racial hierarchy found expression in a book written by Hinton R. Helper of North Carolina, who would become a chief Republican antislavery polemicist. Describing his visit to California in his *The Land of Gold*, published in 1855, Helper wrote of the inhabitants of a small coastal town north of San Francisco: "Bodega contains not more than four hundred inhabitants, including 'Digger' Indians, 'niggers,' and dogs, the last by far the most useful and decent of the concern." Of the Chinese, Helper charged that the "semibarbarians" had no more right to

Perspectives, 1990, ed. Marlon K. Hom et al. (San Francisco: Chinese Historical Society of America, 1990), pp. 28–29, 31–32.

43 Quoted in Takaki, *Iron Cages*, p. 14.

44 Alexander Saxton, *The Indispensable Enemy: Labor and the Anti-Chinese Movement in California* (Berkeley and Los Angeles: University of California Press, 1971), pp. 19–45; and idem, *The Rise and Fall of the White Republic: Class Politics and Mass Culture in Nineteenth Century America* (London: Verso, 1990). See also Luther W. Spoehr, "Sambo and the Heathen Chinee: Californians' Racial Stereotypes in the Late 1870s," *Pacific Historical Review* 42, no. 2 (May 1973): 185–204; and Miller, *Unwelcome Immigrant*.

be in California than "flocks of blackbirds have in a wheat field," and he offered his view of American race relations: "No inferior race of men can exist in these United States without becoming subordinate to the will of the Anglo-Americans. . . . It is so with the Negroes in the South; it is so with the Irish in the North; it is so with the Indians in New England; and it will be so with the Chinese in California."[45] Within months after the end of the Civil War, the *New York Times* warned of allied dangers: "We have four millions of degraded negroes in the South . . . and if there were to be a flood-tide of Chinese population—a population befouled with all the social vices, with no knowledge or appreciation of free institutions or constitutional liberty, with heathenish souls and heathenish propensities . . . we should be prepared to bid farewell to republicanism."[46] In popular culture, the stereotype character of the "heathen chinee" made its debut in American theater by way of the blackface minstrel shows, and Chinese were paired with black sambos in Wild West melodramas.[47]

The institutionalization of Africans and Asians as the Other, as nonwhites, was embraced in American law and proposed legislation. California's state assembly passed two companion bills excluding from the state both Chinese and African Americans, modeled on the black codes of midwestern states.[48] In 1854, Justice Charles J. Murray delivered the California Supreme Court's ruling on *The People v. George W. Hall*, in which Hall, a white man, was convicted of murder based upon the testimony of Chinese witnesses. Murray outlined the precedents that established that "no black or mulatto person, or Indian, shall be allowed to give evidence in favor of, or against a white man," and

45 Saxton, *Indispensable Enemy*, p. 18; and Caldwell, "Negroization of the Chinese Stereotype," p. 127.

46 Cited in Ronald Takaki, *Strangers from a Different Shore: A History of Asian Americans* (Boston: Little, Brown & Co., 1989), pp. 100–101.

47 Saxton, *Indispensable Enemy*, p. 20.

48 Ibid., pp. 19–20. For comparisons of Chinese and African American intelligence, see U.S. Congress, Senate, *Report of the Joint Special Committee to Investigate Chinese Immigration*, 44th Cong., 2d sess., 1877, pp. 942, 1133–34.

he considered the generic meaning of the terms "black" and "white." The words, Murray contended, were oppositional, and "black" meant "nonwhite," and "white" excluded all persons of color. In addition, the intent of the law was to shield white men "from the testimony of the degraded and demoralized caste" and to protect the very foundations of the state from the "actual and present danger" of "a race of people whom nature has marked as inferior, and who are incapable of progress or intellectual development beyond a certain point . . . differing in language, opinions, color, and physical conformation; between whom and ourselves nature has placed an impassable difference."[49] The Chinese testimony thus was inadmissible, and Hall's conviction was reversed.

Like exclusion, antimiscegenation laws helped to maintain the boundary between white and nonwhite. Virginia banned interracial marriages in 1691.[50] Besides withholding state sanction of interracial cohabitation, antimiscegenation laws sought to prevent race mixing and the creation of "hybrid races" and the "contamination" and lowering of the superior by the inferior race. The issue of Chinese and white parents, predicted John F. Miller at California's 1878 constitutional convention, would be "a hybrid of the most despicable, a mongrel of the most detestable that has ever afflicted the earth." California enacted its antimiscegenation law two years later, prohibiting marriages between whites and nonwhites, "negro, mulatto, or Mongolian."[51] Based on the same reasons for antimiscegenation laws, African, Asian, and Ameri-

49 Quoted in Wu, "*Chink!*" pp. 36–43.

50 George M. Fredrickson, *The Arrogance of Race: Historical Perspectives on Slavery, Racism, and Social Inequality* (Middletown: Wesleyan University Press, 1988), p. 196. Cf. Takaki, *Strangers from a Different Shore*, p. 101, who, like Winthrop Jordan, claims that a 1664 Maryland law that discouraged the marriage of "Negro slaves" with "freeborne English women" by imposing a penalty requiring such women and their children to be consigned into slavery should be viewed as a ban on interracial marriage. Fredrickson, however, argues that before the 1690s, bans on interracial unions were largely class as opposed to race-based.

51 Takaki, *Strangers from a Different Shore*, pp. 101–2.

can Indian children were excluded in 1860 from California's public schools designated for whites, and the state's superintendent of public instruction had the power to deny state funds to schools that violated the law. Nonwhite children attended separate schools established at public expense.[52]

Asian laborers might have been ideal replacements for African slaves because they were productive and incapable of becoming citizens, but they were also useful in that they were neither white nor black. Although some believed that the addition of yet another group of people to society would only add to the complexity and hence difficulty of race relations, others saw the entrance of Asians as a way to insulate whites from blacks. Asians were simultaneously members of the nonwhite Other, despite their sometime official classification as white, and an intermediate group between white and black. The foundations of that social hierarchy can be found in the economic relations of the plantation system. Franklin Knight informs us that in nineteenth-century Cuba, Asians were classified as whites, yet "their conditions of labor tended to be identical to those of slaves," and on plantations with a mixed labor force, Asians "bridged the gap between black and white," assisting slaves in the fields and factories but, unlike slaves, performing simple semiskilled tasks and handling machines.[53]

In Louisiana before the 1870 census, Chinese were counted as whites in the absence of a separate category for people who were neither white nor black.[54] Despite that classification, whites perceived Asians as belonging to the economic, if not social, caste assigned to Africans. In 1927, taking up a Chinese American

52 Elmer Clarence Sandmeyer, *The Anti-Chinese Movement in California* (Urbana: University of Illinois Press, 1973), p. 50; Victor Low, *The Unimpressible Race: A Century of Educational Struggle by the Chinese in San Francisco* (San Francisco: East/West Publishing Co., 1982), pp. 6–37; and Charles M. Wollenberg, *All Deliberate Speed: Segregation and Exclusion in California Schools, 1855–1975* (Berkeley and Los Angeles: University of California Press, 1976), pp. 30, 31, 39–43.

53 Knight, *Slave Society*, p. 71.

54 Cohen, *Chinese in the Post–Civil War South*, p. 167.

challenge by Gong Lum to Mississippi's Jim Crow schools, the U.S. Supreme Court, citing its 1896 landmark decision *Plessy v. Ferguson*, which set forth the "separate but equal" doctrine, affirmed the state supreme court's ruling that Chinese were nonwhite and hence "colored" and thus could be barred from schools reserved for whites. A Chinese man who married an African American woman during the 1930s recalled: "Before 1942, the Chinese had no status in Mississippi whatever. They were considered on the same status as the Negro. If a Chinese man *did* have a woman, it *had* to be a Negro." Mississippi planter William Alexander Percy described Delta society in his autobiography, *Lanterns on the Levee*, published in 1941: "Small Chinese storekeepers are almost as ubiquitous as in the South Seas. Barred from social intercourse with the whites, they smuggle through wives from China or, more frequently, breed lawfully or otherwise with the Negro."[55]

The Chinese, however, occupied an ambiguous position racially, as reflected in Louisiana's census. In 1860, Chinese were classified as whites; in 1870, they were listed as Chinese; in 1880, children of Chinese men and non-Chinese women were classed as Chinese; but in 1900, all of those children were reclassified as blacks or whites and only those born in China or with two Chinese parents were listed as Chinese.[56] In Mississippi, according to sociologist James W. Loewen, the Chinese were initially assigned "a near-Negro position" with no more legal rights or political power, but neither whites nor blacks "quite thought of them *as* Negroes," and they later served in some respects "as middlemen between white and black."[57] In fact, that function both mediated and advanced the prevailing social relations.

55 Loewen, *Mississippi Chinese*, pp. 59, 61, 66–68.
56 Cohen, *Chinese in the Post–Civil War South*, pp. 167–68. Sociologists Omi and Winant point out that racial classification is "an intensely political process" and is not a mere academic exercise but denies or provides access to resources and opportunities (Omi and Winant, *Racial Formation*, pp. 3–4).
57 Loewen, *Mississippi Chinese*, p. 60. Similarly, the biracial offspring of Africans, Europeans, and American Indians occupied an ambiguous social

In 1925, two months after the founding of A. Philip Randolph's Brotherhood of Sleeping Car Porters, the Pullman Company hired Filipinos to serve on its private cars as attendants, cooks, and busboys. African Americans, who had for more than fifty years worked in those capacities, were henceforth relegated to the position of porter and denied mobility to easier, more-lucrative positions. At first, the Brotherhood called Filipinos "scab labor" and sought their elimination from Pullman lines; however, during its most desperate years, the 1930s, the Brotherhood, unlike the racist American Federation of Labor that had excluded both Africans and Asians, recognized the hand of capital in dividing workers and saw the common plight of black and yellow: "We wish it understood," explained a policy statement, "that the Brotherhood has nothing against Filipinos. They have been used against the unionization of Pullman porters just as Negroes have been used against the unionization of white workers. . . . We will take in Filipinos as members. . . . We want our Filipino brothers to understand that it is necessary for them to join the Brotherhood in order to help secure conditions and wages which they too will benefit from."[58]

Amid such examples of solidarity, African Americans were severely tested by the capitalist system, which deliberately pitted African against Asian workers, whereby Asians were used to discipline African workers and to depress their wages. The root cause of African and Asian American oppression was further clouded by mutual ethnocentrism and prejudice that frequently devolved from the ideas and practices of the master class. It is not surprising, therefore, that some African Americans, like Howard University professor Kelly Miller, saw a danger in linking the

and legal position in the South. See Adele Logan Alexander, *Ambiguous Lives: Free Women of Color in Rural Georgia, 1789–1879* (Fayetteville: University of Arkansas Press, 1991).

58 Barbara M. Posadas, "The Hierarchy of Color and Psychological Adjustment in an Industrial Environment: Filipinos, the Pullman Company, and the Brotherhood of Sleeping Car Porters," *Labor History* 23, no. 3 (1982): 363.

claims of African and Asian Americans. "The Negro is an American citizen whose American residence and citizenry reach further back than the great majority of the white race," wrote Miller. "He has from the beginning contributed a full share of the glory and grandeur of America and his claims to patrimony are his just and rightful due. The Japanese, on the other hand, is the eleventh hour comer, and is claiming the privilege of those who have borne the heat and burden of the day."[59]

What is surprising, instead, was the extent and degree of solidarity felt by African Americans toward Asian Americans. The *Chicago Defender* explained that Chinese and Japanese learned from racist America, having been "taught to scorn the Race or lose the little footing they may now boast," and Mary Church Terrell believed that Japanese shunned African Americans in an attempt to avoid the stigma of inferiority that whites had placed upon blacks.[60] And despite dismay over Asian American ethnocentrism, African Americans steadfastly realized that the enemy was white supremacy and that anti-Asianism was anti-Africanism in another guise. Thus, in 1906 and 1907, when the San Francisco school board ruled that Japanese children had to attend "Oriental schools" and when President Theodore Roosevelt intervened to avoid an international incident, the *Colored American Magazine* declared: "We are with the President in the California muddle, for as California would treat the Japanese she would also treat the Negroes. It is not that we desire to attend schools with the whites at all, per se, but the principle involved in the attempt to classify us as inferiors—not because we are necessarily inferior, but on the grounds of color—forms the crux of our protest."[61]

The Philippine–American war, like many of America's imperialist wars, provided an extraordinary test for American minori-

59 Kelly Miller, *The Everlasting Stain* (Washington, D.C.: Associated Publishers, 1924), p. 163.

60 David J. Hellwig, "Afro-American Reactions to the Japanese and the Anti-Japanese Movement, 1906–1924," *Phylon* 38, no. 1 (March 1977): 103.

61 *The Colored American Magazine* 12, no. 3 (March 1907): 169.

ties. The late nineteenth century, America's period of manifest destiny and expansionism overseas, was a time of severe repression at home for African Americans. Shouldering the white man's burden was an opportunity for making domestic claims and gains, but at the expense of peoples of color with whom African Americans identified: the Cubans, Puerto Ricans, and Filipinos. Bishop Henry M. Turner of the African Methodist Episcopal church characterized the U.S. presence in the Philippines as "an unholy war of conquest" against "a feeble band of sable patriots," and Frederick L. McGhee, a founder of the Niagara Movement, observed that America was out "to rule earth's inferior races, and if they object make war upon them," and thus concluded that African Americans could not support the war against the Filipinos.[62] From the Philippines, an African American soldier wrote home to Milwaukee, where his letter was published in the *Wisconsin Weekly Advocate* on May 17, 1900:

I have mingled freely with the natives and have had talks with American colored men here in business and who have lived here for years, in order to learn of them the cause of their [Filipino] dissatisfaction and the reason for this insurrection, and I must confess they have a just grievance. . . . [Americans] began to apply home treatment for colored peoples: cursed them as damned niggers, steal [from] and ravish them, rob them on the street of their small change, take from the fruit vendors whatever suited their fancy, and kick the poor unfortunate if he complained, desecrate their church property, and after fighting began, looted everything in sight, burning, robbing the graves.

I have seen with my own eyes carcasses lying bare in the boiling sun, the results of raids on receptacles for the dead in search of diamonds. The [white] troops, thinking we would be proud to emulate their conduct. . . . One fellow . . . told me how some fellows he knew had cut off

---

62 Willard B. Gatewood, Jr., *"Smoked Yankees" and the Struggle for Empire: Letters from Negro Soldiers, 1898–1902* (Urbana: University of Illinois Press, 1971), p. 13; and William Loren Katz, *The Black West* (Seattle: Open Hand Publishing, 1987), pp. 323–24. On African American soldiers and the Vietnam War, see Byron G. Fiman, Jonathan F. Borus, and M. Duncan Stanton, "Black–White and American–Vietnamese Relations among Soldiers in Vietnam," *Journal of Social Issues* 31, no. 4 (1975): 39–48.

a native woman's arm in order to get a fine inlaid bracelet. . . . They talked with impunity of "niggers" to our soldiers, never once thinking that they were talking to home "niggers" and should they be brought to remember that at home this is the same vile epithet they hurl at us, they beg pardon and make some effiminate [sic] excuse about what the Filipino is called.

I want to say right here that if it were not for the sake of the 10,000,000 black people in the United States, God alone knows on which side of the subject I would be.

General Robert P. Hughes, a commander in the Philippines, entertained some doubt over "which side of the subject" African American troops fell when he reported: "The darkey troops . . . mixed with the natives at once. Whenever they came together they became great friends." And according to a contemporary report, white troops deserted because they found the Army irksome, whereas black troops deserted "for the purpose of joining the insurgents," whose cause they saw as the struggle of all colored people against white domination. Perhaps the most famous African American deserter was David Fagan of the Twenty-fourth Infantry, who joined the Filipino freedom fighters and fought the Yankee imperialists for two years.[63] After the war—the war in which General "Howlin' Jake" Smith ordered his men to "kill and burn, kill and burn, the more you kill and the more you burn the more you please me" and the war that cost over 600,000 Filipino lives for the sake of "civilizing" those who remained—about 500 African Americans, many of whom had married Filipino women, chose to stay in the Philippines.[64]

Asians, like African Americans, resisted their exploitation and subjugation, and in the shared struggle for equality secured the blessings of democracy for all peoples. On this point, we must be

63 Gatewood, *"Smoked Yankees,"* pp. 14, 15.

64 Luzviminda Francisco, "The First Vietnam: The Philippine–American War, 1899–1902," in *Letters in Exile: An Introductory Reader on the History of Pilipinos in America,* ed. Jesse Quinsaat (Los Angeles: UCLA Asian American Studies Center, 1976), pp. 15, 19; and Gatewood, *"Smoked Yankees,"* p. 15.

clear. Inclusion, human dignity, and civil rights are not "black issues," nor are they gains for one group made at the expense of another. Likewise, the democratization of America fought for by African and Asian Americans was advantageous for both groups. The "separate but equal" doctrine of *Plessy v. Ferguson*, for instance, was a basis for the 1927 case *Gong Lum v. Rice*, and both were cited as precedents in the 1954 *Brown v. Board of Education* decision.[65] In addition to those parallel and conjoining struggles for freedom, African and Asian American lives converge like rivers through time. In full knowledge of intergroup conflicts and hatreds among America's minorities and their sources and functions, I will recall here only acts of antiracialism and solidarity between Asian and African Americans.[66]

During the late 1840s and early 1850s, African Americans gathered with Chinese and whites at San Francisco's Washerwoman's Bay to wash clothes, and relations between Chinese and Africans were apparently friendly. William Newby, a prominent African American leader in the city, reported to Frederick Douglass "that the Chinese were the most mistreated group in the state and that blacks were the only people who did not abuse them." Both shared with Indians, Newby pointed out, the "same civil rights disabilities," insofar as they were denied the franchise and debarred from the courts.[67] In 1869, the first Japanese settlers arrived in California and established the Wakamatsu Tea and Silk Farm Colony near Sacramento. The colony failed, but among that

---

65 Richard Kluger, *Simple Justice: The History of* Brown v. Board of Education *and Black America's Struggle for Equality* (New York: Vintage Books, 1975), pp. 120–22, 191, 423, 448, 554, 565–66, 670, 703–4.

66 On African and Asian American conflicts, see Arnold Shankman's three publications: "'Asiatic Ogre' or 'Desirable Citizen'? The Image of Japanese Americans in the Afro-American Press, 1867–1933," *Pacific Historical Review* 46, no. 4 (November 1977): 567–87; "Black on Yellow: Afro-Americans View Chinese-Americans," *Phylon* 39, no. 1 (Spring 1978): 1–17; and *Ambivalent Friends: Afro-Americans View the Immigrant* (Westport: Greenwood Press, 1982).

67 Rudolph M. Lapp, *Blacks in Gold Rush California* (New Haven: Yale University Press, 1977), pp. 104–5.

group of adventurers was Masumizu Kuninosuke, who married an African American woman, had three daughters and a son, and operated a fish store in Sacramento for many years.[68] Sacramento Chinese shared their church with African Americans for some time during the nineteenth century, and in San Francisco, Jean Ng, an African American married to a Chinese American, was buried in a Chinese cemetery. In 1913, Charley Sing, a Mobile, Alabama, Chinese laundryman, tried to get permission to marry Lillie Lambert, an African American.[69] A Filipino band made sweet music under the baton of its African American conductor, Walter Loving, at the San Francisco Panama-Pacific International Exposition in 1915, and touring African American musicians sometimes stayed at Chinese-owned lodging houses in San Francisco.[70] In 1927, Lemon Lee Sing, a sixty-eight-year-old Chinese laundryman in New York City, sought permission to adopt Firman Smith, an abandoned African American child he had found sleeping in a hallway. Sing fed and clothed Firman, enrolled him in school, and ultimately won from the courts custody of the child.[71] Sam Lee, a Chinese restaurant owner in Washington, D.C., refused to fire one of his African American employees, despite threats on his life, while in Chicago, in 1929, a Chinese restaurant was dynamited for serving African Americans.[72]

Many of us, Asian and Pacific Americans, several generations native-born, came of age during America's imperialist war in

68 Bill Hosokawa, *Nisei: The Quiet Americans* (New York: William Morrow, 1969), pp. 31–33.

69 Lapp, *Blacks in Gold Rush California*, pp. 104–5, 109–10; Douglas Daniels, *Pioneer Urbanites: A Social and Cultural History of Black San Francisco* (Philadelphia: Temple University Press, 1980), p. 97; and Shankman, *Ambivalent Friends*, pp. 31–32. On marriages between Africans and Asians in the South, see Loewen, *Mississippi Chinese*, pp. 135–53; Cohen, *Chinese in the Post–Civil War South*, pp. 149–72; and Doris Black, "The Black Chinese," *Sepia*, December 1975, pp. 19–24.

70 Kenneth G. Goode, *California's Black Pioneers: A Brief Historical Survey* (Santa Barbara: McNally & Loftin, 1974), p. 110; and Shankman, *Ambivalent Friends*, p. 30.

71 Shankman, "Black on Yellow," pp. 15–16.

72 Ibid., p. 16.

Vietnam and the African American freedom struggle of the 1960s. Many of us found our identity by reading Franz Fanon and Malcolm X, Cheikh Anta Diop and W. E. B. Du Bois, Leopold Senghor and Langston Hughes. Many more of us, however, have migrated to the United States since 1965; we came of age in Reagan's America, the era of yuppies and yappies, and wasn't that the time when history came to an end?—announced, significantly, by an Asian American.[73] During fall semester 1990, I asked my Asian American students with whom they felt a closer kinship: African or European Americans? They almost universally expressed affinity with whites, and I recalled how in 1944, amid strident, anti-Japanese wartime propaganda and concentration camps for Japanese Americans, the *Negro Digest* conducted a poll among its readers. To the question, "Should negroes discriminate against Japanese?" 66 percent in the North and West and 53 percent in the South answered "No."[74] During spring semester 1991, I asked my Asian American students the same question, and all of them claimed kinship with African Americans, and I recalled how in 1960, Yuri Kochiyama, born in San Pedro, California, and interned during the war at the Jerome concentration camp in Arkansas, and her husband, a veteran of World War II, enrolled in the Harlem Freedom School established by Malcolm X to learn African American history and to engage in the struggle for civil rights.[75]

We are a kindred people, African and Asian Americans. We share a history of migration, cultural interaction, and trade. We share a history of colonization, oppression and exploitation, and

73 Francis Fukuyama, "The End of History?" *National Interest* 16 (Summer 1989): 3–18. The symbol of a man of color, particularly a man of Japanese ancestry, schooled in the West proclaiming "the triumph of the West" added substance to the finality of that "triumph," especially to those dubbed by Allan Bloom "we faithful defenders of the Western Alliance" (Allan Bloom, "Responses to Fukuyama," *National Interest* 16 [Summer 1989]: 19).

74 *Negro Digest*, September 1944, p. 66.

75 Yuri Kochiyama, "Because Movement Work Is Contagious," *Gidra*, 1990, pp. 6, 10.

parallel and mutual struggles for freedom. We are a kindred people, forged in the fire of white supremacy and tempered in the water of resistance. Yet that kinship has been obscured from our range of vision, and that common cause, turned into a competition for access and resources. We have not yet realized the full meaning of Du Bois's poetic insight: "The stars of dark Andromeda belong up there in the great heaven that hangs above this tortured world. Despite the crude and cruel motives behind her shame and exposure, her degradation and enchaining, the fire and freedom of black Africa, with the uncurbed might of her consort Asia, are indispensable to the fertilizing of the universal soil of mankind, which Europe alone never would nor could give this aching world."[76]

Is yellow black or white? In 1914, Takao Ozawa, a Japanese national, filed for naturalization on the basis of his over twenty-eight-year residence in the United States and the degree of his "Americanization." Further, Ozawa contended, Asians were not specifically excluded under the naturalization laws, and thus he should be considered a "free white person." The U.S. Supreme Court rendered its decision on November 13, 1922, rejecting Ozawa's application and claim. Only whites and Africans were accorded the privilege of naturalization, wrote Associate Justice George Sutherland, and although the founding fathers might not have contemplated Asians within the meaning of either black or white, it was evident that they were not included within the category of "free white persons." Ruled Sutherland: "the appellant is clearly of a race which is not Caucasian, and therefore belongs entirely outside the zone on the negative side."[77] The marginaliza-

76 W. E. B. Du Bois, *The World and Africa, An Inquiry into the Part Which Africa Has Played in World History* (New York: International Publishers, 1965), p. 260.

77 Frank F. Chuman, *The Bamboo People: The Law and Japanese-Americans* (Del Mar, Calif.: Publisher's Inc., 1976), pp. 70–71. See also Yuji Ichioka, *The Issei: The World of the First Generation Japanese Immigrants, 1885–1924* (New York: Free Press, 1988), pp. 210–26.

tion of Asians—"entirely outside the zone"—was accompanied by their negation as "nonwhites"—"on the negative side"—in this institutionalization of the racial state. Yellow is not white.

But yellow is not black either, and the question posed is, in a real sense, a false and mystifying proposition. The question is only valid within the meanings given to and played out in the American racial formation, relations that have been posited as a black and white dyad. There are other options. Whites considered Asians "as blacks" or, at the very least, as replacements for blacks in the post–Civil War South, but whites imported Chinese precisely because they were not blacks and were thus perpetual aliens, who could never vote. Similarly, whites upheld Asians as "near-whites" or "whiter than whites" in the model minority stereotype, and yet Asians experienced and continue to face white racism "like blacks" in educational and occupational barriers and ceilings and in anti-Asian abuse and physical violence. Further, in both instances, Asians were used to "discipline" African Americans (and other minorities according to the model minority stereotype). That marginalization of Asians, in fact, within a black and white racial formation, "disciplines" both Africans and Asians and constitutes the essential site of Asian American oppression. By seeing only black and white, the presence and absence of all color, whites render Asians, American Indians, and Latinos invisible, ignoring the gradations and complexities of the full spectrum between the racial poles. At the same time, Asians share with Africans the status and repression of nonwhites—as the Other—and therein lies the debilitating aspect of Asian–African antipathy and the liberating nature of African–Asian unity.

On November 27, 1991, about 1,200 people gathered outside Los Angeles City Hall to participate in a prayer vigil sponsored by the African–Korean American Christian Alliance, a group formed the previous month. A newspaper reporter described the "almost surreal" scene:

Elderly Korean American women twirling and dancing with homeless men in front of the podium. Koreans and street people in a human chain, holding hands but not looking at each other. Shoes and clothing ruined by cow manure, which had been freshly spread over the rally grounds in an unfortunate oversight. Alliance co-chair Rev. Hee Min Park startled rally-goers when he began quoting from Martin Luther King's famous "I have a dream" speech. Black homeless people listened in stunned silence at first, as the pastor's voice with a heavy immigrant accent filled the slain black minister's familiar words. Then a few began chanting "Amen" in response to Park's litany.[78]

Park's articulation of King's dream reminds me of Maxine Hong Kingston's version of the story of Ts'ai Yen, a Han poetess kidnapped by "barbarians," in her book *The Woman Warrior*. Although she had lived among them for twelve years, Ts'ai Yen still considered the people primitive, until one evening, while inside her tent, she heard "music tremble and rise like desert wind." Night after night the barbarians blew on their flutes, and try as she might, Ts'ai Yen could not block out the sound. "Then, out of Ts'ai Yen's tent, which was apart from the others, the barbarians heard a woman's voice singing, as if to her babies, a song so high and clear, it matched the flutes." After she was ransomed, Ts'ai Yen brought her songs back to her people, who sang them to their own instruments. Concluded Kingston, "They translated well."[79]

78 *Korea Times*, December 9, 1991. In Los Angeles, after a meeting between the Korean American Grocers Association and several African American gang leaders on May 25, 1992, the merchants announced plans to hire gang members, and a participant in the negotiations reported a "total bond between the two groups," which included the widely feared gangs the Bloods and the Crips (*Asian Week*, May 29, 1992; and *Korea Times*, June 8, 1992).

79 Maxine Hong Kingston, *The Woman Warrior: Memoirs of a Girlhood among Ghosts* (New York: Alfred A. Knopf, 1976), pp. 241–43.

3

Recentering Women

Y O U must not tell anyone,' my mother said, 'what I am about to tell you. In China your father had a sister who killed herself. She jumped into the family well. We say that your father has all brothers because it is as if she had never been born.'"[1] Thus began Maxine Hong Kingston's story "No Name Woman" in her 1975 book, *The Woman Warrior: Memoirs of a Girlhood among Ghosts.* Kingston's narrator tells the story of her aunt, who committed suicide after having given birth to a girl, conceived not of her husband, who had gone to sojourn in Gold Mountain, but of another man. The story is rich with symbolism and lays the foundation for Kingston's entire collection of "talk stories," explicating the position of women in Chinese and Chinese American culture.

The aunt, this "no name woman," like all other "no name women," existed on the margins of Asian culture, dominated by a patriarchy that held that "it was better to raise geese than girls." Even in death she was punished by being deliberately forgotten, unconnected to the living—the descent line—and became a "wandering ghost," who was "always hungry, always needing," begging or stealing food from other ghosts, who had living kin to give them gifts of food and money.

The aunt, this "no name woman," was expunged from the family record, "as if she had never been born," and even her name was erased from memory, like all the countless other "no name women," who fail to appear in the pages of history books "as if

1 Kingston, *Woman Warrior*, p. 3.

they had never been born." Her illegitimate child, too, who died with her, could not have been included within the circle of kin, because she posed a severe critique of male dominance, having been conceived out of either rape or defiance of "female chastity."

The aunt, this "no name woman," defied exclusion, and her story passed from mother to daughter, albeit in secret and out of earshot of the narrator's father. And the aunt's memory haunts Kingston's narrator: "her ghost [is] drawn to me because now, after fifty years of neglect, I alone devote pages of paper to her, though not origamied into houses and clothes." Still, the telling and recording were acts of resistance, and the paper, however fragile and brittle, gives reality to the figurative hand that reaches from the depths of the family well to touch us, her kin, today.

Asian American history is replete with the deeds of men. Women constitute a forgotten factor in Asian American history. They have "no name." During Korea's Yi dynasty (1392–1910), women had no names of their own. They were identified relative to men, as so-and-so's daughter, so-and-so's wife, and so-and-so's mother. When she married, not her name but her family name was entered into her husband's family registry, and her name was removed from her family registry, where only the name of her husband was recorded.[2] Having no name thus meant being defined in relation to men, and having no name meant erasure and ostracism.

The exclusion of Asian women from the "pages of paper" is not without meaning or effect. Their omission serves to bolster a system of male dominance, a system of privilege and oppression. "The scholarly disciplines, like society at large, are dominated by those on the inside," wrote political scientist Jo Freeman. "They reflect a desire to explain, justify, and maintain the status quo of human and institutional relationships. The result is a consistency of approach that is almost stifling." The inclusion of women on

2 Yung-Chung Kim, ed. and trans., *Women of Korea: A History from Ancient Times to 1945* (Seoul, Korea: Ewha Woman's University Press, 1976), pp. 85–86.

those "pages of paper"—their recentering—challenges those relations of power and presents a truer account of our collective past. "A feminist perspective is practical as well as theoretical," concluded Freeman; "it illuminates possibilities for the future as well as criticizes the limitations of the present."[3]

This project, this recentering of women, subverts the social relations of patriarchy and, at the same time, deconstructs the body of knowledge upon which those relations of power are built. Historian Connie Young Yu wrote of two kinds of histories: one written by outsiders about Asian Americans; the other recorded in the collective memories of Asian Americans, "what we learn in the family chain of generations." Within the pages of the former, Yu noted, Asians were frequently absent or caricatured, but within the latter Asians had faces, names, and identities. "Our grandmothers are our historical links," she wrote, and although "family papers, photographs, old trunks that have traveled across the ocean several times filled with clothes, letters, and mementos provide a documentary on our immigration," her grandmother, mother, and other women "fill in the narrative." "I keep looking at the artifacts of the past: the photograph of my grandmother when she was an innocent young bride and the sad face in the news photo taken on Angel Island," recalled Yu. "I visit the immigration barracks from time to time. . . . I see the view of sky and water from the window out of which my grandmother gazed. My mother told me how, after visiting hours, she would walk to the ferry and turn back to see her mother waving to her from this window. . . . When I leave the building, emerging from the darkness into the glaring sunlight of the island, I too turn back to look at my grandmother's window."[4] That backward glance, to her grandmother, linked their lives, and her grandmother's window opened for Yu her past.

3 Jo Freeman, ed., *Women: A Feminist Perspective* (Palo Alto, Calif.: Mayfield Publishing, 1975), pp. xix–xx.

4 Connie Young Yu, "The World of Our Grandmothers," in *Making Waves: An Anthology of Writings by and about Asian American Women*, ed. Asian Women United of California (Boston: Beacon Press, 1989), pp. 33–42.

Pioneering historian Gerda Lerner explained that this project of recentering women was not a simple act of taking women from the margins of history and fitting them "into the empty spaces" of men's history. After all, she declared, "women are and always have been at least half of mankind and most of the time have been the majority of mankind"; in fact, "the truth is that history, as written and perceived up to now, is the history of a minority, who may well turn out to be the 'subgroup.'"[5] At the same time, recentering Asian women in American history is a particularly thorny problem, because of the demographics of Asian migration. Women were barely present in the bachelor society that typified much of the early period of Asian American history.[6] Chinese women, for instance, comprised only 7.2 percent of the Chinese in America in 1870 and a mere 3.6 percent in 1890; Japanese women constituted 4 percent of the Japanese population on the U.S. mainland in 1900 and 12.6 percent in 1910; of all the Filipinos admitted into California between 1920 and 1929, only 6.7 percent were women; Korean women comprised 25 percent of the Koreans on the mainland in 1920 and 34 percent in 1930; and of the 474 Asian Indians in America in 1909, none were women.[7] Given those statistics, how could one write a woman-centered

5 Gerda Lerner, "Placing Women in History: Definitions and Challenges," *Feminist Studies* 3, no. 1/2 (Fall 1975): 12–13.

6 See George Anthony Peffer, "From under the Sojourner's Shadow: A Historiographical Study of Chinese Female Immigration to America, 1852–1882," *Journal of American Ethnic History* 2, no. 3 (Spring 1992): 41–67, for a critical review of the sojourner thesis and its influence on Chinese women's history.

7 Sucheng Chan, "The Exclusion of Chinese Women, 1870–1943," in *Entry Denied: Exclusion and the Chinese Community in America, 1882–1943*, ed. Sucheng Chan (Philadelphia: Temple University Press, 1991), p. 94; Yamato Ichihashi, *Japanese in the United States* (Stanford: Stanford University Press, 1932), p. 72; *Facts about Filipino Immigration into California*, State of California, Department of Industrial Relations, Special Bulletin no. 3 (San Francisco, 1930), p. 32; Takaki, *Strangers from a Different Shore*, p. 273; and Karen Leonard, "Marriage and Family Life among Early Asian Indian Immigrants," in *From India to America: A Brief History of Immigration; Problems of Discrimination; Admission and Assimilation*, ed. S. Chandrasekhar (La Jolla: Population Review Publications, 1982), p. 67.

history—"the majority's past," in Lerner's words—and remain faithful to the historical realities?

Asian men in America were not solitary figures moving in splendid isolation but were intimately connected to women in Asia, like the "no name" aunt of Kingston's narrator, who built and maintained the solid world of family and community. Recentering women extends the range of Asian American history, from bachelor societies in Hawaii and the U.S. mainland to the villages and households in Asia, in an intricate and dynamic pattern of relations. Transcending American exceptionalism is but one of the consequences of a woman-centered history. While Asian American historiography might have begun with Europeans and European Americans imagining and witnessing Asia, the primary contexts of Asian American history, it might be argued, comprise that entrance of Asians into the European consciousness, together with the intersection of Asians with Africans and the agency of generative societies in Asia, where women held up half the sky.

Europe's feminization of Asia, its taking possession, working over, and penetration of Asia, was preceded and paralleled by Asian men's subjugation of Asian women. Europe's intellect and vigor in contrast to Asia's sensuality and softness were the counterparts of the Asian "yang," or male attributes of light, strength, agency, and the endowments of the "firm nature of heaven," as opposed to "yin," or female traits of dark, weak, passive, and the "yielding nature of the earth." Although those tenth-century B.C.E. cosmological foundations were originally conceived of as equal and complementary, they were reborn as hierarchical relations, as the heavens rule over the earth, in the teachings of Confucius and his disciples and became the dominant ideology perhaps from the second century B.C.E.[8]

Those socially defined attributions of gender and gender relations were presented to women as "virtues," like women's bound feet, a practice begun during the Sung dynasty (960–1279), which

8 Elisabeth Croll, *Feminism and Socialism in China* (London: Routledge & Kegan Paul, 1978), p. 12.

were deified as paragons of feminine beauty and worshipped in cults of the "golden lotus" and "golden lily." Throughout her life, the ideal woman was subject to her father as a child, her husband when married, and her sons when widowed, and she was taught the four "virtues": first, a woman should know her place in the universe and behave in compliance with the natural order of things; second, she should guard her words and not chatter too much or bore others; third, she must be clean and adorn herself to please men; and fourth, she should not shirk from her household duties.[9]

As for the cult of the "golden lotus," the poet felt inadequate when confronted with the matchless beauty of bound feet:

> *Anointed with fragrance, she takes lotus steps;*
> *Though often sad, she steps with swift lightness.*
> *She dances like the wind, leaving no physical trace. . . .*
> *Look at them in the palm of your hand,*
> *So wondrously small that they defy description.*[10]

Women frequently saw their bound feet in a different light. "I was inflicted with the pain of footbinding when I was seven years old," remembered a woman. "I was an active child who liked to jump about, but from then on my free and optimistic nature vanished. . . . My feet felt on fire and I couldn't sleep; Mother struck me for crying . . . I tried to hide but was forced to walk on my feet." There was a saying, "for every pair of bound feet a bucket full of tears."[11] The practice, among certain classes and ethnicities of Chinese women, secured their dependence upon men and served to confine them within the household gates. During the 1890s, reformists and poets criticized footbinding as repressive and obsolete and formed the Unbound-Feet Society and Natural Foot Society beginning in 1892. Still, footbinding continued, es-

9 Ibid., pp. 13, 14, 19.
10 Ibid., p. 19.
11 Ibid.

pecially in certain rural areas, well into the first few decades of the twentieth century.[12]

Although Chinese men depicted Chinese women as weak, timid, and sexually available, they also saw them as dangerous, powerful, and sexually insatiable. Historian Joanna F. Handlin points out that the cults of footbinding, chastity, and virginity and the rules that oppressed women were the reactions of men to women's resistance—to "the aggressive behavior of women"—and to economic necessity and women's expanded opportunities brought about by the urbanization and industrialization of the nineteenth century.[13] Some of that "aggression" was displayed by women in their participation in the Taiping rebellion (1851–64), begun in Guangxi and Guangdong provinces. The Taiping rebels called for equality between men and women and for an end to Confucian status ethics, footbinding, and polygamy. "Because they were so active," a historian wrote, "Taiping women bared their large (unbound) feet and preferred to wear pants instead of skirts. Their odd appearance—large feet, red-turbaned heads, and pants—probably caused the 'civilized' people of the Chinese empire to regard them as an inferior race vastly different from the Han people, a race somewhere between monkeys and human beings on the evolutionary chain. But it was precisely these women who fought even more bravely than the men."[14]

Nameless, except for her identification as "third daughter of the Su family," Sanniang Su led a Taiping army of 2,000 troops against the Qing government, and the Taiping women's forces numbered over 10,000 by 1853. A Qing official, sent to assess the situation at Nanjing, the Taiping capital, recommended to his su-

12 Ibid., pp. 45–51.

13 Joanna F. Handlin, "Lu K'un's New Audience: The Influence of Women's Literacy on Sixteenth-Century Thought," in *Women in Chinese Society*, ed. Margery Wolf and Roxane Witke (Stanford: Stanford University Press, 1975), p. 14.

14 Kazuko Ono, *Chinese Women in a Century of Revolution, 1850–1950*, ed. Joshua A. Fogel (Stanford: Stanford University Press, 1989), p. 8.

periors: "After we recapture the city, all the Guangxi women should be executed. Absolutely no leniency or mercy should be shown them. For they have been just as courageous and fierce as male soldiers in defending the city."[15] In the territories they captured, the Taipings prohibited footbinding, and Guangxi women inspected and forcibly removed the restricting cloth, inflicting corporal punishment on women who failed to unbind their feet. Unbound feet served the purposes of both women's liberation and increasing her capacity for manual labor, which benefited an authoritarian state. Speculating upon the impact of Taiping liberalization, historian Kazuko Ono asked: "Were there no women who relished their first encounter with the outside world after having been virtually imprisoned at home because of the traditional dictate that 'women must not go past the gate'? And, however strenuous the forced labor, were there no women who felt joy in being able to chat together while working?"[16] The Taiping Heavenly Kingdom of Great Peace came to an end in 1864 at the hands of the Qing government and foreign powers, but the great peasant war that had engulfed much of the area from which the majority of Chinese migrants to America came began the emancipation of Chinese women—these "big-footed barbarian women"—who had instigated the drive for their own liberation.

Marriage resistance was another way by which women sought self-determination in Guangdong Province from the early nineteenth to the early twentieth century. Some women in the rural areas of the Canton delta refused to marry and organized themselves into sisterhoods after having undergone a hairdressing ritual and taken a vow; others engaged in "spirit marriage" (marriage to a deceased man) or "compensation marriage" (marriage with monetary compensation to avoid cohabitation with her husband), which granted to the principals the status accorded to married women and the comforts of remembrance after death

15 Ibid., pp. 8–9, 10.
16 Ibid., pp. 13–14.

and enabled them to retain their earnings and avoid the necessity for sex and reproduction. Although marriage resistance was likely limited to comparatively few women and confined to certain localities in the province, it was widely known among the Cantonese and was particularly important among villages where most of the men had gone and left behind mainly women and children.[17]

Many girls lived in women's houses until they married or took the vows of spinsterhood, and they formed a cohort of "sisters," who moved about freely in public, visiting temples or attending theater performances and festivals in large groups. For girls, the houses were an important agent of socialization, where information, instruction, and secrets were passed on, contributing in some cases "to a vigorous anti-marital bias among unmarried girls." Married women sometimes joined these sisterhoods to prevent their husbands from taking on concubines or to flee confinement and loneliness for the relative freedom and sisterly support of the women's houses. Other women cited their fear of becoming a "slave of men," a "human propagation machine," or a hostage in marriage to the "wrong type" of man as their reason for entering the sisterhoods. Still others expressed a preference for lesbianism, and some professed celibacy as a religious principle or as an insurance against rape.[18] Underlying these divergent reasons for marriage resistance was a singular desire for the self-definition of women, apart from the men, who had sought to define and control so much of their lives.[19]

17 Marjorie Topley, "Marriage Resistance in Rural Kwangtung," in *Women in Chinese Society*, ed. Wolf and Witke, pp. 67–68, 72–73; and Janice E. Stockard, *Daughters of the Canton Delta: Marriage Patterns and Economic Strategies in South China, 1860–1930* (Stanford: Stanford University Press, 1989). For a gossipy account of celibate Chinese women in Malaysia, see Sit Yin Fong, *Tales of Chinatown* (Singapore: Heinemann Asia, 1983), pp. 111–17.

18 Topley, "Marriage Resistance," pp. 73–74, 76–77, 79; and Stockard, *Daughters*, pp. 32–37, 40, 46.

19 Although marriage resistance might have been oppositional to patriarchal repression, it frequently conformed to patriarchy's ideals and institu-

Women who had married migrant men were virtual widows, having to serve their husbands' parents and remain sexually faithful to distant men, who were free to engage the service of prostitutes or take on other wives. Toishan folk songs capture some of those women's anguish:

> *You bid farewell to the village well, setting out*
> *   overseas.*
> *It has been eight years, or is it already ten, that*
> *   you haven't thought of home?*
> *Willow branches are brilliant, fields exuberantly*
> *   green;*
> *Inside her bedroom, the young woman's bosom*
> *   is filled with frustration.*

> *I am still young, with a husband, yet a widow.*
> *The pillow is cold, so frightening.*
> *Thoughts swirl inside my mind, chaotic like hemp*
> *   fibers;*
> *Separated by thousands of miles, how can I reach*
> *   him?*
> *Thinking of him tenderly—*
> *I toss and turn, to no avail.*
> *He is far away, at the edge of the sky by the*
> *   clouds;*
> *I long for his return, especially since it's midnight*
> *   now.*

> *O, don't ever marry a daughter to a man from*
> *   Gold Mountain;*
> *Lonely and sad, her only companion is her*
> *   cooking pot!*

tions. Thus, its various forms might have been both resistance and acquiescence. For a critical review of the literature and personal narratives, see Vanessa Chien, "Unravelling Popular Spinsterhood in the Canton Delta: Marriage Resistance Re-imagined" (B.A. thesis, Amherst College, 1992).

My husband, because of poverty, has gone to
   Gold Mountain.
With only a petty sum of capital, he cannot make
   the journey home.
The road to Gold Mountain is extremely perilous
   and difficult;
At home, in grief and pain, my longing eyes
   piercing through the horizon, waiting.
No way is life better than farming at home:
Toiling for half a year, relaxing the rest;
You greet your parents in the mornings,
You are with your wife at nights.
Everyone is happy, smiles all over their faces;
Festivals, parties, New Year's Eve celebrations—
You and me, hu   nd wife, O, how amorous
   will that be!

Although many wives must have missed their husbands, and husbands their wives, the women in China did not simply retire to their bedrooms "filled with frustration," nor were their only companions their cooking pots. They labored in home, field, and factory, they joined and led rebel and smuggler groups, and they banded together as sisters and helped forge a growing feminist consciousness that coalesced with the 1898 Reform Movement, which proposed women's education and an end to the practice of footbinding as part of a program of national reconciliation and reconstruction.[21]

Glimpses of that selfsame yearning for individual freedom can be seen among the first, extraordinary women who ventured forth to America. Unlike most Asian men, who migrated to America to gain the resources needed to establish patriarchal households,

20 Marlon Kau Hom, "Some Cantonese Folksongs on the American Experience," *Western Folklore* 42, no. 2 (April 1983): 129–30.

21 Ono, *Chinese Women*, pp. 23–46. Despite its advocacy of some aspects of women's liberation, the 1898 Reform Movement can hardly be called a feminist movement.

some of the first women who migrated to America sought to flee gender oppression and gain a measure of independence. In that sense, women's migration was a form of resistance. The first Chinese woman in Hawaii and California was probably Marie Seise, the only name by which we know her today, as listed in the Trinity Episcopal Church records in San Francisco. Seise ran away from home in Guangzhou to escape being sold into slavery, married a Portuguese sailor in Macao, and became a domestic servant to an American family following the death of her husband at sea. Seise was taken to Hawaii by that family in 1837, where she remained for six years, and after returning to China, she entered into the service of the Charles V. Gillespie household and accompanied that family to California in 1848.[22]

Maria Hwang, a Korean woman, left her husband to go to Hawaii, because despite her objections, her husband had taken a concubine. One day she defiantly announced to him: "I am no longer going to live with you, I am going to take my three children to America and educate them. *I shall become a wonderful woman!*" (emphasis added). Hwang signed a labor contract with the Hawaii Sugar Planters' Association and took her daughter, two sons, and sister-in-law to a sugar plantation on the island of Maui. The women worked in the fields during the day and mended, ironed, and washed clothing at night and on Sundays, saving for the children's education. One of her sons eventually earned a degree from Hamilton Law College in Chicago, but he was prevented from practicing law because he was not, and could not become, a U.S. citizen. He joined the women picking grapes in California's vineyards and later became an herbalist.[23]

Another Korean woman told of her strong desire to flee con-

22 Tin-Yuke Char, comp. and ed., *The Sandalwood Mountains: Readings and Stories of the Early Chinese in Hawaii* (Honolulu: University Press of Hawaii, 1975), pp. 42–44; and Judy Yung, *Chinese Women of America: A Pictorial History* (Seattle: University of Washington Press, 1986), p. 14.

23 Harold Hakwon Sunoo and Sonia Shinn Sunoo, "The Heritage of the First Korean Women Immigrants in the United States: 1903–1924," *Korean Christian Scholars Journal* 2 (Spring 1977): 152–55.

finement within the walls of her father's home. Her only information about the world outside was gleaned during her
occasional trips to the marketplace accompanied by a servant girl.
One day at the market, she learned about "picture brides." "Ah,
marriage!" she thought. "Then I could get to America! That land
of freedom with streets paved of gold . . . !" That dream became
an obsession, and she eventually managed to make her way to
Pusan City, a distance of about thirty miles, where she contacted
a broker, who helped her pick a husband from among pictures of
four men in America. After waiting for two years, she received a
letter from her prospective husband, who explained that he could
not save the money required for her passage to the United States
and thus asked to be released from their engagement. "Cancel?
Now I was really a doomed woman!" she recalled. "Had I not already promised myself to him? This is more like a 'divorce'! Oh,
now my brazen 'marriage' and 'cancellation' must be revealed to
my family! How can I survive the Hell I'm certain to face?"

Instead of living with that humiliation, she wrote to her "in-
laws," asking them to take her in as their daughter-in-law. "I was
determined to go there even if I should die and turn into a devil!"
she remembered. "A few days later, a servant announced the arrival of a traveler to our home. I recognized the name to be that
of my 'father-in-law'! He did not identify himself as such to my
parents, but I knew who he was immediately. I was overjoyed! He
had come to get me! I immediately went to my room and got my
few possessions together and tied it neatly in a cloth bundle. Finally, I would escape the cruelty of my family!" When the stranger
got up to leave, she made herself ready: "My cloth bundle bal-
anced on my head, my long braided hair reaching to my ankles
with a red ribbon trailing behind, I stood ready behind him at the
gate. That was the last my family saw of me. I had nothing to say
to my family, but I do remember their shocked and surprised
expressions as I left, also echoes of their scolding voices." She
served her in-laws while waiting for her husband, but just when
he had saved enough to send for her, her father-in-law died, and
as wife of the eldest son, she had to serve as chief mourner for

three years, the period of mourning. Having fulfilled her filial duty, she arrived in Spokane in 1919, where she met her husband, was whisked off to a farm in Montana, worked there alongside her husband, and reared ten children. Her husband died a month before the birth of their tenth child.[24]

Women's migration to America was sometimes prompted by a desire for freedom; their migration was also induced and orchestrated by men for their profit and exploitation. Sociologist Lucie Cheng has argued that the issue of prostitution's morality has obscured the fact that prostitutes had economic functions as laborers, who were simultaneously exploited as cheap workers and advanced the exploitation of men insofar as they helped to perpetuate the system of migrant labor that featured men unencumbered with the costs of families or the costs of the reproduction of laborers.[25] However, prostitution's economic function should not obscure the fact that the exploitation of Asian women in America was also an extension of social relations in Asia, where patriarchy controlled women's bodies and lives. A prostitute's contract, for example, clearly illustrates the nature of that control. "Because, coming from China to San Francisco, she became indebted to her mistress for passage," an 1873 contract read, "Ah Ho herself asks Mr. Yee Kwan to advance for her $630, for which Ah Ho distinctly agrees to give her body to Mr. Yee for service of prostitution for a term of four years."[26]

In nineteenth-century Guangdong Province, where wars, population pressures, and Western imperialism wreaked political and economic havoc with people's lives, women's prostitution was an alternative to infanticide, abandonment, and the selling of daughters. Working mainly in the cities, prostitutes helped to support the patriarchal family with their earnings. A Qing government re-

24 Ibid., pp. 149–52.
25 Lucie Cheng, "Free, Indentured, Enslaved: Chinese Prostitutes in Nineteenth-Century America," in *Labor Immigration under Capitalism*, ed. Cheng and Bonacich, pp. 402–34.
26 U.S. Congress, Senate, *Some Reasons for Chinese Exclusion*, 57th Cong., 1st sess., 1902, Document no. 137, p. 19.

port estimated that each prostitute in Canton sustained ten family members; likewise, a prostitute in San Francisco sent as much as $200 or $300 to her family in China over a seven-month period.[27] But not all prostitutes earned wages, and many simply worked for their owners, who kept all of their earnings and exploited them further in manual labor as seamstresses, cooks, and washer-women. Prostitutes ran away, married their patrons, committed suicide, or died of disease and abuse. In 1870, the *California Alta* reported that the bodies of Chinese women had been discarded on San Francisco's streets. We know very little about the children of prostitutes, some of whom might have escaped the brothel for the anonymity of communities in other cities or states.[28]

Like Chinese women, many of the first Japanese women in America were lured, tricked, and forced into prostitution by men and were appendages of an organized traffic that flowed from Japan to China and Southeast Asia from the 1870s. Tales of easy wealth frequently enticed women into accompanying men to America, like Waka Yamada, who traveled with a man to Seattle in 1902, believing his account of riches, only to be forced into prostitution under the name of "Oyae of Arabia." The following year, she fled to San Francisco but was again thrust into a China-town brothel. She escaped a second time and succeeded in return-ing to Japan, where she educated herself and became a noted writer and critic. Some of the men leaders of the Japanese migrant community, like Genji Hasegawa, derived their fortunes from the labor of prostitutes, prompting a prostitute to remark: "From the way I see them [people in general], they're all whores. Whores without human feelings. . . . And people at large, in apparent glee, respect male whores who have power."[29]

Those "male whores," of course, built reputations, businesses, and communities and inscribed their names and deeds in histories

27 Cheng, "Free, Indentured, Enslaved," pp. 403, 405.

28 Ibid., pp. 417, 419.

29 Yuji Ichioka, "*Ameyuki-san*: Japanese Prostitutes in Nineteenth-Century America," *Amerasia Journal* 4, no. 1 (1977): 3–4, 8, 11–12, 17.

that slighted and marginalized the selfsame women who had been instrumental in their rise to power. Recentering women in Asian American history, as we have seen, stretches the boundaries of that past to encompass both the bachelor societies in the United States and their counterpart communities of women in Asia. Recentering women also resurrects gender as a prominent social category, perceives social change as a product of gender relations, and posits a new chronology that reflects more faithfully the position of women within the social formation. Ultimately, as historian Joan Kelly has written, a feminist history is a history of power relations rooted in the relations of production. "Surely a dominant reason for studying the social relation of the sexes is political," declared Kelly. "To understand the interests, aside from the personal interests of individual men, that are served by the retention of an unequal sexual order is in itself liberating. It detaches an age-old injustice from the blind operation of social forces and places it in the realm of choice. This is why we look to the organization of the productive forces of society to understand the shape and structure of the domestic order to which women have been primarily attached."[30]

Applying that framework to the Asian American experience, we would understand the maintenance of patriarchy and women's resistance against its claims to be a principal motive force in history, and we would periodize that history in accord with the evolution of that dialectic, its stages, transitions, and transformations. Thus, for example, instead of the male-centered periodization scheme of migration and settlement, with women fitted "into the empty spaces," a feminist periodization might highlight the loosening of patriarchy's grip wrought by urbanization and industrialization, Western imperialism, and the resurgence of nationalism within Asia, along with the contradictions and opportunities presented to women under capitalism in Hawaii and the American West. For many women in Asia, those transforma-

30 Joan Kelly-Gadol, "The Social Relation of the Sexes: Methodological Implications of Women's History," *Signs* 1, no. 4 (1976): 822.

tions occurred during the late nineteenth century, when masses of women moved from rural field to urban factory and forged a nationalism that sought to revitalize the nation by espousing Western modernization and, at the same time, resisting Western hegemony.[31]

The extraordinary life and career of Jin Qiu (1875–1907) helps to illustrate those changes that marked a historic shift within the relations between men and women in China. A child of the gentry, Qiu studied and wrote poetry, rode horses, learned to wield a sword, drank wine, and grew up into "a talented, unconventional, and strong-willed young woman, accustomed to having her own way." She delayed her marriage until twenty-one and spent an unhappy eight years of marriage with a spoiled man and wastrel. She, however, enjoyed a circle of women friends, with whom she wrote poetry, discussed politics, and drank, but her seemingly meaningless life contrasted with the momentous events of the day, including the 1898 Reform Movement, the Boxer Rebellion, and the occupation of Beijing by Western troops in 1900. Fearing that China was on the verge of extinction because of Western imperialism, Qiu left her husband and children in 1904 to study in Japan and devoted her life to education, feminism, and revolution. Qiu demanded that women enjoy the same freedom as men but blamed women for having failed to resist men's oppression and proposed that women perform male tasks traditionally valued by society to achieve liberation. Qiu followed her own advice and dressed in men's clothing, carried a short sword, and practiced bomb-making and marksmanship, all masculine roles—the martial, self-sacrificing, superhuman, and tragic hero—familiar in Chinese romance.

In 1906, Qiu sailed with fellow radicals to Shanghai, a center of the women's movement, where she fiercely denounced the

31 Kumari Jayawardena, *Feminism and Nationalism in the Third World* (London: Zed Books, 1986), shows the contradictions of imperialism and nationalism vis-à-vis feminism and argues that feminism was not imposed by Europe but arose within the historical and material circumstances of Asian societies, aided by important infusions of European thought.

"black prison" created by women's "darkness and ignorance" and by Confucianism and men's treatment of women as "horses and cattle" or as playthings. Like her contemporary feminists, Qiu targeted footbinding, arranged marriages, enforced chastity, and confinement, and stressed education as a means by which women would liberate themselves from the prisons that confined them. But foremost, women's freedom would be achieved through revolution and national liberation, Qiu believed, and she actualized those aims as principal of the Ming-tao Girls' School and organizer of a Restoration Army. A student remembered Qiu wearing a man's long gown and black leather shoes, with her hair combed back into a queue, riding horseback astride, and ordering the girls in military drills. Her intense commitment to revolution led to her capture by government troops, her refusal to confess under torture, and finally her execution on July 15, 1907. Qiu's life and death testify to the independence and strength of an iconoclastic woman but also reveal how when women assume positions usually reserved for men, they have to take on men's characteristics to elicit respect from society.[32] In addition, women had to show themselves virtuous both within and without the domestic sphere, submerging their sexual identity to the identity and will of men.

In India, British colonization gave rise, in the nineteenth century, to the social reform movement and, in the twentieth century, to the nationalist movement. Like their counterparts in China, these two historic agencies of social and political transformation were stimulated by Western imperialism and compelled a reexamination of the incongruity of national liberation and women's bondage. The social reform movement, which laid the intellectual

32 Mary Backus Rankin, "The Emergence of Women at the End of the Ch'ing: The Case of Ch'iu Chin," in *Women in Chinese Society*, ed. Wolf and Witke, pp. 39–66. See Elizabeth Castelli, "'I Will Make Mary Male': Pieties of the Body and Gender Transformation of Christian Women in Late Antiquity," in *Body Guards: The Cultural Politics of Gender Ambiguity*, ed. Julia Epstein and Kristina Straub (New York: Routledge, 1991), pp. 46–47; and Nancy Schuster, "Changing the Female Body: Wise Women and the Bodhisattva Career in Some *Maharatnakutasutras*," *Journal of the International Association of Buddhist Studies* 4, no. 1 (1981): 24–69.

foundations of modern India, sought to eradicate practices such as the *sati* ("truly devoted wife," or a woman who joined her husband on his funeral pyre),[33] the ill-treatment of widows, the ban on widow remarriage, polygamy, child marriage, and the denial of property rights and education for women. Social change and national liberation would be achieved, the reformers held, through women's equality and education. They were proven correct during the decades before World War II, when women joined mass nationalist movements, including its Gandhian phase, and formed the nationwide All India Women's Conference in 1927, which helped to influence the passage of liberalizing laws, from social legislation to employment and trade issues.[34]

The convergence of Western (and Chinese and Japanese) imperialism, social reformation, and nationalism in Korea during the late nineteenth century similarly led to the rise of a woman's movement. The period, known as the "enlightenment era," witnessed movements directed at the creation of a new society, such as the Tonghak Movement led by Che'u Ch'oe (1824–64), who pronounced the failure of old values and delineated a new creed named Tonghak, or "Eastern learning," as opposed to Catholicism, called Sohak, or "Western learning." Tonghak envisioned a new social order in which there would be equality regardless of social class or sex and called for an end to the power of the rich over the poor, and of men over women. Although Ch'oe was executed in 1864, his teachings spread rapidly, especially among the peasants, who rose up in revolt between 1884 and 1894, and his ideas of nationalism and women's liberation informed a feminism

33 Gayatri Chakravorty Spivak has shown the sometimes contradictory subject-positions of women under patriarchy and imperialism. While the *sati*, for example, subjugated women, it was also the object of British contempt of Indian culture, who believed it to exemplify Indian barbarism (Robert Young, *White Mythologies: Writing History and the West* [London: Routledge, 1990], pp. 163–64).

34 Neera Desai and Maithreyi Krishnaraj, *Women and Society in India* (Delhi: Ajanta Publications, 1987), pp. 38–41, 336–38.

that sought to foster women's abilities for the development of a modern Korea.[35]

Ok-kyong Yi and Helen Kim were two remarkable women who helped forge a feminist movement whose full potential was stunted by an entrenched conservatism and Japanese colonialism. Yi was born in Korea in 1870, married at sixteen, bore a son, saw her husband take a concubine when she was nineteen, and studied foreign languages with private tutors. In 1907, as president of the Society for Women's Education, she promoted adult education, questioned the separation of men from women, considered women's health issues, and debated the country's economic future. Under her leadership, the society established a school for girls, published a women's educational journal, and offered life insurance to women. Helen Kim earned her doctorate in education from Columbia University in 1931, becoming the first Korean woman Ph.D., and later became the first Korean president of Ewha Woman's University, founded in 1886 by missionary Mary Fitch Scranton. Kim's dissertation, "Rural Education for the Regeneration of Korea," studied Korea's rural areas, where illiteracy, poverty, and disease were rampant and where the future of a new Korea lay. Despite Korea's colonization, wrote Kim, "a people politically and economically ruined is not a people destroyed. Sometimes when one is lowest in the dust he sees the stars most clearly. . . . Only as the individual becomes fully possessed of the spiritual inheritance of his race does he reach full development." The regeneration of Korea, Kim argued, was predicated upon the creation of a strong Korean identity shaped through education and a respect for Korean history and culture. The link between women's advancement and national liberation was graphically shown at Kim's alma mater, Ewha Woman's University, where the students stopped studying at 3 p.m. every day to pray for national independence.[36]

35 Kim, *Women of Korea*, pp. 243–45.
36 Ibid., pp. 251–54, 256–60.

In America, the transformation of patriarchy was similarly prompted by changes in women's role in the relations of production under capitalism and in the struggle for an ethnic identity amid racism and domestic "colonization."[37] Sociologist Evelyn Nakano Glenn observed that Japanese American women entered into domestic service during the first few decades of the twentieth century because of economic necessity and because of their determination to gain a measure of independence despite their husbands' opposition. Unlike in Japan, where the household was the unit of production, observed Nakano Glenn, in America the individual was the productive unit, earning wages outside the household. And even though those wages were frequently pooled within a family, women's earnings and access to social networks outside the family helped them to ameliorate men's authority within the household. Thus, although Mrs. Takagi bemoaned "killing" herself by working forty to sixty hours per week as a domestic servant, she concluded: "I'm glad to be able to do that. I'm so lucky to be in the United States. In Japan, I wouldn't have had the chance as a woman." However, having to work in both the wage labor and the domestic spheres and being relegated to menial and low-paying jobs attenuated women's gains. Women's employment, consequently, was both liberating and oppressive; it gave women greater independence but also saddled them with a double burden as producers and unpaid household workers under men's authority.[38]

Asian women in America shared with their sisters in parts of colonized Asia the twin oppressions of sex and race, and they discerned a connection between the rising social and national movements in Asia and their own cause of liberation in this country.

37 For a useful synopsis of Asian American women's history, see Sucheta Mazumdar, "General Introduction: A Woman-Centered Perspective on Asian American History," in *Making Waves*, ed. Asian Women United of California, pp. 1–22.

38 Evelyn Nakano Glenn, "The Dialectics of Wage Work: Japanese-American Women and Domestic Service, 1905–1940," in *Labor Immigration under Capitalism*, ed. Cheng and Bonacich, pp. 470–514.

Chinese Americans, like their feminist contemporaries in China, sought an end to footbinding, polygamy, and prostitution and promoted women's health care and education. In 1902, a newspaper reporter described Jinqin Xue, a sixteen-year-old who had come to Berkeley to study: "Her goal, upon completion of her studies, is to return to China to advocate women's education and to free Chinese women of thousand-year-old traditional bindings." When she revisited the Bay Area as a leading feminist, Xue spoke before hundreds of San Francisco Chinatown residents on "the role of Chinese women and the need to abolish outdated Chinese customs and emulate the West." When the revolutionary heroine Jin Qiu was executed in 1907, she was mourned and eulogized by Chinese American women, and women in the Young China Society promoted women's rights along with the 1911 Chinese Revolution, contributing money, jewelry, bandages and medicines, and garments to the war effort.[39] Many Chinese Americans realized that China's liberation from Western imperialism paralleled and intersected with their freedom from America's domestic colonization of them, and their liberation as a race would be signaled by women's entry and full equality.

That recognition of connections took the form of a Third World identity during the 1960s as articulated in the civil rights, student, and feminist movements of that period. Merle Woo, a writer and participant in those social movements, in an open letter to her mother, dissected her Third World identity and her relationship with her mother. Despite what she called her mother's self-hatred and isolation and the chasms between them caused by their separate identities, Woo noted their connection as Asian American women and as mother and daughter: "Because of your life," wrote Woo, "because of the physical security you have given me: my education, my full stomach, my clothed and starched

39 Judy Yung, "The Social Awakening of Chinese American Women as Reported in *Chung Sai Yat Po*, 1900–1911," in *Unequal Sisters: A Multicultural Reader in U.S. Women's History*, ed. Ellen Carol DuBois and Vicki L. Ruiz (New York: Routledge, 1990), pp. 195–207.

back, my piano and dancing lessons—all those gifts you never received—I saw myself as having worth; now I begin to love myself more, see our potential, and fight for just that kind of social change that will affirm me, my race, my sex, my heritage. And while I affirm myself, Ma, I affirm you." As for her life's work, Woo called herself an Asian American feminist or a yellow feminist, "because race and sex are an integral part of me," and she saw her struggle against racism and sexism as a unifying cause for Third World women: "In loving ourselves for who we are—American women of color—we can make a vision for the future where we are free to fulfill our human potential. This new framework will not support repression, hatred, exploitation and isolation, but will be a human and beautiful framework, created in a community, bonded not by color, sex or class, but by love and the common goal for the liberation of mind, heart, and spirit."[40]

Inclusion of women within that kind of historical community, a history "bonded not by color, sex or class," finally means remembering women's names, recalling their lives, and hearing their voices. The purposes of women's history are "to restore women to history and to restore our history to women."[41] If, at the general level, recentering women involves revising periodization to reflect more closely women's position within the social relations, at the personal level, recentering women draws up a chronology based upon the passages of individual women's lives. Mary Paik Lee has given us a remarkable account of her life in *Quiet Odyssey: A Pioneer Korean Woman in America*, published in 1990 and ably edited and introduced by historian Sucheng Chan.[42]

Born Paik Kuang Sun on August 17, 1900, Mary Paik Lee wrote

40 Merle Woo, "Letter to Ma," in *This Bridge Called My Back: Writings by Radical Women of Color*, ed. Cherríe Moraga and Gloria Anzaldúa (New York: Kitchen Table, Women of Color Press, 1983), pp. 140–47.

41 Kelly-Gadol, "Social Relation of the Sexes," p. 809.

42 The following account of Lee's life is taken from Mary Paik Lee, *Quiet Odyssey: A Pioneer Korean Woman in America*, ed. Sucheng Chan (Seattle: University of Washington Press, 1990), pp. 5–9, 12, 14–16, 19–20, 23–24, 27, 33, 44, 50–51, 54–56, 58–59, 61–62, 66–67, 77–79, 83, 92, 94–98, 100, 103, 111–12, 116, 121, 124, 127, 134.

about some of her earliest recollections of childhood. "Although I do not remember the faces of my paternal grandparents," began Lee, "two experiences remain in my memory. The first is waiting for my grandfather to come home in the late afternoon. He left home early every morning before I was awake to attend to his business in the village marketplace. I always sat on the front steps, impatiently waiting for his return. As soon as he turned the corner a block away, I would run out to meet him. He would pick me up in his arms, laughing and pretending not to know why I was searching his pockets. He always had *yut* candy and other surprises for me. I can still hear his laughter and jolly voice." Lee's second memory was that of her grandmother, who strapped her on her back one morning and took her to her classroom. "As we entered the room, I looked over her shoulder and saw a large room full of girls who rose to sing a song, perhaps in greeting to their teacher. Grandmother spoke for several minutes and then dismissed the class. That is my only remembrance of her."

Colonization was the first source of dislocation in Lee's life. While waiting for her grandfather one afternoon in 1905, Lee was startled by two Japanese officers, who ordered the Paik family to leave their home. "Although the news was no surprise to them [the Paik family], it must have felt as though the sky had fallen on us," wrote Lee. Migration, flight from colonization, was the second major fracture in Lee's life. To escape the Japanese, her father signed a contract with Hawaii's sugar planters, and on board the ship that took her family to the islands, Lee recalled being miserable for several days, until a kindly Chinese cook gave her "a wonderful-tasting bowl of hot noodles" that drove away her seasickness. Life in Hawaii was hard. "We lived in a grass hut, slept on the ground, and had to start from scratch to get every household item." Feeling desperate, Lee's father borrowed money to take the family to California, believing that there would be more opportunities in the Golden State.

Labor migration was a dominant feature of Lee's life in America. Seeking better wages, the family moved, within the space of ten years, from San Francisco to Riverside to Claremont to Co-

lusa to Roberts Island near Stockton to Idria south of San Jose
and to Willows, where Lee met and married Hung Man Lee
(H. M.) in 1919. Family members worked as a group, blurring the
vertical hierarchies of men and women, adults and children, and
the horizontal domestic and external spheres. While her father
worked with Korean, Chinese, Japanese, and Mexican men in
Riverside's citrus groves, Lee's mother cooked for about thirty
single men, making their breakfast at 5 a.m., packing their
lunches, and serving them supper at 7 p.m. Because of the work,
her mother had to cut her "long, thick black hair that touched the
ground," which, wrote Lee, "must have caused her much grief to
lose her beautiful hair, but she never complained." Lee helped
with domestic chores, looked after her baby brother, and also
served the single men by heating bathwater for them at 6 p.m. On
weekends, with her elder brother, she collected firewood and
sorted through the meat scraps that the butchers had thrown out
as unfit for human consumption.

Lee understood the value of her labor, even as a child, to the
family's well-being and survival. As an eleven-year-old, "my
stomach ached for lack of food, and I had severe cramps," she remembered. "One evening the pain was so bad I got up to fill myself with water. . . . As I neared the kitchen, I saw Father and
Mother sitting across from each other at the table holding hands,
with tears flowing down their faces. I realized then how much agony they were suffering, and that my own feelings were as nothing
compared with theirs." That recognition, recalled Lee, "awakened me to the realities of life." To help her family, Lee worked for
a dollar a week as a domestic servant in the home of her school
principal, after school and all day on the weekends. Later, when
she was fifteen years old, Lee left her family in Idria to work as a
domestic in the home of a white family in nearby Hollister, enabling her to attend high school but making her feel guilty for
having left her mother, who had just given birth to her eighth
child. After completing just one year of high school, Lee rejoined
her family weak, sick, very tired, and weighing only ninety-eight
pounds.

Racism was a third source of dislocation in Lee's life. When her family left Hawaii for California, she recalled seeing white people for the first time as she and her family walked down the gangplank at San Francisco. "They laughed at us and spit in our faces; one man kicked up Mother's skirt and called us names we couldn't understand. . . . I was so upset." In Riverside, Lee was sent to school. "My first day at school was a very frightening experience," she recalled. "As we entered the schoolyard, several girls formed a ring around us, singing a song and dancing in a circle. When they stopped, each one came over to me and hit me in the neck, hurting and frightening me." They stopped when a tall woman with "bright yellow hair and big blue eyes" interceded, but this woman was "a fearful sight" to Lee, who had never seen a white person that close before. "I turned around, ran all the way home, and hid in our shack."

Lee had unpleasant memories about being asked if she were human, about being barred from entering a church by a man who told her, "I don't want dirty Japs in my church," and about feeling a "chilling" atmosphere in school, where no one befriended her except Margaret Finch, whose mother told Lee, "Don't you dare go into my house. I don't want dirty Japs walking around in my home." She remembered a high school history teacher who talked about "stinking Chinks and dirty Japs" when referring to China and Japan, and who taunted Lee, whom he knew to be Korean, by telling the class that Korea was "a wild, savage country that had been civilized by the 'Japs.'"

But Lee's father had told her something she has "never forgotten": "although girls and women were supposed to be soft and obedient," he said, "they should also learn to think like men and make correct judgments. He told me to speak up when the occasion demanded and to stand up for what is right. That advice gave me strength in later life." After marrying at the age of eighteen, Lee and H. M. moved to Anaheim, where they operated a produce stand. A white man came to their stand one day, obviously drunk, and slapped Lee hard on the back saying loudly, "Hi Mary!" "I was so surprised and annoyed that I turned around and hit him as

hard as I could on his back and said, 'Hi Charlie!'" Lee recalled.
Two days later, the man returned to apologize and to ask Lee why
she had called him "Charlie." Lee asked him to first explain why
he had called her "Mary," to which he replied, "I thought all you
Jap women were Mary," prompting Lee to retort: "The reason I
called you Charlie is because people like you always call all Oriental men by that name."

White racism against all people of color led Lee to understand
the common bond among the objects of that oppression. As a
child in Riverside, Lee noticed that Koreans, Chinese, Japanese,
and Mexicans lived in segregated camps outside the town, and she
remembered sifting through the butcher scraps with Mexican
children. She attended school with Mexican children and enjoyed
sharing the delicious tamales made by the mothers of those children. When she saw a motion picture for the first time as a
fourteen-year-old, Lee recalled that when the cowboy characters
in the film laughed as they shot an old Chinese man, "I was so
shocked, I vowed I would never go to see the pictures again." After Pearl Harbor, Lee remembered how her Japanese neighbors
and friends were taken away and how, upon her and H. M.'s re-
tirement from farming in 1950, she lived and befriended Mexican
and African Americans in Los Angeles, because "due to our mutual problems, all minorities felt a sympathetic bond with one
another."

Intervening, amid the dislocations of colonization, labor migration, and racism, were family, culture, and an abiding belief in her
essential humanity. Mary Paik Lee's life seems to have had
smooth transitions from childhood to adulthood and marriage to
motherhood and to old age, marked by burying her parents, husband, son, and siblings. And although work was an all-pervasive
subtext, family was the prominent text, and although gender relations helped to define her identity as a woman, racism appeared
as influential in shaping her identity as a woman and a person of
color. Finally, despite gaining American citizenship in 1960, Lee's
national identity transcended the borders of the state; in closing
her reflections upon her "quiet odyssey," Lee chose a story that

resonated with America's promise, but she evoked it in a distinctly Asian voice: "On the first day of March 1919, thirty-three brave Korean patriots signed their names on the Korean Declaration of Independence, knowing full well they would be killed by the Japanese soldiers. Every year, on the first day of March, we remember their courage and their sacrifices as well as Korea's independence."

Women's recentering, their inclusion within our "community of memory," has only just begun. This project leads us to the following conclusions: recentering women extends the interpretive and geographic boundaries of Asian American history and identity— Asian America's bachelor society was neither exclusively male nor splendidly isolated from Asia; recentering women positions gender as a prominent social category in determining relations of power and trajectories of social change—race and class are neither the sole nor principal determinants of Asian American history and culture; recentering women suggests a new periodization for Asian American history—a feminist account of the past destabilizes the patriarchal categories of sojourners and settlers and the centrality of the exclusion laws, including the 1875 Page Law, which barred Asian women's immigration, and instead pivots on feminism's rise in Asia and America about the turn of the century; recentering women blurs the distinction between internal and external spheres—wage and domestic labor both oppressed and liberated women, exploiting them as workers but also sharpening their claims within the patriarchal household;[43] recentering women underscores the complexity of social relations—the location, functioning, and challenging of power involve class, gender, and race, exemplified in the consciousness of an oppressed class as workers, as women, and as women of color; finally, recentering women allows us to hear the voices of the majority of human-

43 That merging of internal and external spheres was illustrated in the life of Mary Paik Lee and documented in the work of sociologist Evelyn Nakano Glenn. See, for example, the latter's *Issei, Nisei, Warbride: Three Generations of Japanese American Women in Domestic Service* (Philadelphia: Temple University Press, 1986), pp. 107–9.

kind—women's names and their "quiet odysseys" have shaped our collective past and destiny.

Of especial interest to me in the rise of women is the nature of women's role in the preservation and transmission of Asian culture, a culture encrusted with patriarchy and women's oppression but also a culture that resisted European American racism and colonization. Is it possible that women, in passing on Asian culture to the next generation, "Americanized" (not in its usual meaning of assimilation or Anglo-conformity, but in the sense of transformation and democratization) that culture by subverting its patriarchal forms and meanings and thereby helped to liberate themselves? The question deserves a book.

We remember the aunt of Kingston's narrator—that "no name woman"—who committed suicide by leaping into the family well with her newborn daughter. The act was not only a fitting revenge for her ostracism but also a last, emphatic claim to permanent membership in the family that had so eagerly marginalized and forgotten her. Despite her mother's admonition—"you must not tell anyone"—the narrator, through the author Kingston, transcribed an oral tradition onto pages of paper, and the story of the "no name woman" was passed on from mother to daughter, from one generation to the next. In truth, calls for recentering women are necessary only because of historians' narrow chauvinism. Women have long known themselves to be at the center. And that claim cannot be denied.

4

Family Album History

ASIAN American history is more than an assemblage of dates, acts, names; it is more than an accounting of the deeds of the famous and wealthy; it is more than an abstraction from the realm of the senses to the reaches of theory and discourse. To be sure, Asian American history is all that, and more. Asian American history, like the histories of other people of color and of women, acquires substance from interpretation and explanation, aspires to speak in the vernacular by including the activities of the ordinary and lowly, and plunges unapologetically into the teeming sea of human experience and daily life.

Asian American history is suffused with optimism: of belief in the human spirit, of certitude in human agency, of an abiding faith in the individual, however mean, and in the power of the human will, however fragile. Even as its pages reveal overweening oppression and formidable constraints, Asian American history bears the indelible imprint of struggles waged, of determined effort—even defiance—of an unbroken tradition of resistance. And although its pages testify undeniably to paralysis and despair, to wills broken and in bondage to others, the history of Asians in America also bears witness to fires unquenched, feet unbound, and spirits that soar.

A family album history is inspired by the strands in Asian American history that reach to those regularly absent from the gallery of "great men," to activities excluded from the inventory of "significant events," and to regions usually ignored by the world of science. Family albums are filled with snapshots of life, of people called family and friend, of events to be remembered and cherished, of places both familiar and exotic. They are especially crammed with the faces of children—the next generation—who offer proof of the persistence of self and community.

A family album history is an emphatically personal account that is often isolated from a social context—an insularity that is both its attraction and its danger—but the events portrayed invariably take place amid poverty and plenty, powerlessness and control, continuity and change. The pictures I include in this family album merely hint at those overarching social relations; nonetheless, my understanding of those relations has assuredly determined the criteria by which I have chosen and arranged this family portrait.

A family album history is crammed with visual stories and encoded messages that reflect and structure and transmit culture and community. And like the oral tradition of "talk story," family albums help to define a personal identity and locate its place within the social order and to connect that person to others, from one generation to the next, like the exchanging of snapshots among family and friends. Sometimes those albums are censored by external forces, such as during World War II, when Japanese Americans burned photographs that might have linked them to Japan, or when administrators restricted and prohibited the documentation of life in America's concentration camps.

In other instances, those albums might present "autobiographical distortions," only recording pleasant memories of the good times and glossing over the bad. Or, in the case of some "picture brides," the photographs of their prospective grooms might have been "fakes," involving pictures of men posing next to cars, giving a false impression of wealth, or snapshots taken when the men were years younger. Still, as pointed out by visual anthropologist Richard Chalfen, the photos, as social documents, reveal both their subjects and their creators, their assumptions, purposes, and meanings.[1]

1 Richard Chalfen, *Turning Leaves: The Photograph Collections of Two*

Finally, two caveats: first, this version of the people in Asian American history is not properly a history. I do not situate people's lives in their time and space and am more interested in mapping an ethnography of relationships traced around the themes of "departures" and "arrivals." Second, I have mixed my metaphors. Although I conceptualize this depiction as a visual representation—a family album—I will, instead, present to you an oral account—a story—assembled from a variety of published oral histories. My metaphorical incongruity is, of course, problematic, insofar as visual and oral documents represent two quite distinctive modes of communication. Having recognized that my presentation is neither "family album" nor "history," let me beg your indulgence and proffer you "word pictures" that will fill your "mind's eye" and make substantial and real the people who inhabit the margins of race and class within American history.

I share with you, in this family album history, a glimpse into the Asian American past through verbal snapshots of faces frozen in time. The word pictures gain us entry into the lives of women and men, an intimate passage into a world best known to them. We are intruders and can only imagine the thread that must link our lives to theirs. But imagine we will, by listening to their voices, because the connections formed, albeit gossamery, can only strengthen our claim to membership in the American community.

Departures

Migrants left kin and home filled with hope and despair. Women fled abusive husbands and an oppressive patriarchy to build new lives for themselves and their children, as evidenced in the memorable declaration of Maria Hwang, who left her husband because he had taken a concubine: "I shall become a wonderful woman!" Men also left Asia, in the words of the poet, "overblown

Japanese American Families (Albuquerque: University of New Mexico Press, 1991), p. 13.

with hope," searching for the path to Gold Mountain.[2] But women and men also sang the migration blues, when leaving, when confronted with the reality of America, and when recalling the memories of childhood and home.[3] "I was married in Japan when I was twenty-two and had one child there," recalled Kane Kozono. "My husband was a farmer, as was my father. My husband came here to the States three years earlier than I did. When he didn't come back to Japan, his parents asked me to go and bring him back. They thought that two of us working for a few years would give us enough money to come home." Kozono despaired of leaving her mother, being an only daughter, but believed that the fortune she would make in America would "help my mother visit the temple with offerings." Before parting, Kozono remembered her conversation with her mother: "I told her not to worry about me, and also said, 'Although I'm going to go to America, please don't feel lonely when I leave you, Mama. Don't let loneliness make you ill. Don't die of it.' She then replied, 'Your husband is there waiting for you, so you'd better go. I'd probably worry about you even if you stayed here with us.' Such was my mother."[4]

Hanayo Inouye remembered leaving her mother at the train station: "'I am going to miss you very much when you leave,'" her mother told her, "'but I'll always be with you. We won't be separated even for a moment.' At first I did not know what she was talking about," admitted Inouye. "Later that night when I was undressing myself to go to sleep, I understood what she meant. I found a piece of the Buddhist altar ornament in the breast of my

2 Poem by Ichiyo, in Kazuo Ito, *Issei: A History of Japanese Immigrants in North America*, trans. Shinichiro Nakamura and Jean S. Gerard (Seattle: Japanese Community Service, 1973), p. 20.

3 "Immigration blues" is the creative term employed by Marlon K. Hom, in his *Songs of Gold Mountain: Cantonese Rhymes from San Francisco Chinatown* (Berkeley and Los Angeles: University of California Press, 1987).

4 Eileen Sunada Sarasohn, ed., *The Issei: Portrait of a Pioneer* (Palo Alto: Pacific Books, 1983), pp. 34–35.

kimono. I was so sad when I left her at the station that I didn't
know it was there. When I found it, I thought, 'She is with me after
all, my mother.'"[5]

The reciprocal of men in America was, typically, women in
Asia. At times, women grieved over the men's departure and la-
mented the period of separation, usually coming during the
springtime of their youth. A Cantonese song expressed a wife's
sorrow:

> *The sailing date approaches in quick pace.*
> *Husband will be off to Gold Mountain.*
> *At first I thought it was all fun and excitement;*
> *Who would see it, in our youthful years, as a*
> *   cruel separation?*
> *But suddenly—*
> *An endless remorse, aroused by his parting.*
> *Husband says he must go; I plead: don't go so*
> *   soon;*
> *Don't leave this young woman all by her*
> *   lonesome self, grief-stricken.*[6]

At other times, wives welcomed men's departure, as shown in this
Cantonese song:

> *Husband: so dumb, second to none;*
> *Wife: wounded with deep resentment.*
> *Foolish and naive, he doesn't know when to have fun;*
> *It's a real bore to be with him at any moment.*
> *Alas! is this called fate?*
> *I am disgusted with the family, everyone.*
> *Had I followed the Western practice and made my own choice,*
> *Never, never would I have agreed to wed a moron.*[7]

5 Ibid., p. 37.
6 Song 40 in Hom, *Songs of Gold Mountain*, p. 119.
7 Song 36 in ibid., p. 115.

And, at still other times, women and families waited in vain for the return of men, who had abandoned them. "My father is a U.S. naval officer—a commander. He met my mother in Da Nang while he was serving in Vietnam," explained Freddy Nguyen. "In August of 1967 my father was sent back to the United States. He promised to come back to Vietnam and take us all to the United States with him but he never came. He kept in touch with us at first but as time went by it was out of sight out of mind. He seemed to grow gradually indifferent to us. Later he got married. My mother loved my father but when he wrote and told her of his marriage she stopped writing to him because she knew it was not going to lead to anything now. She let him be happy with his new world."[8]

Departures frequently evoked nostalgic memories of the "old world," of childhood and home. "Well, we were poor but it wasn't really that bad because we owned land," explained a Filipino migrant. "We planted some bananas and sweet potatoes. . . . Sometimes we had enough bananas or sweet potatoes or corn to trade with people who subsisted on fishing. They bartered their fish for our corn or rice. . . . This was the way we lived in that small village . . . a beautiful thing, yeah."[9] Another migrant similarly recalled: "There are so many beautiful things that as a Vietnamese I remember, very sentimental. We had very good relations with our neighbors. We visited each other almost daily. When we had good things to eat, we would offer them to our neighbors, and they did that for us. We were not relatives, but we liked each other; we were like relatives."[10]

That secure sense of belonging and of community, however, was sometimes shaken by death, famine, and betrayal. A Viet-

8 Joanna C. Scott, *Indochina's Refugees: Oral Histories from Laos, Cambodia and Vietnam* (Jefferson, N.C.: McFarland & Co., 1989), p. 22.

9 Joan May T. Cordova and Alexis S. Canillo, eds., *Voices: A Filipino American Oral History* (Stockton: Filipino Oral History Project, 1984).

10 James M. Freeman, *Hearts of Sorrow: Vietnamese-American Lives* (Stanford: Stanford University Press, 1989), p. 89.

namese migrant remembered moving from town to town after the death of his father. "My mother," he recalled, "brought her eight children from one city to another to get what we needed. She worked very hard to raise us, and finally we came to a fishing village. My mother is feminine, but she has the spirit of a man; she can do everything, and she's resourceful."[11] Lilac Chen described her abbreviated childhood: "I was six when I came to this country [America] in 1893. My worthless father gambled every cent away, and so, left us poor." One day, her father told her he would take her by ferry to visit her grandmother. As they left, Chen's mother began crying, and "I couldn't understand why she should cry if I go to see Grandma. She gave me a new toothbrush and a new washrag in a blue bag when I left her. When I saw her cry I said, 'Don't cry, Mother, I'm just going to see Grandma and be right back.'" Instead, her father locked her in a cabin, once on board the ferry, and sold her to a woman. "I kicked and screamed and screamed and they wouldn't open the door till after some time, you see, I suppose he had made his bargain and had left the steamer. Then they opened the door and let me out and I went up and down, up and down, here and there, couldn't find him. And he had left me, you see, with a strange woman." The woman took Chen to Shanghai, where another woman claimed her and took her to San Francisco.[12]

Migrants frequently came to America as children and teenagers. Bing Fai Chow joined his older brother and uncle in California in 1921 as a mere ten-year-old. "Coming here wasn't my choice," explained Chow. "My family, especially my father, wanted me to come and help my brother out—to work and send money back to them in China. So it wasn't my own choosing. I wouldn't say I've been happy here, because I had to leave friends

11 Ibid., p. 90.
12 Victor G. Nee and Brett de Bary Nee, *Longtime Californ': A Documentary Study of an American Chinatown* (Boston: Houghton Mifflin, 1974), pp. 84–85.

and family in China. But I wasn't unhappy. I don't regret it either."[13] Sixteen-year-old Masuo Akizuki arrived in San Francisco in 1912, "because my father asked me to come join him in the United States. When I left Japan, my mother told me to help my father, and I promised her that he would come home within five years." The promise was kept.[14]

Fourteen-year-old Hieu survived a harrowing twenty-six-day boat journey across the South China Sea before arriving in America in 1980. Hieu described leaving his mother and father: "I'm sure she wanted to hug me," recalled Hieu of his mother, "and I wanted to hug both my mother and father, but I couldn't because there were a lot of people on the street. To this day I deeply regret not having the chance to really say good-bye to them." Hieu, his older brother and younger sister, and eleven other refugees boarded a twenty-nine-foot boat in the early morning darkness. After four days at sea and running low on fuel and food, the refugees headed for land, having had their pleas for help ignored by several large passenger ships, one of which sailed on into the night while its passengers danced. As they neared an island, "suddenly shots rang out, hitting the prow of the boat, shattering splinters of wood, sending smoke into the air. . . . The next shots ripped into the cabin. The captain's daughter was hit in the neck and died almost instantly." The refugees somehow managed to pull away from the island, but after twenty minutes their boat ran out of fuel and they drifted for twenty days. "Never in my life will I forget those 20 days and nights," said Hieu. "It's hard to speak of them, sometimes, but they are seared in my memory forever. . . . During that period, I came not to care whether the world, or life, continued. . . . When the pain, the anger, the sadness, the hunger came to be too much to bear, I'd scream as long and loud as I could." Once again, ships, "too numerous to count," with most

13 Jeff Gillenkirk and James Motlow, *Bitter Melon: Stories from the Last Rural Chinese Town in America* (Seattle: University of Washington Press, 1987), p. 61.

14 Steven Misawa, ed., *Beginnings: Japanese Americans in San Jose* (San Jose: Japanese American Community Senior Service, 1981), p. 12.

avoiding them "pointedly," passed the refugees until on the twenty-sixth day, a freighter stopped to rescue Hieu and his companions.[15]

Departures in America, as the result of another war, World War II, were sometimes just as final and sorrowful as departures in Asia. Mary Tsukamoto recalled the military orders that forced Japanese Americans to leave their homes for concentration camps in May of 1942. "I remember Mrs. Kuima, whose son was thirty-two years old and retarded," she said. "They had five other boys, but she took care of this boy at home. The welfare office said No, she couldn't take him, that the families have to institutionalize a child like that. It was a very tragic thing for me to have to tell her, and I remember going out to the field—she was hoeing strawberries—and I told her what they told us, that you can't take your son with you. And so she cried, and I cried with her. A few days before they were evacuated they came to take him away to an institution. . . . It was only about a month after we got to Fresno Assembly Center that they sent us a wire saying he died. All these years she loved him and took care of him, he only knew Japanese and ate Japanese food. I was thinking of the family; they got over it quietly; they endured it."[16]

Takae Washizu remembered another kind of departure or would-be departure in America before World War II. "Many wives deserted their husbands in those days," recalled Washizu. "There were many ads about finding wives in the newspapers at that time. I wanted to run away from my husband, for he was too old and too small-minded for me to communicate with, but I couldn't leave my children. I couldn't trust my husband to raise the children; besides I didn't have anyplace to go. I was just patient and dreamed about my children's bright future."[17]

Victimized by patriarchy, traumatized by war and inhumanity,

15 Freeman, *Hearts of Sorrow*, pp. 320–35.

16 John Tateishi, *And Justice for All: An Oral History of the Japanese American Detention Camps* (New York: Random House, 1984), pp. 8–9.

17 Sarasohn, *Issei*, pp. 112–13.

and called to America for their labor, children grew quickly old and adults older, and their pictures, dog-eared and sepia-tinged, gathered dust and were, on occasion, roughly torn from the pages of the family album. A Vietnamese poet offered the following trenchant reflection: "I remember crying twice in my lifetime. The first time was when my father hit me. The second time was when I left my country."[18]

Arrivals

"It was cold. I was there on the pier all by myself, hungry and afraid," recalled a Filipino migrant. "You know, you are all alone in a strange country. You don't know anybody. And you're just 17 years old. I saw a restaurant nearby, and I only had 50 centavos. That's all the money I had. I was hungry so I decided to go in but hesitated because there were a lot of people. I saw a man at the counter and said, 'Sir, I'm hungry. I'd like to buy one piece of bread.' 'Huh? What do you want, boy?' I said, 'I would like to buy one piece of bread. I'm hungry.' 'Okay.' So he went to the kitchen for two slices of bread and gave them to me. I gave him my 50 centavos. 'What's this? What kind of money is this?' 'Sir, that's Filipino money.' 'You can't use this here. Go on. Take the bread. Get away!' "[19]

A nineteen-year-old Korean woman accompanied her mother, her two brothers, and her mother's sister-in-law to Hawaii between 1903 and 1905. "At first we were unaware that we had been 'sold' as laborers," she began, speaking about the contract her mother had signed with the Hawaiian Sugar Planters' Association. "We were told that money was unnecessary so my mother exchanged the money for gold pieces before we left for 'America.' . . . When we arrived we were immediately sent to a labor camp on a sugar plantation in Maui. My mother, sister-in-law, and older brother were sent to the fields, while my younger

18 Freeman, *Hearts of Sorrow*, p. 423.
19 Cordova and Canillo, *Voices*.

brother was sent to school. Inasmuch as I was a teenager, I was told to stay away from the 'bad' plantation workers." Although unused to a life of field labor, the family members completed their period of contract and moved to Honolulu. "If all of us worked hard and pooled together our total earnings, it came to about $50.00 a month, barely enough to feed and clothe the five of us. We cooked on the porch, using coal oil and when we cooked in the fields, I gathered the wood. We had to carry water in vessels from water faucets scattered here and there in the camp area." To supplement their income, the women sewed shirts for twenty-five cents and scrubbed, ironed, and mended clothes for five cents apiece.[20]

"I came to the Golden Mountain in 1921, when I was twenty-one years old," began Yow Wong. "My father had been here for about fifteen years before. He'd worked in Mexico first, doing fieldwork, then found out that wages were higher in the U.S. and came over here. . . . My grandfather didn't want my father to come; he felt the work here was too hard, that he'd be better off in China. That happened with my *great*-great-grandfather too. He told my great-grandfather not to come over. You see, my great-great-grandfather had been to Golden Mountain before." Wong sailed from Hong Kong to San Francisco crowded together with other migrants. "We slept in bunkbeds in one large room, everyone kind of sleeping together. There were very few women on board. Those that were they kept separated from the men. They ate at different times, in different rooms. They slept in different rooms. We hardly ever got to see the women on board." On arrival, Wong was held at Angel Island Immigration Station for two months before he was cleared for admittance.[21]

Moola Singh migrated to America from the Punjab in 1911 with the intention of bringing over his wife when he had saved enough money for her fare. "She good, nice looking, healthy, but

20 Sunoo and Sunoo, "Heritage of First Korean Women Immigrants," pp. 152–55.
21 Gillenkirk and Motlow, *Bitter Melon*, p. 44.

she love," remembered Singh. "You know love, person no eat, worry, then maybe die. Mother wrote one time letter, 'she sick, you gotta come home.' Then I write her letter from Arizona, to her I say, 'I'm coming, don't worry, I be there.'" But she died before Singh could return. "Lots of time I dream," he said, "she come close to me, she's with me now you know. No, she don't want come close, she go round, round no come close in my dream . . . that's a life gone."[22]

Women's arrival ensured the physical survival of Asian America because of their reproductive powers and, equally important, because of their productive powers, enabling the leap from subsistence to surplus product for most working-class Asians. Despite their efforts to mitigate sexism, Asian women labored within a resistant patriarchy that constrained them as prostitutes and as wives. "One man tried to make love to someone else's wife," recalled Takae Washizu. "Having been refused by her, he killed her child by pushing the child into a hole where there was a motor. Another man, who also tried to seduce one mother in vain, cut her daughter's hand. Mr. and Mrs. Toshiba's child was kidnapped while they were working on a farm. Mrs. Toshiba had also rejected one man who tried to make love to her."[23] Some women fled abusive husbands for other men or took on secret lovers. Sadae Takizawa was shocked to see advertisements in Japanese newspapers offering rewards for "catching eloped couples. The reward was twenty-five dollars or something. I saw such ads in the paper every day. . . . Even married women ran away with other men."[24] A *hole hole bushi* (work song) sung by women in Hawaii suggested:

> *Tomorrow is Sunday, right?*
> *Come over and visit.*
> *My husband will be out*

22 Karen Leonard, "Immigrant Punjabis in Early Twentieth-Century California," in *Social and Gender Boundaries in the United States*, ed. Sucheng Chan (Lewiston, N.Y.: Edwin Mellen Press, 1989), pp. 108–9.

23 Sarasohn, *Issei*, p. 113.

24 Ibid., p. 130.

watering cane
And I'll be home alone.[25]

Frequently outnumbered, Asian American women labored both inside and outside the home, reared children, and created permanent communities, oftentimes in distant and isolated places. A nineteen-year-old Filipino high school graduate and teacher left for America in 1930 with her husband. Because of the depression, he was forced to drop out of the University of California, Berkeley, and they "worked picking pears and peaches and all kinds of fruit," the "only place we could go for a job." "We lived in a bunkhouse without a floor. The bed was on the ground. We had one son, Ted, and we were the only family there. Sometimes my husband would work in Lodi and leave us in Fairfield. Ted and I were so scared. So what I did was let Ted stay inside, in bed, while I was outside, just keeping watch in case someone would come around. I didn't even sleep that night because I was protecting Ted. But then we were brave. We were ready for any circumstances."[26]

Nand Kaur Singh, one of the few South Asian women in America before World War II, remembered her first impression of her new home, an isolated apple orchard in Utah. "When we got there it was 11 at night. We went for a walk. . . . And then I started crying. I said, 'What's wrong with India?' And he said, 'You will like it here soon.' I had come from a village where I was surrounded by family and friends," explained Singh, "and here there was no one but my husband, who worked hard all day. . . . There were none of my countrywomen to speak with, and it was against our custom to talk with men who were not related."[27] Tsuru Yamauchi described her first impression of the plantation camp she was to call home: "You couldn't see anything but cane and some mountains. I felt lost without my parents and sisters. Here you

25 Franklin S. Odo and Harry Minoru Urata, "Hole Hole Bushi: Songs of Hawaii's Japanese Immigrants," *Mana* (Hawaii ed.) 6, no. 1 (1981): 73.
26 Cordova and Canillo, *Voices.*
27 Takaki, *Strangers from a Different Shore*, pp. 308–9.

couldn't see anything, no view, no landscape, just fields and hills. Ah, such a place. The sun was already going down. I thought, 'Is Hawaii a place like this?' "[28]

Arrivals of a special sort involved migration and marriage, epitomized by the plucky picture brides. Rikae Inouye described a picture bride who, when the boat anchored, "took out a picture from her kimono sleeve and said to me, 'Mrs. Inouye, will you let me know if you see this face?' She was darling. Putting the picture back into her kimono sleeve, she went out to the deck. The men who had come to pick up their brides were there. It was like that. I felt they were bold." Some brides were disappointed with their grooms. "The picture brides were full of ambition, expectation, and dreams," noted Ai Miyasaki. "None knew what their husbands were like except by the photos. I wondered how many would be saddened and disillusioned. There were many." "One woman met her husband in San Francisco," recalled Minejiro Shibata, "and she claimed that the man was different from her husband in the picture. He looked more handsome in his retouched picture. . . . The pictures retouched by the photographer looked better than the actual brides and grooms, and they were disappointed with one another."[29]

A Filipino recalled a forbidden arrival, his marriage to a white woman. Because of California's antimiscegenation law, the couple had to go to Vancouver to get married. Unfortunately, the date they selected was December 9, 1941, and Japan's attack on Pearl Harbor threatened to cancel their planned journey to Canada. "We went anyway," he recalled. "On December 8 we left for Vancouver. Boy, there was a black-out on our way. We were in Eugene, Oregon at about one in the morning when they wouldn't let us go through town without an escort. All the lights were off and some kind of cellophane was put on the headlights so that they

28 Ethnic Studies Oral History Project and the United Okinawan Association of Hawaii, *Uchinanchu: A History of Okinawans in Hawaii* (Honolulu: Ethnic Studies Program, University of Hawaii, 1981), p. 488.
29 Sarasohn, *Issei*, pp. 51, 55, 107.

couldn't be viewed from the air. The Chief of Police in Eugene asked me why we were going to Vancouver. 'I'm going to get married over there,' I told him. 'Why don't you get married in California?' he asked. 'Well, sir, you know there are laws that won't allow Caucasians and Orientals to get married in California.' 'Are you an American citizen?' 'No, sir, I know you have laws also that won't allow us to be American citizens.' Well, he didn't say anything more. Anyway, he gave us a guide who sat down on the hood of our car to guide us until we were out of the town. We just went ahead and drove after that. . . . That was our wedding and honeymoon."[30]

Births signaled the arrival of families, permanence, and the next generation. "When I was having a baby," remembered Kane Kozono, "I couldn't go to a doctor because I didn't have the money to do so. My husband boiled the water for me, and I delivered the baby and cut the navel string by myself while my husband took up the baby and gave it the first bath. I did it all by myself like that with the help of my husband. When we were working on a hops ranch, the house where we lived was such a dirty place! I remember the dirty mattresses there. It was not a kind of place you want a doctor or a midwife to come to."[31] While births signaled the formation of communities, childbearing also exacerbated some women's bondage. A Korean picture bride spoke of her permanently deferred dream of furthering her education: "When I received the picture, I sent mine," she recalled. "The arrangements did not take long. After I arrived I did not want to marry and do housework. I wanted to go East and study. But since my husband was fairly old, he did not want to let me go. Besides, I got pregnant every year. As the Kor[e]an saying goes, 'Before the sparrow has chicks, she will readily fly when she is shot at; but after she has her chicks, nothing can keep her away from her nest.'"[32]

30 Cordova and Canillo, *Voices*.

31 Sarasohn, *Issei*, p. 126.

32 Sun Bin Yim, "Korean Immigrant Women in Early Twentieth-Century America," in *Making Waves*, ed. Asian Women United of California, p. 53.

Births sometimes represented both an arrival and a departure. Emi Somekawa, a nurse at Tule Lake concentration camp during World War II, told about a woman who had a serious heart condition and who spent most of her time in bed, under medication, during her final months of pregnancy. She gave birth to a healthy, though premature, baby, but she lapsed into a coma for ten days and had to be placed under an oxygen tent. "One day her husband came and said that he just couldn't stand watching [her] breathing, a very labored type of breathing, day after day. Would we please take her out of her misery." Somekawa recalled being shocked at his request but agreed to consult with the physician, who was willing to comply with the husband's wishes. "And so then we talked about it and I think it was the next day the husband came back again with his family. This was her fifth pregnancy. . . . They all came. He had made his decision; this was what he was going to do. So he talked to the doctor again, who told me to fix up a fourth of morphine. So I was there. There was a teaspoon there with some water in it, and the father told each child to give the mother a sip of water, and after the last child gave the sip of water, the father did the same thing, and then he was ready for the morphine. That was it. That was it. Right away, the oxygen tent was removed and she just went to sleep. You know, I feel this might have been a legitimate thing to do for a woman in that condition. But I still feel that if we were not in camp, that there might have been some other treatment."[33]

Arrivals imply experiencing a new sense of place, of home. For Asians, that sensibility, that space, could not be assumed but had to be struggled for, because of the nature of migrant labor and the anti-Asian movement that sought, depending upon the time and participants, to exclude and eradicate all traces of Asians in America. In Shawn Wong's exquisite novel *Homebase*, the narrator, Rainsford Chan, searches for the town for which he was named, the place where his great-grandfather first settled in America. "Rainsford doesn't exist anymore. There's no record of

33 Tateishi, *And Justice for All*, pp. 149–50.

it ever having existed, but I've heard stories about it," he says. "I've spent many days hiking and skiing through the Sierra Nevada looking for it. I've never found exactly where it was, but I'm almost sure I've seen it or passed by it on one of those days." Still, Rainsford, California, is his place, his homebase, insists Chan. "This chronicling of my life should be given the name of a place . . . after 125 years of our life here," he reasons, "we are old enough to haunt this land like an Indian who laid down to rest and his body became the outline of the horizon. See his head reclining, that peak is his nose, that cliff his chin, and his folded arms are summits."[34]

Twenty-five miles from Sacramento, Chinese migrants built Locke, "the most visible monument to the extraordinary efforts made by the Chinese to develop agriculture in California and establish communities in rural America."[35] Ping Lee described how his father, Bing Lee, and other merchants approached George Locke, a landowner, for land to build Locke. "They went up to see George Locke . . . and talked about it. No problem. You can always build back to the levee this way . . . then continue on this way and build a town. Then they shook hands about how much rent. This is all history now, exactly what they did. They never changed their mind. It's how the town was built, in 1914."[36] Soon, the town had a restaurant, boardinghouse, dry-goods store, hardware store, two gambling halls, and a town hall that eventually became a Chinese-language school. "In the past, the whites would attack you with stones when you walked through some of these towns," recalled Bing Fai Chow. "We never dared to walk on the streets alone then—except in Locke. This was our place."[37]

Outside "our place" during the 1920s and 1930s, Asians were fair game. "White people used to call us 'Jap,'" said Shoichi Fukuda. "When kids looked at us, they used to call us 'Chink.'"

34 Shawn Wong, *Homebase* (New York: Plume, 1979), pp. 1–2, 94, 95.
35 From the "Introduction" by Sucheng Chan, in Gillenkirk and Motlow's *Bitter Melon*, p. 18.
36 Gillenkirk and Motlow, *Bitter Melon*, pp. 33–34.
37 Chan, "Introduction," in ibid., p. 24.

Choichi Nitta added: "There was so much anti-Japanese feeling in those days! They called us 'Japs' and threw things at us. When I made a trip to Marysville to look for land, someone threw rocks. It took strong determination to decide to buy land and live here permanently."[38] "In those days," recalled Jose Sarmiento, "Filipinos were followed in the streets, with people calling them all kinds of names, like 'go-go,' and 'monkey,' and such. One time I was followed by a Cadillac with four kids, about 19 or 20. They followed me from where I worked; they followed me and they called me names, even though I did nothing." His tormentors trailed Sarmiento to his house, at which point he rushed inside, took a butcher knife, and ran after the car, chasing them away. Sarmiento also recalled being taken into custody in San Francisco because the police were looking for suspects in a missing-person case. "I never even heard of her [the missing person] before, but I was Filipino so I was a suspect, so they took me to the police station. And while I was down there, they questioned me, and they kept telling me that I was a liar. So they beat me up—the policeman beat me up."[39]

Within Asian American communities—"our place"—scattered from the islands of Hawaii to the U.S. mainland, in rural farming communities and urban Chinatowns, Japantowns, Manilatowns, Koreatowns, Little Saigons, migrants became settlers, parents worked for the sake of the children, and youngsters played with their Barbie dolls and watched television. "I felt we were growing up in an all-American way," said a thirty-two-year-old Korean woman. "The whole family used to watch Lawrence Welk every Saturday. I thought we had a very typical upbringing. . . . I decided I was as American as anyone else. We recited the Pledge of Allegiance every day before class. We sang 'America the Beautiful' before class began, from first to sixth grade. We ate very American things—spaghetti, hot dogs. But whenever we had a family get to-

38 Sarasohn, *Issei*, pp. 63, 64.
39 Roberto V. Vallangca, *Pinoy: The First Wave* (San Francisco: Strawberry Hill Press, 1977), pp. 96–97.

gether, we would have Korean food. My mother would make Korean marinaded beef, and it would be charbroiled. . . . We always had my grandmother's broiled beef, and of course, kimchee."[40]

"I would go to a playground right behind my mother's place," recalled Lisa Mah of her childhood in San Francisco Chinatown, "and one image I have, I think this is my most basic image of what mother love means, was one day when I saw an old village woman there. . . . She had short, straight hair, very crudely combed, no curve in it, just straight hair pushed across her head with a little barrette holding it. She carried a baby on her back in one of those criss-cross holders. . . . Well, there was a small child with the woman, as well as the one which was on her back. The other kid was sucking a lollipop, and suddenly he dropped it in the sand. I was watching this very carefully. Dropped his lollipop in the sand, and of course he started screaming, and I felt it too, I was thinking, 'Dropped it in the sand. That's the end of the lollipop.' . . . But anyway the mother picked up the lollipop and licked it all off, both sides, very thoroughly. Then she spat out the sand and gave the lollipop back to the kid. That's what I remember." Mah concluded: "I feel more at home in Chinatown than anywhere else. Chinatown always felt like a community to me. Of course, I have to recognize that this is based on my own vision and my own very selective way of seeing and feeling the world. A lot of times I realize I'm actually lonely here. But it's as if people here just live their lives, and it's a life that has reality to me. Not that it's a rich life, maybe it is rich. I don't know how to describe it, but life feels real here in Chinatown."[41]

In his early twenties and alone, Roberto Vallangca had a Chinese classmate named Jim Sue, who invited him to Chinatown to eat after school. "He often asked me 'How come you look like Chinese,' and I just laughed," remembered Vallangca. "He was a nice fellow and I always answered him that it was good that I looked Chinese, otherwise we would not be such good friends." One Saturday night, Sue invited Vallangca to attend a dance with him at the Chinese Y.M.C.A. in San Francisco Chinatown. Vallangca feared he would not be let into the dance, because he was not Chinese, but Sue assured him that he would take care of everything. Sue changed Vallangca's name to "Ben Lee," advised him not to say a word, and ushered Vallangca past the door. "The hall was crowded and there were lots of beautiful girls with their dates," recalled Vallangca. "The band began to play and Jim patted my hand reassuringly as he got up to dance. I did not know any girls there so I just watched the dancers. The band was good, playing new songs and dance pieces of the thirties . . . everyone seemed to really enjoy themselves as there was much laughter." The first dance after midnight was designated "ladies' choice," and as the band began playing "When the Moon Comes over the Mountain," "everybody clapped their hands and the ladies started to walk toward the boys of their choice. To my surprise, a smiling Chinese girl walked toward me, her long hair in tendrils and her body swaying to the music as she approached. I was nearly petrified, but out of politeness, I got up, very conscious of the situation. . . . She started talking to me in Chinese. I just smiled, nodding as she talked to me. As she kept talking, I made my steps wider and danced with the tempo of the music, heading nearer to the orchestra, which would drown out her voice and my pretended replies. It was heavenly dancing with her, although I was quite nervous, but finally the music stopped. As I walked her slowly back to her seat, I told her that I wished the music had not stopped but she just laughed. When we finally reached her seat, she asked me if I spoke any Chinese since I had not answered her in Chinese during the dance. I probably blushed but I instinct[ive]ly answered her that I did not speak Chinese as I was born in Hawaii and the family did not speak Chinese at home. So she apologized for speaking in Chinese and sat down. I again politely thanked her for the dance and went back to where Jim was sitting. He smiled and teased me but he was glad I had finally danced, and especially with such a beautiful girl."[42]

V. Ishikawa remembered the picnics in the farming community of Del Rey, California. "We always went to the foothills for the picnics. . . . We went about 10:00 or so in the morning. . . . They always took soda water but our own lunches, everybody had their own lunches, you know *bento*. . . . The games . . . we always just ran. . . . The parents all ran too, the old ladies did spoon races where they run and carry something in a spoon and try not to drop it. There prizes were very menial, pencils, tablets . . . and we were glad to get the pencils, we didn't get much in those days, it was really something."[43] "I remember many happy experiences as a member of a Women's Club," reminisced a Filipina. "There were five or six women who got together and organized a Women's Club. Gradually as the years went by, that club increased in membership. Yes, being part of this group made my life happy because of all the social activities we became involved with. We had dances and programs or banquets. Those were the only happy get-togethers we had in those days."[44]

Family gatherings frequently centered around special occasions and food. A South Asian woman described her family's evening meal: "It is a hearty Gujarati-Indian meal, since the whole family has this one full meal together."[45] Tony Hom observed that "food always seemed to be a central part of the family. . . . Food is *the* main gathering point around the table. Mother would spend the entire day preparing, with my grandfather helping. It brought them together."[46] Food also linked the living with the dead.

42 Vallangca, *Pinoy*, pp. 63–65.

43 David Mas Masumoto, *Country Voices: The Oral History of a Japanese American Family Farm Community* (Del Rey, Calif.: Inaka Countryside Publications, 1987), pp. 100–101.

44 Cordova and Canillo, *Voices*.

45 Suvarna Thaker, "The Quality of Life of Asian Indian Women in the Motel Industry," *South Asia Bulletin* 2, no. 1 (Spring 1982): 70.

46 Lee, *Asian American Experiences*, p. 152.

"Whenever I visit my mother during a Chinese holiday and she has the special food and settings out to honor our ancestors," remembered Sue Jean Lee Suettinger, "I always light some incense, kowtow several times and kneel before pictures of my ancestors." Suettinger described her family's twice yearly visit to her grandparents' grave as "a way for my family to get together. We would bring a chicken . . . roast pork, and a slice of pork fat and some sweet cakes to the cemetery. Then there are oranges and apples. First we trim the grass around the grave markers, clean them off with water, then we place flowers and the food, and light candles and incense by the graves, offer them the food and then pour three tea cups of Johnny Walker Red on the ground. The food and whiskey is symbolic; it is our way of offering them a special meal each year to honor and remember them, so they won't go hungry. Then we burn paper money, lots of it. . . . And we bring along a cassette of Chinese music which we play, so that my grandparents can enjoy the music while they are eating."[47]

Reunions were arrivals of a different sort, sometimes taking place in Asia, when fathers returned from America. May Low was reared by her mother in a village near Canton. "Until I was twelve years old, I never saw my father," said Low. "I just knew the pictures he had been sending all along. In 1945, when I was twelve, we left the village and went to Hong Kong. Then all of a sudden one day my mother told us we were going down to the pier to pick up our father. She just said, 'This is your father,' and we welcomed him, took him home, and I offered him tea and sort of officially greeted him and called him 'Father.' I remember he was like a stranger at first. But a nice stranger that I had met, he seemed to be a very nice man."[48] At other times, reunions took place in America, where wives rejoined their husbands and children their fathers. In a twist on the story of men in America, who supported wives in Asia, eighteen-year-old Rose Eng joined her husband in Boston in 1929. After World War II, her husband returned to

47 Ibid., p. 164.
48 Nee and Nee, *Longtime Californ'*, p. 173.

China, married another woman, and subsisted on the remittances of his wife in America. "When my husband went back to China," said Eng, "he took a second wife, and she had a daughter by him. As he didn't have a son, the family adopted one. So I would send money back—several hundred dollars a year—to support these two children until they were full grown. To that end, I feel as though I have fulfilled my obligation to him and his family."[49]

Literary scholar Elaine H. Kim recalled seeing her half sister for the first time at the age of twenty. Kim had been born in New York City and grew up in Maryland, while her half sister was born and reared in Korea. "Because we are sisters," wrote Kim, "I am always haunted by her stories, feeling that we were like a pair of twins separated by accident. I could have been the one imprisoned for 'anti-Japanese thoughts,' the one married off to a man I had never met, the one drinking in the fragrance of cucumbers I could not afford to eat. I might have known nothing about American racism. In turn, she could have been the 'Chink' or the 'Jap' on the school playground, the one with the full stomach and the saddle shoes, diagramming English sentences for homework, ears stinging from being asked by teachers to stand in front of the room to tell her classmates 'what you are.'"[50] That transposition of image and reality often applied to the stiff portraits included within the family album. The photograph of a South Asian mother-in-law and daughter-in-law, for example, revealed a relationship of subservience of the latter to the former if taken in India, but in America, where the daughter-in-law was a vital economic producer, her status was equal to or higher than that of her mother-in-law, although she was still far from being an equal partner with her husband.[51] The point is, the picture's setting frequently determines its story and meaning.

Another determinant of a picture's narration is its photogra-

49 Lee, *Asian American Experiences*, p. 140.
50 Elaine H. Kim, "War Story," in *Making Waves*, ed. Asian Women United of California, pp. 82–83.
51 Thaker, "Quality of Life of Asian Indian Women," pp. 71–72.

pher's vantage point. Arrival at old age affords an extended vista of life in its totality and in its multiplicity of appearances, changing with the seasons of light. "A man should have historical faith," asserted Kengo Tajima. "That is not only the history of the old people, but particularly the history of our various backgrounds, the culture that is behind us." "I believe children and grandchildren must know the way their grandparents walked," reflected Osuke Takizawa. "The Sansei [third generation] and the Yonsei [fourth generation] should know their grandparents' history. . . . You are a homeless dog without your identity. Though we are U.S. citizens, we are Japanese. The color of our faces and so on. . . . Losing identity is the same as losing money: you lose your way of life."[52]

In retrospect, arrivals, like departures, can be accompanied by feelings of joy and pain. Looking at a photograph, Osuke Takizawa observed: "These people were from my neighborhood and from the same village as mine. This man is dead, this man is dead, and this man was the owner of an inn. He was thrown off a horse and died. I'm the only survivor among these people." Sadae Takizawa, his wife, added: "It is a joy to live for eighty-eight years. However, you can't help feeling lonely after all of your friends have died."[53] Although the photographs sometimes evoke a painful recognition of a severance, they also prompt a remembrance of a union. They document individuals who once lived, loved, worked, and created; they reanimate men, women, and children who forged an identity, culture, and community; and they tell stories about a people who were linked in an ethnography of relationships, a discourse of arrivals and departures.

Those grounds—the places of departures and arrivals—marked the lives of individuals and communities, like our ancestral gravesites, which reach from Asia to America, from the past to the present. Life's passages of birth, marriage, and death were snapped and fastened within the family album; likewise, a

52 Sarasohn, *Issei*, pp. 275, 277.
53 Ibid., pp. 274–75.

people's history of migration and settlement was recorded and put into the family album. Jam-packed with the faces of our history, the family album—our "community of memory"—expands daily with the new faces of our future.

I close this family album history with the summation of an elderly Filipino immigrant. "I was sometimes homesick for the Philippines," he admitted. "It was always hard because you never forget the place where you were born and all your childhood experiences. Wherever you go, they will always be there in your mind. . . . Yet I accomplished what I really wanted: adventures and learning a lot of things. Then, I dream about my own family. I feel that I have accomplished something great because the kids, even though we went through a lot, are doing good. It makes me feel that I have accomplished something because they have accomplished something worthwhile in their lives. I'm proud of all of them because they have their degrees. Mom and I are proud of our kids because they are on their own. . . . I cannot complain because my wife is here, my kids, my grandkids. What more can I ask for, huh?"[54]

54 Cordova and Canillo, *Voices*.

5

Perils of the Body and Mind

O N a plateau of rock bathed in light radiating from the Cross—that symbol in which alone Christians win their victories—stand allegorical figures of the civilised nations," noted the explanation accompanying a painting commissioned by Kaiser Wilhelm II of Germany. Austria, England, France, Germany, Italy, Russia, and "the smaller civilised States" are represented in the painting as women in martial garb, all looking, with varying degrees of interest and resolve, toward an approaching "calamity which menaces them." Leading that group of women, the winged archangel Michael holds in his right hand "a flaming sword. His countenance is turned towards the female group, his features reflect grave energy, and his outstretched left hand, which points to the approaching horror, also emphasises the invitation to prepare for the sacred conflict."

Beneath the rocky plateau extends "the vast plain of civilised Europe. A majestic stream gushes across it. Lines of mountains bound the horizon, and in the valley cities are discerned, in the midst of which tower churches of various creeds." But over the peaceful landscape "clouds of calamity are rolling up," explained the caption. "Dark pitchy vapours obscure the sky. The path trodden by the invaders in their onward career is marked by a sea of flames proceeding from a burning city. Dense clouds of smoke twisting into the form of hellish, distorted faces ascend from the conflagration. The threatening danger in the form of Buddha is enthroned in this sombre framework. A Chinese dragon, which at the same time represents the demon of Destruction, carries this heathen idol. In an awful onset the powers of darkness draw nearer to the banks of the protecting stream. Only a little while, and that stream is no longer a barrier." Beneath the original painting, completed in 1895, Wilhelm II had inscribed the legend: "Nations of Europe, defend your holiest possession."[1]

The "yellow peril," defined by historian Roger Daniels as "this irrational fear of Oriental conquest, with its racist and sex-fantasy overtones,"[2] was probably coined by Wilhelm II and popularized through his much discussed painting, which became the most influential political illustration of the late nineteenth century. The kaiser sent reproductions of the picture, copied in oils, to some of his European royal peers and to America's President William McKinley, who would soon engage the Asiatic dragon in the Philippines. But the origins of the idea of the yellow peril can be found within the European imagination long before its articulation by Wilhelm II, perhaps as early as the fifth century B.C.E., arising from the conflict between Greeks and Persians, or in the thirteenth century C.E., when the Mongols devastated portions of eastern Europe "swarming like locusts over the face of the earth."[3]

Marco Polo, from his travels to Cathay in 1275, described a "swarming," bestial Mongol army that was mechanical (nonhuman) and fanatical (superhuman) in its devotion to conquest and to the Great Khan. "They are brave in battle," wrote Polo of Mongol soldiers, "almost to desperation, setting little value upon their lives, and exposing themselves without hesitation to all manner of danger. Their disposition is cruel. They are capable of supporting every kind of privation, and when there is a necessity for it, can live for a month on the milk of their mares, and upon such wild animals as they may chance to catch. . . . The men are habituated

1 Reproduction of painting and explanation in *The Review of Reviews* (London), December 1895, pp. 474–75.

2 Roger Daniels, *Concentration Camps: North America, Japanese in the United States and Canada during World War II* (Malabar, Fla.: Robert E. Krieger Publishing, 1981), p. 29.

3 Friar William of Rubruck, as quoted in Campbell, *Witness*, pp. 88–89.

to remain on horseback during two days and two nights without dismounting; sleeping in that situation whilst their horses graze." Polo then warned of the peril they posed: "No people upon earth can surpass them in fortitude under difficulties, nor show greater patience under wants of every kind. They are perfectly obedient to their chiefs, and are maintained at small expense. From these qualities, so essential to the formation of soldiers, it is, that they are fitted to subdue the world, as in fact they have done in regard to a considerable portion of it."[4]

Fundamentally, however, the idea of the yellow peril does not derive solely from the alleged threat posed by Asians to Europeans and their "holiest possessions"—civilization and Christianity—but from nonwhite people, as a collective group, and their contestation of white supremacy. Further, the idea of the yellow peril is both a means of defining the European identity and a justification for European expansion and colonization, expounded most vehemently at the height of imperialism and at the start of Third World nationalism and decolonization. Finally, although conceptualized as a global contest between the white and the nonwhite "races" of humankind, the idea of the yellow peril is also bound by the time and place of the nation-state in which it arises and is thereby shaped by the particulars of that history and culture. In America, Europeans encountered indigenous peoples—imagined "Indians" or Asiatic offshoots—who might have been "noble savages" (hence feminized and rendered harmless), but who also threatened the body and mind (hence masculinized).

Europe's frontier in America, at the fringes of incorporation but just as surely a disputed border, was a site of struggle between the tender, English transplants and the wild, native stock. With widespread illness and a dwindling food supply, the Jamestown settlers came perilously close to extinction in the fall of 1607. "It pleased God (in our extremity)," wrote John Smith, "To move the Indians to bring us Corne, ere it was halfe ripe, to refresh us, when we

4 *Travels of Marco Polo*, p. 128.

rather expected . . . they would destroy us." And another leader of the colony cited divine intervention as the reason for its deliverance: "If it had not pleased God to have put a terrour in the Savages heart," he claimed, "we had all perished by those wild and cruell Pagans, being in that weake estate as we were."[5]

Even before their arrival on America's shore, the English believed that the wilderness and its beasts, including the Indian, had to be cleared and subdued before the colonists could realize "New Canaan." As the first English colonists were preparing to embark for Roanoke Island, George Peckham published in London *A True Report, of the late discoveries, . . . of the Newfound Landes*, in which he reasoned that colonization would be "profitable to the adventurers in perticular, beneficial to the Savages, and a matter to be attained without any great daunger or difficultie." Nonetheless, he predicted, "the Savages . . . will not be heerewithall satisfied, but barbarously wyll goe about to practise violence either in repelling the Christians from theyr Portes and safe Landinges or in withstanding them afterwardes to enjoye the rights for which both painfully and lawfully they have adventured themselves thether; Then in such a case," he concluded, "I holde it no breache of equitye for the Christians to defende themselves, to pursue revenge with force, and to doo whatsoever is necessary for attayning of theyr safety; For it is allowable by all Lawes in such distresses, to resist violence with violence."[6]

William Bradford, the leader of Plymouth Colony, declared of his Pilgrim band: "What could they see but a hideous and desolate wilderness, full of wild beasts and wild men." And he wrote that the English had settled the "desolate wilderness" in the full expectation of the "continual danger of the savage people, who are cruel, barbarous, and most treacherous," with dispositions that made "the very bowels of men to grate within them and make

5 Gary B. Nash, *Red, White, and Black: The Peoples of Early America* (Englewood Cliffs, N.J.: Prentice-Hall, 1974), p. 56.
6 Ibid., p. 42.

the weak to quake and tremble."[7] In Virginia, after the war of 1622, in which one-third of the English settlers died, "an unambiguously negative image of the Indian pervaded the Virginian mentality," and descriptions such as "perfidious," "cunning," "barbarous," "liars," "of no constancy or trust," and "lesse capable than children of sixe or seaven yeares old, and lesse apt and ingenious," were used for the Indians, who were henceforth beyond the reach of redemption and thus targeted for elimination.[8]

The English, wrote historian Roy Harvey Pearce, saw the Indian as everything they abhorred and strived not to become. Indians were savage, barbarous, and a feature of the "hideous and desolate wilderness"; the Puritans were civil, Christian, and were on an "errand into the wilderness" to clear the forests and build a "city on the hill" that would "shine like a beacon" to a dark and decadent world. The Puritan identity, thus, was measured against its antithesis and was deemed virtuous through the eradication of its Other.[9] Or, according to Gary B. Nash, Indians "were a psychological obstacle since while they remained 'savages' they threatened the identity of individual Puritans and the collective success of the Puritan Way."[10] The Puritan determination to destroy the Pequots in 1637, consequently, was a way of expiating self-doubt and guilt by ridding America of "Satan's agents," but it was also a way of mending rifts within the Puritan community and refocusing the energies of the elect upon securing the promised land.[11] By confronting those external perils to the body and mind, the community mitigated its internal dissensions and found its collective identity and sense of direction and resolve.

American history, as told by the founding fathers, was a pro-

7 Drinnon, *Facing West*, p. 14; and Nash, *Red, White, and Black*, p. 77.
8 Nash, *Red, White, and Black*, pp. 61–63.
9 Roy Harvey Pearce, *Savagism and Civilization: A Study of the Indian and the American Mind* (Baltimore: Johns Hopkins University Press, 1965), pp. 3–49.
10 Nash, *Red, White, and Black*, p. 83.
11 Ibid., p. 86.

gressive account of triumph over the perils of the forests and its beasts, of change from a lesser to a greater good, of growth from the simple to the complex, of evolution from savagism to civilization. America's Indians stood in the way of progress and, in fact, represented the past. "To study him [the Indian] was to study the past," wrote Pearce. "To kill him was to kill the past. History would thus be the key to the moral worth of cultures; the history of American civilization would thus be conceived of as three-dimensional, progressing from past to present, from east to west, from lower to higher."[12] In addition, those historical dimensions related directly to the confrontation between whites and Asians, in that Indians were widely seen as descendants of Asians,[13] and in that America's westward march continued into the Pacific, extending to Asia, where the "Far East" became the nation's "Far West."[14]

In 1853, when Horatio Greenough's sculpture *Rescue Group* was erected on the Capitol's East Front steps, the outcome of the contest between settler and Indian was no longer in question. The sculpture depicts a cowering white woman clutching her baby while being threatened by an Indian with upraised tomahawk, but looming large behind the savage stands a white giant, who locks the Indian's arms in a viselike grip, rendering him helpless. Greenough reportedly described his famous work as showing "the peril of the American wilderness, the ferocity of our Indians, and the superiority of the white-man, and why and how civilization crowded the Indian from his soil."[15] But after the conquest of the

12 Pearce, *Savagism and Civilization*, pp. 48–49.

13 Ibid., pp. 24–25. Los Angeles police officer Edward Duran Ayres, before a 1942 grand jury investigating "criminal tendencies" among Chicano youth, testified that the Indian blood of Mexicans, having derived from Asians, left them with an "utter disregard for the value of life" that typified Asians (Matt S. Meier and Feliciano Rivera, eds., *Readings on La Raza: The Twentieth Century* [New York: Hill & Wang, 1974], p. 128).

14 From John Hay's reflections. See also Walter LaFeber, *The New Empire: An Interpretation of American Expansion, 1860–1898* (Ithaca: Cornell University Press, 1963), p. 5.

15 Drinnon, *Facing West*, pp. 119–21.

wilderness, new perils awaited the nation in the American South, where a black majority threatened the slavocracy.[16]

The very success of slavery led to disquiet among some of the South's rulers, because as the number of slaves multiplied through importation and reproduction, the likelihood of insurrection similarly increased among those enchained within a system of human bondage that bred resistance. Virginia's William Byrd congratulated the earl of Egmont in 1736 for the prohibition of slavery in Georgia: "They import so many Negroes hither," he wrote, "that I fear this Colony will some time or other be confirmed by the Name of New Guinea. I am sensible of many bad consequences of multiplying these Ethiopians amongst us." Slavery, Byrd contended, made whites lazy, and their increased numbers made slaves "insolent," resulting in "the necessity of being severe." But those "private mischiefs" were nothing compared "to the publick danger. We have already at least 10,000 Men of these descendants of Ham fit to bear Arms, and their Numbers increase every day as well by birth as Importation." Should a leader arise among the bondsmen, warned Byrd, "such a man might be dreadfully mischievous before any opposition could be formed against him, and tinge our Rivers as wide as they are with blood."[17]

Indeed, there was ample cause for alarm. Because slaves were employed in all sorts of tasks, they posed an impediment to free workers, who sometimes competed with unfree laborers for the same jobs. Whites complained that the competition was unfair (in arguments that portended claims made against Asians during the nineteenth century) because Africans did not have to maintain their upkeep, while Europeans had families to support. After it was first proposed that slaves in Charleston be prohibited from serving for hire as porters, carters, or fishermen in 1737, owners were charged a weekly sum for hiring out their slaves as carters

16 I am indebted to a student of mine, Moon-Ho Jung, for pointing out this source of the yellow peril in a Cornell history seminar held in the spring of 1991.

17 Wood, *Black Majority*, p. 224.

and porters, and an annual fee of five pounds was levied on African fishermen. Another source of anxiety was miscegenation, because while "pure" white children helped to even the dangerous racial balance, mulatto children "increased the ranks of the slaves and served as a reminder of the Europeans' precarious social and genetic position." Chiding those who would commit racial suicide, the *South Carolina Gazette* published a poem in 1732 entitled "The Cameleon Lover." Whites with a predilection for African lovers, being "Stain'd with the Tincture of the Sooty Sin," might very well "imbibe the Blackness of their Charmer's Skin," the poem warned. Underlying that discourse on miscegenation was the mounting fear of and preoccupation with rape. "Individual rape if committed by a black man," historian Peter H. Wood pointed out, "was suggestive of social overthrow, just as broad upheaval had implications of personal rape. . . . The increasing white obsession with physical violence, therefore, must be taken as an integral part of the white minority's wider struggle for social control."[18]

White fears of the black majority in South Carolina were fully realized with the Stono rebellion of 1739. On Sunday, September 9, about twenty slaves led by Jemmy broke into Hutchenson's store, took small arms and powder, killed the proprietors, and plundered and burned houses in their path. Other slaves joined the group, which soon swelled to between fifty and a hundred, and with drums beating and banner raised, they shouted "Liberty!" as they marched toward Spanish Florida. Although the planters routed and scattered the band by nightfall, it took a month to finally quell the uprising, and apprehension among whites continued long after a reporter declared an end to the peril in mid-October, "the Rebellious Negros are quite stopt from doing any further Mischief," he wrote, "many of them having been put to the most cruel Death." A year later, an Englishman reflected on the scar left by Stono and predicted: "Such dreadful Work, it is to be feared, we may hear more in Time," because "if it is considered

18 Ibid., pp. 228, 233–38.

how vastly disproportionate the Number of white Men is to theirs: So that at best, the Inhabitants cannot live without perpetually guarding their own Safety, now become so precarious."[19]

Stono was followed by the great slave rebellions led by Gabriel in 1800 and Nat Turner in 1831, both in Virginia, and historians have documented the incidences and varieties of resistance. "While there is a difference of opinion as to the prevalence of discontent among the slaves," wrote historian Herbert Aptheker, "one finds very nearly unanimous agreement concerning the widespread fear of servile rebellion."[20] That fear was inspired by both domestic and international manifestations of slave resistance to white rule, especially the stirrings among the French West Indian slaves during the 1790s that culminated with the successful 1794 revolution in Haiti led by Toussaint L'Ouverture, Jean-Jacques Dessalines, and Henri Christophe. Thomas Jefferson, writing on the eve of the Haitian revolution, confessed: "I become daily more & more convinced that all the West India Islands will remain in the hands of the people of colour, & a total expulsion of the whites sooner or later will take place. It is high time we should foresee the bloody scenes which our children certainly, and possibly ourselves (south of the Potomac), have to wade through, & try to avert them."[21]

That recognition, on the part of whites on either side of the Potomac, helped to define their identity as whites in the face of the nonwhite peril. "The Europeans' response to this 'precarious' situation was desperate and effectual," wrote Wood about the aftermath of the Stono rebellion. "Confronting at last the actual possibility of widespread revolution, bickering factions were able to cooperate in ways which maintained the English slave colony and determined many aspects of Negro existence for generations to come."[22] And historian Eugene D. Genovese concluded that the

19 Ibid., pp. 308–23.
20 Herbert Aptheker, *American Negro Slave Revolts* (New York: International Publishers, 1983), p. 18.
21 Ibid., pp. 41–42.
22 Wood, *Black Majority*, p. 323.

"pervasive fear of slave revolt" during the nineteenth century, whether real or imagined, enabled the forging of an identity of interest between the slaveholders of the South and their northern Democratic party allies, who conspired to stifle abolitionism and northern freedom and democracy.[23]

In the postbellum period, that domestic fear of African American resistance to white supremacy would eventually merge with the international fear of the yellow peril, as exemplified in the government surveillance of African American leaders and organizations after World War I. Bureau of Investigation (forerunner of the FBI) agent R. W. Finch reported the contents of a speech by Marcus Garvey delivered in Harlem in December 1918. Garvey declared, noted the agent, "that Japan was combining with the Negro race to overthrow the white race because the blackman was not getting justice in this country (United States). That it was time for the blackman to mob[i]lize his forces against these former white masters who were not giving the blackman a square deal." J. J. Hannigan, commandant of the Twelfth Naval District headquartered in San Francisco, wrote to the director of the Office of Naval Intelligence on December 3, 1921. In that weekly report on the activities of the Japanese and of Garvey's Universal Negro Improvement Association (UNIA), Hannigan charged that UNIA's real purpose was to rouse "racial and political hatred against the Whites and against the existing American government. . . . Furthermore, it communicates with 'colored races' other than the black. The Japanese agents are playing an important part of the role, and evidently there are Hindus who are busily engaged in aiding the novel and disastrous propaganda." Hannigan wrote that a UNIA supporter stated: "All Negroes—indeed all other colored peoples as well—should wake up to the wrongs done to them, planned against them, by the white race and should rise and stand up in a solid body against the whites. You know there are more colored peoples than whites, but all these colored people are under the white man's foot. Why, the colored people all taken together, which numbers about four times as many as the whites, will not forever remain under the slavery of the whites. . . . Just look at Japan and what she has done and will do. The Japanese are only one of the many colored races; she has done wonders in her own political and industrial improvements. Why, any other colored race can do what Japan has done if they only try."[24]

While Germany and her fellow European states looked eastward, as depicted in Wilhelm II's painting, America faced west to confront the pagan and barbarous yellow peril. America's perception of that yellow peril was colored by the Republic's earlier fears of the wilderness and its beasts and the South's black majority, and all three formed a historical continuum insofar as they imperiled and helped define the white identity. But other anxieties troubled the nation during the late nineteenth and early twentieth centuries, the period of the yellow peril's modern rise. These included urbanization, immigration, poverty, class conflict, deep divisions between North and South, East and West, and the depressions of 1873 and 1893. Also, the end of the frontier—the determinant of American history and culture, according to historian Frederick Jackson Turner and others—witnessed in the 1890 census, prefigured a new social order. "The census takers of 1890 informed us that they could no longer find any frontier upon this continent," wrote Woodrow Wilson in 1902. "We had not pondered their report a single decade before we made new frontiers for ourselves beyond the seas, accounting the 7,000 miles of ocean that lie between us and the Philippine Islands no more than the 3,000 which once lay between us and the coasts of the Pacific."[25]

24 Robert A. Hill, ed., *The Marcus Garvey and Universal Negro Improvement Association Papers*, 7 vols. to date (Berkeley and Los Angeles: University of California Press, 1983–90), 1:312, 4:235.

25 D. Michael Shafer, ed., *The Legacy: The Vietnam War in the American Imagination* (Boston: Beacon Press, 1990), p. 11.

Repression at home, of immigrants, workers, socialists, African Americans, and women, complemented America's expansion abroad and created, in the words of historian Walter LaFeber, the "new empire."[26] In the pursuit of that empire, there arose "a vastly increased emphasis on race," aligning white America with the European colonial powers and African Americans with other people of color in the Third World, prompting W. E. B. Du Bois's well-known insight: "The problem of the twentieth century is the problem of the color-line."[27] Domestic crises and expansion abroad demanded "an identity as well as an identity of interest"[28] that excluded America's racial and ethnic minorities and helped create transnational identities of white and nonwhite.

The idea of the yellow peril contributed to those global identities. English historian Charles H. Pearson was perhaps the most influential architect of the modern yellow peril. His book *National Life and Character*, published in 1893, ostensibly inspired Wilhelm II's call to European nations to defend their faith and home and articulated the intellectual foundations of the modern danger.[29] Pearson's vision was global. Whites, he maintained, had expanded to the farthest reaches of the temperate zones and no more frontiers remained except in the tropics, where a densely populated band of black and yellow peoples lived and where whites could not settle permanently. At the same time, whites desired tropical products and thus colonized those areas, bringing technology and medicines that enabled more efficient production, but also lengthening the lives of nonwhites and introducing them to Western science and industry. The inevitable result, predicted Pearson, would be a tremendous population explosion among the peoples of color and a dramatic increase in their power, marshaled and led by Asians. The resurgent masses, he

26 LaFeber, *New Empire*.
27 Nell Irvin Painter, *Standing at Armageddon: The United States, 1877–1919* (New York: W. W. Norton, 1987), p. 168.
28 Ibid., p. 390.
29 Richard Austin Thompson, *The Yellow Peril, 1890–1924* (New York: Arno Press, 1978), p. 4.

warned, would challenge white rule and would spread and expand beyond the tropical band into the temperate, more desirable zones, and thereby threaten the very heart of the white homeland.[30]

Brooks Adams, descendant of two U.S. presidents and born of a bedrock Yankee family renowned for public service, constructed an American version of the yellow peril that underscored a global economic competition and provided an intellectual rationale for imperialism. Like Pearson, Adams believed that European imperialism had stirred recumbent Asia, but he went on to explain that the extraction of Asia's wealth, which enriched the metropoles and impoverished the colonies, resulted in cheap labor among Asia's masses, with the consequence that Asian manufactures and goods would compete with and ultimately supplant European products. "The cheapest form of labour is thus being bred on a gigantic scale," argued Adams, and as competition intensifies, "nature begins to sift the economic minds themselves, culling a favoured aristocracy of the craftiest and the subtlest types; choosing, for example, the Armenian in Byzantium, the Marwari in India, and the Jew in London." Eventually, the "centre of exchanges" will pass from Europe to Asia, because of the "progressive law of civilization" by which vigorous, tenacious barbarians supersede bloated, opulent civilized peoples. Imperialism, westward expansion, and colonialism will toughen soft America, tame the Asiatic economic beast, and reverse the "progressive law of civilization."[31] Adams's study, wrote historian Charles A. Beard, should be counted among "the outstanding documents of intellectual history in the United States and, in a way, the Western World," and Adams's contemporaries such as Theodore Roosevelt, Alfred T. Mahan, and Homer Lea urged American expansion on the basis of his organic analogy about the birth, rise, decline,

30 Ibid., pp. 18–21.
31 Brooks Adams, *The Law of Civilization and Decay: An Essay on History* (New York: Macmillan, 1895), pp. 286–93.

and revitalization of civilizations.[32] The global themes of imperialism, migration, and economic competition set forth by Pearson and Adams laid the foundation for "yellow perilism."

Thirteen years before Pearson's account, Pierton W. Dooner published an American rendition of the movement of yellow peoples from the tropics into the white heartland titled *Last Days of the Republic*. Although clearly contrived, Dooner's account was called "deductive history" by its author, who claimed that the evidence all pointed to the inevitability of his conclusions, having been derived from a process no different from the multiplication of two numbers.[33] "Servile to the last degree," wrote Dooner of the Chinese, "they seemed to be a people ordained by nature to be the servants of all mankind." But that "eminently peaceful, industrious and law-abiding" people, having suffered prejudice in California, had developed an "unwholesome spirit, seconded by a consuming avarice, and directed by a most incredible cunning [and had] laid the foundation of a scheme of conquest unparalleled in the history of the human race." The plan involved immigration spurred by a growing demand for cheap labor until California's industries were dependent upon the coolie. "The coil of the Asiatic serpent," explained Dooner, "was gradually encircling the entire body of the victim, now virtually within its grasp," and California became "the distributing point whence the institution of Coolieism should be extended throughout the whole Republic."[34]

Meanwhile, China, with its "immense population of four hundred and seventy-five millions of souls," had been awakened from

32 Charles A. Beard, "Introduction," in Adams's *Law of Civilization and Decay*, p. vii; and Thompson, *Yellow Peril*, p. 27. See Homer Lea, *The Valor of Ignorance* (New York: Harper & Brothers, 1909).

33 Pierton W. Dooner, *Last Days of the Republic* (San Francisco: Alta California Publishing, 1880), preface and chapter 5. Another in the genre of "future history" is Marsden Manson, *The Yellow Peril in Action: A Possible Chapter in History* (San Francisco: n.p., 1907).

34 Dooner, *Last Days*, pp. 15, 17–18, 96–97.

its slumber by Europe and America, learned from the West science, industry, and modern warfare, and looked to the United States as a nation ready for the taking, rent as it was by a diverse population of immigrants, internal divisions, and conflicts.[35] At first, the Chinese gained control of the nation's industries through their labor monopoly, then they won political office through the ballot, and finally they raised an army and engaged in open insurrection, whereby the "swarming horde" swept away the "brave defenders." Like Marco Polo's Mongols, the Chinese soldier had few wants and could endure much privation, which in turn kindled "the native ferocity of the soldier into a furious and ungovernable flame of action." Matched against that vast army which acted as one was a divided, complacent America. "Forever occupied and diverted by its factions and its politicians, in their local intrigues for the acquisition of political power," wrote Dooner, "the Ship of State sailed proudly on, too blinded by her preoccupation and too reliant in her strength to bestow a thought upon the perils of the sea. . . . Too late! She was hurled, helpless and struggling, to ruin and annihilation; and as she sank, engulfed, she carried with her the prestige of a race."[36]

Dooner's prophecy was dented by the course of history when, in 1882, two years after the publication of his *Last Days*, the U.S. Congress passed the Chinese Exclusion Act restricting Chinese immigration, and when, in 1895, Japan defeated China. But his basic message about the Asian threat and America's vulnerability continued to ring true, especially with the rise of a predatory, imperialist Japan coupled with Japanese migration to America, which succeeded Chinese migration and reached a peak during the first decade of the twentieth century. Daniels points to a significant escalation of yellow peril rhetoric following Japan's defeat of Russia in 1905, led by the newspapers owned by William Randolph Hearst but beginning with their rival the *San Francisco Chronicle* in February 1905, before the end of the Russo-Japanese

35 Ibid., pp. 145–63.
36 Ibid., pp. 209, 245–52, 256–58.

War. The outcome of that war, the first defeat of a white power by a nonwhite nation in modern times, "undoubtedly stimulated nationalism and resistance to colonialism" in Asia, wrote Daniels, and "in Europe, and particularly in the United States, it greatly stimulated fears of conquest by Asia."[37]

Although those anxieties were especially potent in America, they transcended national borders and helped to define a global racial formation that complemented and buttressed the economic and political world-system, comprised of a core and periphery divided along the racial and geographical lines of Pearson's original formulation. Although the genesis of America's problem lay on the Pacific Coast, wrote Montaville Flowers in 1917, the "Japanese question" was really a world problem. His book *The Japanese Conquest of American Opinion* was dedicated, accordingly, "To the boys and girls of our high schools [and] the young men and women of our colleges upon whose American spirit and whose knowledge of the great world problems of our time depends the preservation of the precious inheritance of the founders and builders of the Republic." The essential struggle, declared Flowers, was a genetic contest over race purity and race survival. America's "original stock" consisted of people from "nations of purest white blood," although "mixed white races" arrived after 1880, diluting the Republic's homogeneity and contributing to its decline. Still, race mixture with the Japanese, by comparison, was even more "radical" and "destroying" and was matched only "when the pure white type marries the pure African type." As surely as Asian immigration will lead to miscegenation, declared Flowers, racial and national decline and dissolution will follow "inter-breeding."[38]

The logic of that twentieth-century racial discourse derived from nineteenth-century Europeans, who had promoted the ascendance of science and Darwinism, industrial development and

37 Daniels, *Concentration Camps*, pp. 10–11, 29–30.
38 Montaville Flowers, *The Japanese Conquest of American Opinion* (New York: George H. Doran Co., 1917), pp. 202, 216, 222–24.

commerce, and imperialism. But it also sought to explain the global subjugation of nonwhite by white and the threats posed to that racial hierarchy by unruly nonwhites in the colonies and by nonwhite migration from the torrid to the temperate zones. The white man's burden had awakened the slumbering colored masses, given them weapons with which to resist the colonizer, and created sea-lanes that brought not only tropical products but also "new barbarians" into the homeland. Like the tarantula hidden among the bunches of bananas, the empire had struck back. "The subjugation of white lands by colored armies may, of course, occur, especially if the white world continues to rend itself with internecine wars," argued white supremacist writer Lothrop Stoddard after World War I. "However, such colored triumphs of arms are less to be dreaded than more enduring conquests like migrations which would swamp whole populations and turn countries now white into colored man's lands irretrievably lost to the white world."[39]

Sociologist Robert E. Park, the doyen of U.S. race relations theory, directed and endorsed a doctoral dissertation entitled "The Japanese Invasion: A Study in the Psychology of Inter-racial Contacts," written by Jesse Frederick Steiner. In the book of that title published in 1917, Steiner argued that "the immigrant invasion from the Orient" posed a grave problem, because the Japanese could not assimilate into American society, making "inevitable the establishment of a color line between the East and the West, no less real than that between the White and the Black."[40] Park

39 Lothrop Stoddard, *The Rising Tide of Color against White World-Supremacy* (New York: Charles Scribner's Sons, 1920), p. vi. Stoddard popularized the racist ideas of Comte Joseph Arthur de Gobineau in America in his *Racial Realities in Europe* (New York: Charles Scribner's Sons, 1924). Another influential racist was Madison Grant, whose book *The Passing of the Great Race; or, the Racial Basis of European History* (New York: Charles Scribner's Sons, 1916), was often cited in Congress in support of restrictive immigration policies.

40 Jesse Frederick Steiner, *The Japanese Invasion: A Study in the Psychology of Inter-racial Contacts* (Chicago: A. C. McClurg & Co., 1917), pp. v–vi.

explained the significance of Steiner's study in his introduction to the book. Modern transportation, communications, and trade had broken down the distance barriers, and the inevitable movement of people from areas of poverty to places of plenty had created "an international and interracial situation that has strained the inherited political order of the United States." When confronted with Asians, whites reacted with race prejudice and antipathies that were "deep-seated, vital, and instinctive impulses." "Race prejudice may be regarded as a spontaneous, more or less instinctive defense-reaction, the practical effect of which is to restrict free competition between races." Interracial amity, proposed Park, depended upon "the extension of the machinery of cooperation and social control," which included racial castes or even slavery, where each race knows "its place" and accepts its status.[41]

But Asians resisted their assigned inferior status, and therein rested the peril to "racial cooperation." In 1920 on the Hawaiian island of Oahu, Japanese and Filipino sugar plantation workers struck for a nonracial wage scale—equal pay for equal work—an eight-week paid maternity leave for women workers, and improved health-care and recreational facilities. The planters declared the strike to be "an attempt on the part of the Japanese to obtain control of the sugar industry" and "a dark conspiracy to Japanize this American territory." A federal commission sent by the U.S. secretary of labor to investigate the causes of the strike concluded, in a secret report, that "Hawaii may have its labor problems . . . but *we believe that the question of National Defense and the necessity to curtail the domination of the alien Japanese in every phase of the Hawaiian life is more important than all the other problems combined.*" Like Dooner's scenario of the spread of Chinese coolieism, the commission described how the Japanese multiplied through "a method of genetal reproduction . . . that will soon overwhelm the Territory numerically, politically and commercially," and alleged that the Japanese had gained

41 Robert E. Park, "Introduction," in ibid., pp. viii, x–xiii.

control over virtually every aspect of Hawaii's economy. Warned the commission: "It may be difficult for the home staying American citizen to visualize the spectre of alien domination which like a thunder cloud in the distance grows larger almost day by day, with the belief that when the infinite patience of this Asiatic Race has reached the point for action the cloud will break and America will wake up to the fact that it has developed within its Territory a race through whose solidarity and maintenance of Asiatic ideals will sweep everything American from the Islands."[42]

The commission's conclusions were supported by military intelligence, which had kept Hawaii's Japanese under surveillance from at least 1918, and by the Bureau of Investigation following the 1920 strike. A 1921 Bureau report described "Japan's program for world supremacy," beginning with the "peaceful invasion" of its migrants into California. If immigration was left unchecked, "the white race, in no long space of time, would be driven from the state, and California eventually become a province of Japan . . . , further, that it would be only a question of time until the entire Pacific coast region would be controlled by the Japanese." Japan schemed to weaken America by fomenting discontent among African Americans, while pursuing its ultimate aim of global conquest: "It is the determined purpose of Japan to amalgamate the entire colored races of the world against the Nordic or white race, with Japan at the head of the coalition, for the purpose of wrestling away the supremacy of the white race and placing such supremacy in the colored peoples under the dominion of Japan." Although apparently "fantastic," the Bureau report conceded, the menace was real and must be taken seriously.[43]

The military in Hawaii, accordingly, planned and prepared for the coming war with Japan at least as early as 1921, when the secretary of war approved a plan that included the internment of en-

42 Gary Y. Okihiro, *Cane Fires: The Anti-Japanese Movement in Hawaii, 1865–1945* (Philadelphia: Temple University Press, 1991), pp. 65–81, 95–97.

43 Ibid., pp. 113–18.

emy aliens. Two years later, Colonel John L. De Witt, who would become the head of the Western Defense Command and a pivotal figure in the mass removal and detention of Japanese Americans on the West Coast, argued for "the establishment of complete military control over the Hawaiian Islands, including its people, supplies, material, etc.," in the event of war with Japan.[44] The idea would lead to the declaration of martial law in Hawaii on December 7, 1941, and to the internment of about 1,400 of Hawaii's Japanese. Fear of the yellow peril on the mainland, following the Pearl Harbor attack, and decades of anti-Asianism that preceded World War II led to the detention of over 110,000 Japanese in America's concentration camps, or at least provided the necessary pretext for the government's declaration of "military necessity."[45] Today we know that the political and military leaders understood that fears of insurrection or invasion on the West Coast were groundless, especially in the summer of 1942, when the detention program began, but we must, I believe, also appreciate the grip that the idea of the yellow peril had on those in charge of Hawaii's defense.

Contrary to most of the literature on anti-Asianism, I do not believe that racism or the idea of the yellow peril is irrational or fantastic; instead, I hold that they are constructed with a purpose in mind and function to sustain the social order. Historian Richard Austin Thompson observed that "the common denominator among yellow perilists was a fear of change," change within the relationship between Europe (and America) and Asia, which was becoming increasingly more intimate and equal.[46] The idea of the yellow peril, as we have seen, helped to define that challenge

44 Ibid., p. 124.

45 See, e.g., Daniels, *Concentration Camps*, pp. 1–73; Jacobus tenBroek, Edward N. Barnhart, and Floyd W. Matson, *Prejudice, War and the Constitution: Causes and Consequences of the Evacuation of the Japanese Americans in World War II* (Berkeley and Los Angeles: University of California Press, 1954), pp. 11–208; and Commission on Wartime Relocation and Internment of Civilians, *Personal Justice Denied* (Washington, D.C.: Government Printing Office, 1982), pp. 27–116.

46 Thompson, *Yellow Peril*, p. 37.

posed by Asia to Europe's dominance and was inscribed within the colonialist discourse as a justification for the imposition of whites over nonwhites, of civilization/Christianity over barbarism/paganism. Like Orientalism, however, yellow peril discourse was hegemonic but not all-powerful, breaking down or changing when confronted with Asian resistance. The fear, whether real or imagined, arose from the fact of the rise of nonwhite peoples and their defiance of white supremacy. And while serving to contain the Other, the idea of the yellow peril also helped to define the white identity, within both a nationalist and an internationalist frame.

Yellow perilism, of course, lives on, just as racism and power contestation continue unabated. Japan's military defeat in 1945 failed to bring an end to the war between white and nonwhite, and the ghosts of Pearl Harbor haunt us still. New warriors, in business suits carrying attaché cases filled with yen, buy political influence in Washington as easily as they buy Rockefeller Center and Pebble Beach, buy and steal technology and America's brightest minds, and gain ready entry into millions of American homes in the form of cars, televisions and stereos, appliances, and computers. In Michael Crichton's best-selling novel (?) *Rising Sun*, America is symbolized as a "small-town girl," a blond "American Beauty long-stemmed rose," who sells herself to "little guys [who] want to fuck a volleyball player." Her tastes and naiveté, like those of Dooner's ship of state, lead to her demise, on the fortysixth floor of the Nakamoto Tower, built by Japanese workers with prefabricated materials brought from Nagasaki (as if rising in revenge from the ashes of atomic destruction), in Japantown, Los Angeles. As aphorisms for the book, Crichton selected: "We are entering a world where the old rules no longer apply," and "Business is war."[47]

Harvard lecturer Robert B. Reich, in a review essay on books published since 1988, including *Agents of Influence, In the Shadow of the Rising Sun, Yen! Japan's New Financial Empire*

47 Michael Crichton, *Rising Sun* (New York: Alfred A. Knopf, 1992).

and Its Threat to America, Japanese Power Game, The Silent War, Pearl Harbor Ghosts, and *The Coming War with Japan,* regretted the thesis of blame explicit within those works, where "it is hard to find much of a plot" in the recent pattern of Japanese investments. Behind the calls for Americans to band together to meet the Japanese challenge was "the real logic—the deep hidden message of these books," which was "to give us a reason to join together . . . as a means of defining ourselves, our interests, our obligations to one another." With the end of the cold war, he concluded, "Japan-as-enemy" supplied Americans with a united identity in a shrinking world and in a time of rapid immigration of nonwhites, growing diversity among America's people, and multiculturalism in the schools, all of which imperiled America's borders and cultural core.[48]

Whether threatening the state through armed insurrection or invasion, the economy through cheap labor and foreign trade, the race through miscegenation and rape, or the culture through paganism and barbarism, nonwhites served as both object and subject in Europe's defense of its holiest possessions. But the yellow peril was not the only enduring icon of white supremacy, nor was it free of ambiguity and contradiction. Europe's colonization of Asia, as foreseen by Pearson, created Asian versions of European polities and economies, under the tutorship of the West. Those copies were ludicrous, flattering, and threatening all at once. They were seen as cheap imitations (mimicries), as products of admiration (as children emulate parents), and as subversions of the original text (grotesque representations of the European identity). Those meanings gave rise to a complementary, benign image of Asians, called today the "model minority."

The concept of the model minority posits a compatibility, if not identity, between key elements of Asian and Anglo-American culture, and thus, instead of deconstructing the European identity, Anglicized Asian culture—the representation—reifies and attests

48 Robert B. Reich, "Is Japan Really out to Get Us?" *New York Times Book Review,* February 9, 1992.

to its original. "At a time when Americans are awash in worry over the plight of racial minorities—one such minority, the nation's 300,000 Chinese-Americans, is winning wealth and respect by dint of its own hard work," declared the December 26, 1966, issue of the *U.S. News & World Report* in the midst of the civil rights movement and African American rebellion in the ghettoes. "In any Chinatown from San Francisco to New York, you discover youngsters at grips with their studies. Crime and delinquency are found to be rather minor in scope. Still being taught in Chinatown is the old idea that people should depend on their own efforts—not a welfare check—in order to reach America's 'promised land.' . . . At a time when it is being proposed that hundreds of billions be spent to uplift Negroes and other minorities, the nation's 300,000 Chinese-Americans are moving ahead on their own—with no help from anyone else." The work ethic, education, family values, and self-help—WASPish attributes represented in Asian American culture—have steered a people from the margins, like all of America's immigrants, to the mainstream, according to the model minority thesis.[49]

While highlighting compatible cultural norms, the model minority stereotype also, at base, positions Asia and America as antipodes, never meeting, as "East is East and West is West." Second-generation Asian Americans, observed a writer in the June 2, 1985, issue of *Parade Magazine*, had to choose between their parents and their country, between Asian and European culture: "It is a question of different values: family responsibility [Asian] vs. individual freedom [European]; personal sacrifice [Asian] vs. the pursuit of happiness [European]; spirituality [Asian] vs. materialism [European]: what Asian-Americans per-

---

49 For a critique of the model minority hypothesis, see Keith Osajima, "Asian Americans as the Model Minority: An Analysis of the Popular Press Image in the 1960s and 1980s," in *Reflections on Shattered Windows: Promises and Prospects for Asian American Studies*, ed. Gary Y. Okihiro et al. (Pullman: Washington State University Press, 1988), pp. 165–74; Takaki, *Strangers from a Different Shore*, pp. 474–84; and Chan, *Asian Americans*, pp. 167–81.

ceive as Asian vs. American." That "cultural tug-of-war," according to the author, alienates Asian parents from their children and can sometimes lead to maladjusted youth. The lesson thus drawn contains a warning: slippages, reversions back to paganism and barbarism, will divide and endanger the family and state and reduce the standing of the offending group.

Like those pliant and persistent constructions of Asian culture, the concepts of the yellow peril and the model minority, although at apparent disjunction, form a seamless continuum. While the yellow peril threatens white supremacy, it also bolsters and gives coherence to a problematic construction: the idea of a unitary "white" identity. Similarly, the model minority fortifies white dominance, or the status quo, but it also poses a challenge to the relationship of majority over minority. The very indices of Asian American "success" can imperil the good order of race relations when the margins lay claim to the privileges of the mainstream. As sociologist Park put it, "The Japanese, the Chinese, they too would be all right in their place, no doubt. That place, if they find it, will be one in which they do not greatly intensify and so embitter the struggle for existence of the white man."[50] But Asians can work too hard, study overmuch, stick together and form a racial bloc, and thereby "flood" our markets and displace workers, "flood" our schools and displace students, and "flood" our land with concentrations of Chinatowns, Japantowns, Koreatowns, Little Saigons, Manilatowns. "Model" Asians exhibit the same singleness of purpose, patience and endurance, cunning, fanaticism, and group loyalty characteristic of Marco Polo's Mongol soldiers, and Asian workers and students, maintaining themselves at little expense and almost robotlike, labor and study for hours on end without human needs for relaxation, fun, and pleasure, and M.I.T. becomes "Made in Taiwan," and "Stop the Yellow Hordes" appears as college campus graffiti, bumper stickers, and political slogans.

The Asian work ethic, family values, self-help, culture and re-

50 Park, "Introduction," p. xiv.

ligiosity, and intermarriage—all elements of the model minority—can also be read as components of the yellow peril. Asian workers can be "diligent" and "slavish," "frugal" and "cheap," "upwardly mobile" and "aggressive," while Asian families and communities can be "mutual aid" and "self-serving" institutions, "inclusive" and "exclusive" groupings, "multicultural enclaves" and "balkanized ghettoes." Asian religious beliefs can be characterized as "transcendentalism" and "paganism," "filial piety" and "superstition," while intermarriage can indicate "assimilation" and "mongrelization," "integration" and "infiltration," and children can be "our second-generation problem" and "our amazing Chinese kids."[51] "Models" can be "perils," and "perils," "models" despite their apparent incongruity.

It seems to me that the yellow peril and the model minority are not poles, denoting opposite representations along a single line, but in fact form a circular relationship that moves in either direction. We might see them as engendered images: the yellow peril denoting a masculine threat of military and sexual conquest, and the model minority symbolizing a feminized position of passivity and malleability. Moving in one direction along the circle, the model minority mitigates the alleged danger of the yellow peril, whereas reversing direction, the model minority, if taken too far, can become the yellow peril. In either swing along the arc, white supremacy is maintained and justified through feminization in one direction and repression in the other.

In 1913, British author Sax Rohmer created a racial archetype in the character of Fu Manchu, "the yellow peril incarnate in one man," who threatened white supremacy. In thirteen novels, three short stories, and one novelette, Rohmer pitted the evil genius against British agent Sir Denis Nayland Smith in a battle of wits, supernatural forces, and science, in which, declared the novels' narrator, "the swamping of the White world by Yellow hordes might well be the price of our failure." Fu Manchu was the first

51 James C. G. Conniff, "Our Amazing Chinese Kids," *Coronet* 39 (December 1955): 31–36.

Asian leader in Anglo-American literature, and he was an imma-
nent presence within the Chinatowns of Britain and America.[52]
Thus, although his ambitions were global and his vast minions remained outside the gates in the periphery, Fu Manchu posed a
peril from within the core, within the European community that
had helped to create him, educate him, and give him technology.

In 1925, author Earl Derr Biggers created a second racial archetype in the character of Charlie Chan. The Hawaii-born detective, an example of upward mobility having risen from
houseboy to the middle class, employs patience, intelligence, and
civility to solve crimes in defense of the social order. Although
brainy, Chan serves under a white superior, and despite being a
family man with numerous children, his devotion to his work pre-
cludes his development as a person. Chan is devoid of emotion
and apologizes for other people's improprieties, both of which are
objects of derision. "Humbly asking pardon to mention it," says
Chan in response to racism, "I detect in your eyes slight flame of
hostility. Quench it, if you will be so kind. Friendly co-operation
are essential between us." Although native born, the pudgy detective is a foreigner, speaking in broken English and serving up
homilies of ancient Chinese wisdom, but he gains membership
within the American community, despite racism, through quiet,
faithful servitude.[53]

Fu Manchu and Charlie Chan, representations of the yellow
peril and model minority, are engendered figures in their bodily
and mental constructions. Fu Manchu is masculine. He is a
leader, speaks impeccable English (no one needs to speak for
him), and poses a martial threat to whites. Charlie Chan is feminine. He is led by a white man, speaks with a broken tongue, and
is docile and polite to a fault. Chan, wrote his creator, "was very

52 William F. Wu, *The Yellow Peril: Chinese Americans in American Fiction, 1850–1940* (Hamden, Conn.: Archon Books, 1982), pp. 164–74. I am
indebted to my student Jane J. Y. Kim, whose seminar paper "Sax Rohmer's
Fu-Manchu: An Artist's Depiction of Yellow Peril," Cornell University, May
1992, helped me understand the author and his pen.
53 Wu, *Yellow Peril*, pp. 174–81.

fat indeed, yet he walked with the light dainty step of a woman." Age accompanied those gendered bodies. Fu Manchu was an adult. Charlie Chan was a child: "His cheeks were as chubby as a baby's, his skin ivory tinted, his black hair close-cropped, his amber eyes slanting," Biggers described the sophomoric detective. Chan's female counterpart, in print and on film, was the "lotus blossom" or "China doll," who was diminutive and deferential, and existed to serve men or the dominant group.

But those aged and gendered figures bore some resemblance, extenuating and mirroring one another in circular fashion. Fu Manchu's masculinity was tempered by femininity. His body was slender, sleek, and feline. His fingers were long, tapered, and clawed. "True masculinity" depends upon energy and order; tyranny was a deviant form of energy and order and was, accordingly, "feminine." Fu Manchu was an oriental despot, a tyrant, a woman. Indeed, like Charlie Chan, Fu Manchu had a female counterpart with whom he merged—the "dragon lady"—who had talons for fingers, plotted revenge, and drew men to their doom with her siren calls. Although feminized, Charlie Chan revealed the strength of mind over body (he solved puzzles with his intellect and could not rely upon his flabby and soft body), exhibited control and equanimity under stress, and impregnated his wife eleven times—all manly virtues. Finally, Fu Manchu was a child, an immature madman, uncontrolled by whites, and thus the yellow peril gone wild, whereas Charlie Chan was an adult, a finished product, schooled and domesticated by whites and thus the yellow peril contained.[54]

54 Nicole Loraux, in her discussion of Herakles of ancient Greek mythology, notes that he was "compulsively masculine" in that he was physically strong and possessed an insatiable sexual appetite, but he was also like a woman insofar as he was fond of warm baths and soft couches. Herakles' femininity, advances Loraux, contained his excessive virility, which threatened to deplete his strength, and accentuated his masculinity (Nicole Loraux, "Herakles: The Super-male and the Feminine," in *Before Sexuality: The Construction of Erotic Experience in the Ancient Greek World*, ed. David M. Halperin, John J. Winkler, and Froma I. Zeitlin [Princeton: Princeton University Press, 1990], pp. 21–52). Fu Manchu's masculinity was tempered by his fem-

Fu Manchu/dragon lady and Charlie Chan/lotus blossom, like their dual genders, were the offspring of a miscegenational union: the interbreeding of Asian and European culture, making them doubly dangerous.[55] Both Fu Manchu and Charlie Chan were steeped in Orientalism but learned from the West, and they challenged and threatened white supremacy, and galvanized and attested to the superiority of Europe. They operated from within the white homeland, within the colonial enclaves of Chinatowns and Hawaii, and hated and envied the West. In the end, Fu Manchu and Charlie Chan, yellow peril and model minority, personified the cunning, sensuality, and mysticism of a feminine Asia (the body) and the intellect, logic, and science of a masculine Europe (the mind).

Nineteenth-century journalist Louis Beck coalesced those two natures into a single person in his representation of Quimbo Appo, ostensibly a San Francisco tea merchant and early resident of New York's Chinatown. Appo, wrote Beck, was a cultivated man, "a man of great intelligence, gifted with a mind whose keenness startled all white men who came in contact with him," and who charmed his associates with his "winning manner." But when drunk, Appo "was a veritable Caliban, dead to all human emotions. At such times he was transformed into a fiend, with an insatiable craving for blood. Woe to the man who crossed the path of Quimbo Appo drunk."[56] Beck's Quimbo Appo possessed manly civility when in control of his faculties and womanly barbarism when freed of inhibitions by alcohol. When stripped of his veneer, his outward charm, "full of interesting reminiscences, bright eyed and smiling," Appo was shown to be, at core, "an inhuman monster, delighting in the worst of crimes" and "a veritable Caliban," who, recalling Shakespeare, was given a language

ininity, enabling the yellow peril's containment, and conversely Charlie Chan's femininity could be exceeded by his masculinity, transforming the model minority into the yellow peril.

55 Thompson, *Yellow Peril*, p. 54.

56 Louis Beck, *New York's Chinatown: An Historical Presentation of Its People and Places* (New York: Bohemia Publishers, 1898), pp. 8–9.

and trained in useful labor by Prospero, but who tried to kill his learned master and rape his master's virginal daughter, Miranda.

During World War II, Gunnar Myrdal, in describing his "American dilemma," agreed with the writer Pearl Buck's contention that the "deep patience" of the world's colored peoples was at an end. "Everywhere among them," she wrote, "there is the same resolve for freedom and equality that white Americans and British have, but it is a grimmer resolve, for it includes the determination to be rid of white rule and exploitation and white race prejudice, and nothing will weaken this will."[57] Myrdal expanded upon Buck's warning, adding that owing to their superior numbers, rapid increase, and industrialization, nonwhites were "bound to become even stronger as time passes." The shrinking white population, Myrdal predicted, "will either have to succumb or to find ways of living on peaceful terms with colored people," else they will face "humiliation and subjugation" when nonwhites become dominant.[58] The "American dilemma," and by extension the white man's dilemma, was the yawning gap between the rhetoric of democracy and equality and the reality of oppression and exploitation and, importantly, the claims of nonwhite peoples to the promise of the American creed. And therein lies the rub and the convergence of the yellow peril and model minority. Those claims, testing the sincerity of the nation's declaration that all men were created equal (a model minority precept), observed Robert E. Park in 1917, broke down the "machinery of cooperation and social control" and unleashed the "instinctive impulses" of racial antipathies (a yellow peril result).[59]

America's Indians and the South's black majority posed perils to white supremacy, but threatened mainly the body, according to some whites. Comparing the Japanese with America's other minorities, Park believed that the Japanese were "more aggressive,

57 Gunnar Myrdal, *An American Dilemma: The Negro Problem and Modern Democracy* (New York: Harper & Brothers, 1944), pp. 1016–17.
58 Ibid., pp. 1017–18.
59 Park, "Introduction," pp. xiii–xiv.

more disposed to test the sincerity of that statement of the Declaration of Independence which declares that all men are equally entitled to 'life, liberty, and the pursuit of happiness.'" In sum, wrote Park, "the difficulty is that the Japanese is still less disposed than the Negro or the Chinese to submit to the regulations of a caste system and to stay in his place."[60] And insofar as they refused to stay in their place, Asians threatened white supremacy and posed perils of the body (the yellow peril) and mind (the model minority).

60 Ibid., p. xiv.

6

Margin as Mainstream

N E W parochialisms abound in the land. To the Right, a parochialism celebrates America's exceptionalism—characterized by Joyce Appleby in her 1992 presidential address to the Organization of American Historians as "America's peculiar form of Eurocentrism"[1]—an exceptionalism that defines and affirms a people by negating others, who form their opposition. The eighteenth-century idea that America represented a break from the European monarchist asylum, declared Appleby, served to unite the disparate colonies against a common foe, but it was also presented as a natural law and universal truth by which others were measured. Similarly, the new parochialism of the late twentieth century offers an adhesive, this time for a fracturing state bursting at the seams with an apparent excess of diversity.

Unlike its parent, however, this new parochialism represents a foreclosure that anchors itself to Europe against the tide of non- and therefore anti-European peoples. The global economy and advanced systems of communication and travel have broken down national borders, even ideological walls, but have reconstructed racial and "tribal" allegiances that enable the survival and competitive edge of those groups.[2] Undergirding the world-system are European or European-like values, ethics, and culture,

1 Joyce Appleby, "Recovering America's Historic Diversity: Beyond Exceptionalism," *Journal of American History* 79, no. 2 (September 1992): 420.

2 Joel Kotkin, *Tribes: How Race, Religion and Identity Determine Success in the New Global Economy* (New York: Random House, 1992).

from capitalism to the English language. In America, Eurocentrists, these new parochialists, proclaim union on the basis of race, language, and culture to counter the perceived threat of nonwhite "racial tribes" and to stifle dissenting voices from within their own ranks—of women, workers, lesbians and gays, and those who would contest the dominant order.

Eurocentrists wax nostalgic for the apparently simpler past: when Egypt was a part of Mediterranean civilization, when Western culture formed the core of a liberal education, and when Americans formed a national consensus.[3] Despite the historical ebb and flow of competing ideologies about America's national character—from the ideals of assimilation to those of pluralism, from homogeneity to heterogeneity, from singularity to diversity—there is, wrapped within that exceptionalist longing for a simpler past, a persistent and pervasive notion about American history and culture: the idea of a unifying mainstream, embraced in the motto "Out of many, one," and in John Jay's definition of America, "one united people . . . descended from the same ancestors."

Steering the ship of state toward the mainstream, toward the central values of the nation, toward the bedrock foundations, holds, for those latter-day restorationists, a return to better times. Besides being free of cultural illiteracy and intellectual impoverishment, the mainstream offers movement, vitality, and clarity, unlike the inert, insipid, and muddy fringes of the margin. The margin, composed of racial minorities, women, the underclass, gays and lesbians, is exhorted to join the mainstream, composed of European Americans, men, the ruling class, heterosexuals. In its stress on racial, gender, class, and sexual inequality, in its insistence on identity and self-definition, the margin has led the nation astray, far from the original formulations that made the Republic great, has created instead balkanized enclaves—ghet-

---

3 See, e.g., Allan Bloom, *The Closing of the American Mind* (New York: Simon & Schuster, 1987); and Arthur M. Schlesinger, *The Disuniting of America* (Knoxville, Tenn.: Whittle Direct Books, 1991).

toes—and, even worse, has stirred up social conflict and "culture wars." Without a center, things have fallen apart.

We know Eurocentrism as consort to the "meanness mania" that ran amok in the Reagan-Bush state, wherein "meanness" involved both selfishness and small-mindedness.[4] We know the new parochialism as the weapon of choice among the born-again, John Wayne gunslingers in their high-noon showdown along the frontiers of Western civilization. We know the new Eurocentrism as the postmodern incarnation of the old exceptionalism, spruced up for the occasion of late capitalism's assault against rebel bases within the heartland of the new world order.

To the Left, another parochialism celebrates a minority's exceptionalism, characterized (and sometimes caricatured) by invention of traditions, affirmation of fragile identities, and exclusion of others, who form their opposition. Like some on the Right who see racial perils and "tribes," some on the Left posit communities—sisterhoods and brotherhoods—that are no less imagined. The ideas that minorities too had heroes and "great" civilizations, that minority scholars can represent and speak for "their" people, that minorities alone possess the virtues that the majority never owned, reflect, rather than reject, their rightist ideological counterparts of racial and ethnic purity, authenticity, and boundaries. Eurocentrism's hegemony can never justify mimetic "isms" that create new hierarchies, privileges, and borderlands, nor should it invoke the same kind of closure witnessed in the neoconservative circling of the wagons.

In truth, ethnic studies began with an alternative vision of American history and culture that was broadly inclusive. It started with the idea that American society consisted not only of Europeans but also of American Indians, Africans, Latinos, and

4 Although coined and applied before the Reagan-Bush years, the term "meanness mania" captures the nation's mood that also characterized the 1980s (Gerald R. Gill, *Meanness Mania: The Changed Mood* [Washington, D.C.: Howard University Press, 1980]).

Asians. It went on to propose that the histories of all of America's people were so intertwined that to leave out any group would result in sizable silences within the overall narrative. It noted a global dimension to the American experience, both in the imperial expansion of European peoples and in the incorporation of America's ethnic minorities. But beyond recapturing historical and contemporary realities and extending the community's reach, ethnic studies fundamentally sought to move the pivot, by fracturing the universalism of white men and by repositioning gender, class, race, and sexuality from the periphery to the core, decentering and recentering the colors and patterns of the old fabric.

What I will suggest in this concluding chapter, albeit in summary fashion, is that racial minorities, specifically Asian Americans, have in the past repeatedly sought inclusion within the American community, within the promise of American democracy, within the ideals of equality and human dignity, and have, just as regularly, been rebuffed and excluded from that company and ideal. What I will suggest further is that racial minorities, in their struggles for inclusion and equality, helped to preserve and advance the very privileges that were denied to them, and thereby democratized the nation for the benefit of all Americans.

Frequently, within the classroom and between the covers of U.S. history textbooks, Asians have been depicted as victims, most prominently as objects of exclusion in the nineteenth-century anti-Chinese movement and as "Americans betrayed" in the twentieth-century concentration camps. The pervasiveness of that portrayal has prompted Roger Daniels to write: "Asians have been more celebrated for what has happened to them than for what they have accomplished."[5] Although first enunciated in 1966, Daniels's assessment of the historical literature remains

---

5 Daniels, *Asian America*, p. 4; and Roger Daniels, "Westerners from the East: Oriental Immigrants Reappraised," *Pacific Historical Review* 36 (1966): 373–83.

largely true in 1992, as evidenced by the fact that books on the anti-Chinese and anti-Japanese movements fill most of the shelf space of Asian American collections.

The Asian "contribution" to American history and culture is the other major focus of multiculturalists, who celebrate Asian labor in the building of America, foremost in the construction of the transcontinental railroad. Chinese men, exemplars of true masculinity and manly virtue, hauled heavy tracks and ties, bored tunnels through granite mountains, and bound the nation with bands of steel. To Asian American men writers like Frank Chin, those railroad men epitomized Asian American manhood: no wimps they, who sweated and cursed, struck for higher wages, and clambered over rock faces and defied death in baskets suspended over ledges.[6] But others have noted that when the picture was taken at Promontory Point, Utah, when the golden spike was driven home, Chinese Americans were left out, just as when they were later pushed out by European immigrants, who rode those rails out West.

Asian American women writers, like Maxine Hong Kingston, have given us a different angle on railroad men, like Ah Goong, her "grandfather of the Sierra Nevada," who, while dangling from a basket one beautiful day, was overcome with sexual desire and ejaculated high above the earth. "He stood up tall and squirted out into space. 'I am fucking the world,' he said. The world's vagina was big, big as the sky, big as a valley. He grew a habit: whenever he was lowered in the basket, his blood rushed to his penis, and he fucked the world."[7] But we also know that Ah Goong's masculine thrust through the most resistant of mountains was an exercise in futility, especially when set against the world's "big as the sky" vagina, and his seed fell on barren ground.

6 See, e.g., his use of the railroad metaphor in Frank Chin, *The Chinaman Pacific & Frisco R.R. Co.* (Minneapolis: Coffee House Press, 1988); and idem, *Donald Duk* (Minneapolis: Coffee House Press, 1991).

7 Maxine Hong Kingston, *China Men* (New York: Ballantine Books, 1977), p. 130.

Asian contributions to American agriculture are nearly as well known as their work on the railroads. Chinese Americans helped drain the lowlands of the Sacramento delta and reclaimed fertile land, helped plant the orchards and vineyards of that Golden State, and "worked the edges," in the words of historian Sandy Lydon, and, like alchemists, turned wasteland and waste products into "Chinese gold."[8] I remember joining a tour group at the Christian Brothers winery in Napa, California, and being told by the guide that the immense limestone cavern in which we stood, where huge oak casks mellowed the juice, was carved out of the mountainside by Chinese workers. He turned majestically toward me as if to make the point, since I was the only Asian face in the crowd, and as the group followed his gaze, I bowed gently and acknowledged the wonder of what my hands had wrought.

Today we know that Asians developed horticultural techniques important for the growing of truck crops, from irrigation sluices to packing sheds, and they formed grower and marketing cooperatives that were so effective that on the eve of World War II, while cultivating only 3.9 percent of California's farmland, Japanese farmers were said to have supplied from 50 to 90 percent of the state's artichokes, cauliflower, celery, cucumbers, green peppers, spinach, strawberries, and tomatoes.[9] We also know of Kinji Ushijima (George Shima), who was dubbed the "potato king" by the press and who controlled 85 percent of California's potato crop, valued at over $18 million in 1920, and of Gim Gong Lue, who was called Florida's "citrus wizard" and who developed a frost-resistant variety of orange that laid the foundation for much

8 Sandy Lydon, *Chinese Gold: The Chinese in the Monterey Bay Region* (Capitola, Calif.: Capitola Book Co., 1985). See also Chan, *Bitter-Sweet Soil.*

9 Hosokawa, *Nisei,* p. 106. See also Masakazu Iwata, "Japanese Immigrants in California Agriculture," *Agricultural History* 36, no. 1 (January 1962): 25–37; and Timothy J. Lukes and Gary Y. Okihiro, *Japanese Legacy: Farming and Community Life in California's Santa Clara Valley* (Cupertino: California History Center, 1985).

of that state's citrus industry.[10] And we are well aware of Hawaiian and Asian contributions to Hawaii's sugar and pineapple industries, mainly as laborers.[11]

Asian American achievements in education have been touted widely during the past several decades, forming a basis for the model minority stereotype, and Asian and Pacific Islander Americans were the fastest growing segment of the population during the decade of the 1980s, increasing by 107.8 percent, compared with 53 percent for "Hispanics," the second fastest growing group, adding to their significance for America's diversity. Despite that rapid growth, Asian and Pacific Islanders number only 7,272,622, or 2.9 percent of America's people, according to the 1990 census, they have regional significance only in the West (including Hawaii) and in the Northeast, and a majority of them have been in the United States only since 1965. Those numbers and the average length of their stay fail to indicate the importance of Asian and Pacific Islanders in America.

The "contributions" approach, it seems to me, misses the true significance of Asians in American history and culture. When compared with the centrality of the founding fathers, the framers of the Constitution, the shapers of American letters and culture, the movers and shakers in the worlds of industry and government, Asian contributions seem trivial, and rightfully so. The majority, defined as those who rule, designed and built the Republic for themselves, while the minority, defined as those separated from power, were consigned to the periphery, where they could exert little influence over the core. In addition, the measure of worth, of significance, hinges upon how contributions affirm or reinforce the established order, the status quo, the very system that domi-

10 Daniels, *Concentration Camps*, p. 8; and Ruthanne Lum McCunn, *Chinese American Portraits: Personal Histories, 1828–1988* (San Francisco: Chronicle Books, 1988), pp. 32–39.

11 Ronald Takaki, *Pau Hana: Plantation Life and Labor in Hawaii, 1835–1920* (Honolulu: University of Hawaii Press, 1983); and Edward D. Beechert, *Working in Hawaii: A Labor History* (Honolulu: University of Hawaii Press, 1985).

nates, oppresses, and exploits minorities, who are then asked to "contribute" to society.

In contrast, acts of resistance, protests against injustice, and insurgency against the established order are quickly labeled divisive, destructive, nationalistic, and self-serving. In that way, the civil rights movement—a social movement that sought to remove barriers, a movement that sought to guarantee and protect the rights of all Americans, a movement that sought a more inclusive society—was depicted as a "Negro" movement, as "their" cause, as for "them." Martin Luther King, Jr., recognized that the struggle for civil rights was a transformative struggle, an act of resistance against the prevailing social order, an attack against society's fundamental institutions and flaws, because of the connections between racism and profits, war and poverty, and he and the movement were watched and treated by the Federal Bureau of Investigation and the U.S. government, in the words of Coretta Scott King, as if they constituted "an alien enemy attack on the United States."[12]

What I would like to suggest is that the deeper significance of Asians, and indeed of all minorities, in America rests in their opposition to the dominant paradigm, their fight against "the power," their efforts to transform, and not simply reform, American society and its structures. Specifically, I am thinking about the challenges posed by Asians to a central tenet of American democracy—equality under the law—but I also have in mind how Asians helped to redefine the meaning of the American identity, to expand it beyond the narrower idea of only white and black, and to move it beyond the confines of the American state and the prescribed behaviors of loyalty and patriotism. In 1910, during testimony before the U.S. Congress, Hawaiian Sugar Planters' Association secretary Royal Mead reported that "the Asiatic has had only an economic value in the social equation. So far as the institutions, laws, customs, and language of the permanent pop-

12 David J. Garrow, *The FBI and Martin Luther King, Jr.* (New York: Penguin Books, 1981), p. 212.

ulation go, his presence is no more felt than is that of the cattle on the ranges."[13] Asians would contest Mead's judgment on the effect of their presence.

Asians were recruited for their labor; their inclusion in America, accordingly, was predicated upon their "economic value in the social equation." When no longer useful, Asians were denied entry into America through the Chinese Exclusion Act of 1882, the Gentlemen's Agreement of 1908, the 1917 and 1924 Immigration Acts, and the Tydings-McDuffie Act of 1934, which excluded Chinese, Japanese, Korean, Asian Indian, and Filipino immigration. The exclusion of Asian women, antimiscegenation statutes in several states, and the 1922 Cable Act, which stripped U.S. citizenship from women who married Asian migrants ("aliens ineligible to citizenship"), restricted the ability of Asians to reproduce and create stable communities, and the 1922 *Ozawa* ruling by the U.S. Supreme Court affirmed earlier decisions that the naturalization laws did not apply to Asians. "The widespread animosity toward the California Chinese," observed students of the anti-Asian movement, "was translated into a broad range of discriminatory legislation designed to drive out those already here and to discourage the immigration of others."[14]

Despite the mainstream's selective construction of the American identity and the foreshortened reach of democracy's embrace, fully encompassing only the core, the aspirations of the periphery could not be forever contained, nor could they be permanently stifled. They took as literal the entitlements of America, even though the guarantees, when first formulated, did not contemplate them. And in the words of Robert E. Park, they were "more disposed to test the sincerity of that statement of the Declaration of Independence which declares that all men are equally entitled to 'life, liberty, and the pursuit of happiness.'" Asians resisted their exclusion and marginalization and thereby enlarged the range and deepened the meaning of American democracy.

13 Okihiro, *Cane Fires*, pp. 16–17.
14 tenBroek et al., *Prejudice, War and the Constitution*, p. 17.

The promise of America offered much hope to Asians. During the late nineteenth century, Chinese invoked an image of George Washington, whose ideals of racial equality were betrayed by the realities of anti-Chinese hostility.[15] After Congress instituted Chinese exclusion in 1882, Yan Phou Lee published a stinging rebuke in the *North American Review*. "No nation can afford to let go its high ideals," warned Lee. "The founders of the American Republic asserted the principle that all men are created equal, and made this fair land a refuge for the whole world. Its manifest destiny, therefore, is to be the teacher and leader of nations in liberty. Its supremacy should be maintained by good faith and righteous dealing, and not by the display of selfishness and greed. But now, looking at the actions of this generation of Americans in their treatment of other races, who can get rid of the idea that that Nation, which Abraham Lincoln said was conceived in liberty, waxed great through oppression, and was really dedicated to the proposition that all men are created to prey on one another? How far this Republic has departed from its high ideal and reversed its traditional policy may be seen in the laws passed against the Chinese."[16]

During the 1909 sugar plantation strike on the island of Oahu, which involved about 7,000 workers, Japanese strikers argued against the racial hierarchies created by the planters: "Is it not a matter of simple justice, and moral duty to give [the] same wages and same treatment to laborers of equal efficiency, irrespective of race, color, creed, nationality, or previous condition of servitude?" Eleven years later, during the 1920 sugar strike, some 3,000 Japanese and Filipino men, women, and children marched through the streets of downtown Honolulu carrying portraits of President Abraham Lincoln, who represented to them the liberator of other plantation workers and the symbol of freedom and

15 See Kevin Scott Wong, "Encountering the Other: Chinese Immigration and Its Impact on Chinese and American Worldviews, 1875–1905" (Ph.D. diss., University of Michigan, 1992), p. 63.

16 Yan Phou Lee, "The Chinese Must Stay," *North American Review* 148, no. 389 (April 1889): 476.

equality. Voicing the reaction of Hawaii's white oligarchy to the strikers, the *Honolulu Star-Bulletin* commented: "Americans do not take kindly to the spectacle of several thousand alien Asiatics parading through the streets with banners flaunting their hatred of Americanism and American institutions and insulting the memory of the greatest American president since Washington."[17]

In Oxnard, California, Japanese and Mexican sugar beet field hands joined together in a historic union, the Japanese-Mexican Labor Association (JMLA), in 1903. Under its president, Kozaburo Baba, the JMLA struck for higher wages and an end to labor contractor commissions and to the company store monopoly. On March 23, a Mexican striker was shot and killed, and two Mexicans and two Japanese were wounded. After negotiations a few days later, the union won most of its demands. Despite its membership exceeding 1,300, or 90 percent of the work force, and despite demonstrating the success of nonracialism and of organizing agricultural workers, the JMLA was refused a charter by the American Federation of Labor, which stipulated that the union had to bar Asians from membership if it were to be granted a charter. The union's secretary, J. M. Lizarras, a Mexican, replied to the AFL's Samuel Gompers: "We would be false [to the Japanese] and to ourselves and to the cause of Unionism, if we . . . accepted privileges for ourselves which are not accorded to them [Asians]." Workers should unite, Lizarras concluded, "without regard to their color or race."[18]

Chinese Americans contested, early on, the exclusion of their children from public education. On August 23, 1859, thirty Chinese parents petitioned the San Francisco Board of Education to establish a primary school for their children. The practice, sanctioned by law, of separate schools for whites and for "col-

---

17 Okihiro, *Cane Fires*, pp. 50, 74.

18 Ichioka, *Issei*, pp. 96–99. The struggle for equality in the workplace was both race- and class-based. Asian workers were exploited by Asian capitalists, and the latter received privileges from the state that were denied the former. See, e.g., Yu, *To Save China, To Save Ourselves*, pp. 165–99.

ored" children derived from the decision to found a "colored school" for African American children in 1854. The board accordingly opened the Chinese School in San Francisco in the fall of 1859, establishing what School Superintendent James Denman called "the only school in the Union that provides a school exclusively for the Chinese learning our language; and there is none other, having in its midst a heathen temple, established and used for the worship of idols, whose worshippers may also enjoy the blessings of the free Common Schools."[19]

To white supremacists, San Francisco's segregated schools were critical to the maintenance of racial purity and were upheld as exemplars of true generosity and enlightenment. An 1885 board of supervisors report explained: "Meanwhile, guard well the doors of our public schools, that they [Chinese children] do not enter. For however hard and stern such a doctrine may sound, it is but the enforcement of the law of self-preservation, the inculcation of the doctrine of true humanity, and an integral part of the enforcement of the iron rule of right by which we hope presently to prove that we can justly and practically defend ourselves from this invasion of Mongolian barbarism."[20] That advice was given in response to a Chinese American effort to integrate the public schools.

In 1884, eight-year-old Mamie Tape, American-born daughter of Chinese migrants Joseph and Mary McGladery Tape, was denied admittance to the Spring Valley Primary School by Principal Jennie Hurley. The Tapes challenged that ruling, and in January 1885, citing the equal protection clause of the Fourteenth Amendment, the court decided in their favor. "To deny a child, born of Chinese parents in this State, entrance to the public schools," wrote the superior court judge, "would be a violation of the law of the state and the Constitution of the United States." The *Tape* decision was affirmed by the state supreme court, but neither rul-

19 Low, *Unimpressible Race*, p. 14.
20 Ibid., p. 59.

ing could hinder the "separate but equal" doctrine that would be established eleven years later in the landmark 1896 U.S. Supreme Court decision of *Plessy v. Ferguson.*

The state passed legislation to skirt the court's ruling by allowing school boards to establish separate schools for Asians. As mandated by the 1885 amendment to Section 1662 of the 1880 Political Code: "Trustees shall have power to exclude children of filthy or vicious habits, or children suffering from contagious or infectious diseases, and also to establish separate schools for children of Mongolian or Chinese descent. When such separate schools are established Chinese or Mongolian children must not be admitted to any other schools." The legislation was praised by San Francisco's school superintendent as "not a question of race prejudice" but "a question of demoralization of one high race by a lower," and on April 13, 1885, Mamie Tape, described by the *Evening Bulletin* as neatly dressed with her hair in "the traditional braid of American children hanging down her back and tied with a ribbon," and her brother Frank joined "four bright Chinese lads" at Rose Thayer's Chinese Primary School on Jackson and Powell streets.[21]

Mary McGladery Tape was unconvinced that the exclusion of her daughter was "not a question of race prejudice." In her letter to the board of education dated April 8, 1885, Tape wrote: "I see that you are going to make all sorts of excuses to keep my child out off the Public Schools. Dear sirs, Will you please tell me! Is it a disgrace to be born Chinese? Didn't God make us all!!! What right! have you to bar my children out of the school because she is a chinese Descend." Tape concluded: "I will let the world see sir What justice there is When it is govern by the Race prejudice men! Just because she is of the Chinese descend, not because she don't dress like you because she does. Just because she is descended of Chinese parents I guess she is more of a American than a good many of you that is going to prewent her being Educated."[22]

21 Ibid., pp. 59–73.
22 Ibid., Appendix D.

In 1920, Hawaii's legislature passed Act 30, which authorized the Department of Public Instruction to issue and revoke operating permits for foreign-language schools, to test and certify language teachers, who were required to have knowledge of the "ideals of democracy, American history and institutions and the English language," and to regulate the curriculum, textbooks, and hours of operation of those schools. Despite the act's regulatory intent, the department applied its provisions toward eliminating the territory's 143 Japanese-language schools, and on December 28, 1922, 87 language schools joined in a petition testing the constitutionality of Act 30. As the litigation moved from territorial circuit court, to the U.S. District Court, to the Ninth Court of Appeals in San Francisco, and finally to the U.S. Supreme Court, Hawaii's legislature tightened controls over the language schools by passing Act 171 in 1923 and Act 152 in 1925.[23]

The Supreme Court rendered a unanimous decision in favor of the Japanese-language school petitioners on February 21, 1927, arguing that despite the "grave problems" of a "large alien population in the Hawaiian Islands," parents had the right to determine the education of their children, and the state had to observe limits in curtailing the rights and powers of individuals.[24] At a mass meeting held the following month, 5,000 supporters of the successful constitutional challenge passed a series of resolutions, including: "we reaffirm our confidence in the friendship and good-will of the American people, and reassert our pride in the fact that our children are American citizens"; and "we emphatically reaffirm our continued loyalty to America and our desire to rear our children as loyal, patriotic and useful citizens of the United States." Kinzaburo Makino, a test case leader, told the gathered throng that the litigation was "the right of a people living in a free democracy to seek legal clarification regarding constitutionality of their laws," but he cautioned, "we must never forget

23 Okihiro, *Cane Fires*, pp. 136–38, 153–54.
24 Kenneth B. O'Brien, Jr., "Education, Americanization and the Supreme Court: The 1920s," *American Quarterly* 13, no. 2 (Summer 1961): 170–71.

that we have to stand up for our rights as guaranteed under the Constitution."[25]

Nine-year-old Martha Lum tried to enroll in the white school in Bolivar County, Mississippi, one morning in 1924. The school superintendent of Rosedale district called the child to his office around noontime to tell her that she was yellow and could not attend school with white children. As a person of color, she had to enroll in the "colored" school. Martha's father, Gong Lum, resolved to fight for his daughter's right to attend the white school, recognizing the inequities that favored the white over the colored school. The case reached the U.S. Supreme Court, where in 1927, in *Gong Lum v. Rice*, Chief Justice William Howard Taft wrote for a unanimous court against Lum: "Were this a new question, it would call for very full argument and consideration; but we think that it is the same question that has been many times decided to be within the constitutional power of the state Legislature to settle, without intervention of the federal courts." Although Taft erred, insofar as *Lum* did not directly challenge school segregation and the legality of school segregation had never been decided upon by the Supreme Court, *Gong Lum v. Rice* was prominently cited, along with *Plessy v. Ferguson*, as a precedent for state-mandated school segregation.[26]

Whereas the struggle for educational equity during the 1920s involved language rights and an end to Jim Crow schools, the demand of the 1960s extended those ideals to higher education and its curriculum. In 1968, at San Francisco State College, the Philippine-American Collegiate Endeavor explained its purpose in its statement of goals and principles: "We seek . . . simply to function as human beings, to control our own lives. Initially, following the myth of the American Dream, we worked to attend predominantly white colleges, but we have learned through direct analysis that it is impossible for our people, so-called minorities,

25 Okihiro, *Cane Fires*, pp. 154–55.
26 Kluger, *Simple Justice*, pp. 120–21.

to function as human beings, in a racist society in which white always comes first. . . . So we have decided to fuse ourselves with the masses of Third World people, which are the majority of the world's people, to create, through struggle, a new humanity, a new humanism, a New World Consciousness, and within that context collectively control our own destinies."[27]

On November 6, the Black Student Union and Third World Liberation Front called for a general strike at San Francisco State, and over a two-month period, from December 1968 to January 1969, police arrested about 600 strikers, more than 50 of whom suffered Mace burns, fractured skulls and other head injuries, ruptured spleens, and broken ribs, hands, arms, and legs. In January, the strike spread across the bay to the University of California, Berkeley, where students demanded, like their San Francisco State counterparts, a Third World College that would study domestic and international dimensions of repression and resistance. "The Third World movement," wrote members of Berkeley's Third World Liberation Front, "was and continues to be a demand of colonized peoples for freedom and self-determination— for the right to control and develop their own economic, political, and social institutions."[28]

In 1992, San Francisco State's School of Ethnic Studies and UC Berkeley's doctoral program in ethnic studies bear witness to the power and influence of those original demands. The numerous ethnic studies programs, faculty, and courses on campuses across America, along with a sustained output of ethnic studies scholarship and resurgent minority student and professional organizations, similarly attest to the efficacy of the "demand of colonized peoples for freedom and self-determination." But it is also impor-

27 Karen Umemoto, "'On Strike!' San Francisco State College Strike, 1968–69: The Role of Asian American Students," *Amerasia Journal* 15, no. 1 (1989): 15.

28 Mike Murase, "Ethnic Studies and Higher Education for Asian Americans," in *Counterpoint: Perspectives on Asian America*, ed. Emma Gee (Los Angeles: UCLA Asian American Studies Center, 1976), p. 208.

tant to recognize that the institutionalization of ethnic studies and the counterstruggle to exclude and mitigate its content and purpose—called "culture wars" today—are a part of a longer history of minority exclusion and inclusion in America.

Besides claiming the promise of America for themselves within the borders of the United States, Asian Americans sought those same freedoms for their people in colonized Asia. Taraknath Das, selected for the Indian civil service, left college in 1905 to help organize Sikh resistance against British rule, or in his words, to become "an itinerant preacher, explaining the economic, educational, and political conditions to the masses of the people." Fleeing arrest, Das joined other Indian dissidents in Japan and in 1906 arrived in Seattle on the advice of a friend, who had told him, "If you want to see the civilized use of machinery, go to America." Das worked in the celery fields of California, attended the University of California, and in 1907 moved to Vancouver, where he became secretary of the newly formed Hindustani Association and published *Free Hindusthan*. Das urged Asian Indian migrants to resist Canadian and American exclusion, seeing them as measures that strengthened British control over Asian Indians, "owing to which the natives of Hindusthan cannot go freely to other parts of the British Empire."[29]

Harassed and kept under surveillance by British and Canadian agents, Das crisscrossed the continent between 1908 and 1910, moving from Vancouver to Seattle, to Northfield, Vermont, to New York, and back to Vancouver, Seattle, and Berkeley. During those years, Das struggled to keep *Free Hindusthan*, described as "revolutionary and anarchical," afloat, lectured on Indian liberation, and worked for the removal of anti-Asian restrictions in Canada and the United States. Das received American citizenship in 1914, was accused of and jailed for conspiring with Russian Bolsheviks to overthrow British colonial rule in India, and was threatened with denaturalization and deportation, but he remained an activist in defense of Asian Indian rights both in Amer-

29 Jensen, *Passage from India*, pp. 165–66.

ica and in India.[30] The activities of Das and other leaders of the
Gadar (rebellion) Movement, like Har Dayal, head of the Gadar
party in San Francisco in 1913, mobilized resistance against British colonial rule in India and also helped shape an Asian Indian
community in America among a widely dispersed people.[31]

Korean nationalists, seeking the overthrow of Japanese colonialism, were inspired by the ideals of American democracy and
self-determination, and many of that movement's leaders were educated and based in the United States. Ch'ang-ho An arrived in
America in 1899 to study, organized a mutual aid society for Koreans in San Francisco, and formed a secret society to train leaders
for the nationalist cause. Yong-man Pak studied at the Hastings
Military Academy in Nebraska, established the Young Korean
Military School in 1909, and headed the Hawaii Korean National
Association. Sung-man Yi (Syngman Rhee) studied at George
Washington University, Harvard, and Princeton, where he received a doctorate in 1910, and became the premier of the Korean
Provisional Government in exile in 1919. The founding principle
of the Korean Independence League, formed in Hawaii in 1919 by
Pak, was "to promote the interests of Koreans everywhere, to de-
velop their knowledge, to lead the minds of Korean societies in the
direction of Democracy, and to train the thoughts of every Korean, in high or low places, in the spirit of liberty."[32]

Korean women played minor roles in the nationalist movement
until the 1919 March First (*mansei*) Movement, when, like their
male counterparts, the Korean Women's Patriotic Society of California and the Korean Women's Relief Society of Hawaii worked
toward Korea's decolonization and independence and promoted
the mutual aid of Korean communities in America. The groups
raised money for the anticolonial struggle, trained nurses for the

30 Ibid., pp. 171–75, 234, 244, 259–64.
31 Jane Singh, "The Gadar Party: Political Expression in an Immigrant
Community," *South Asia Bulletin* 2, no. 1 (Spring 1982): 29–38.
32 Kingsley K. Lyu, "Korean Nationalist Activities in Hawaii and the
Continental United States, 1900–1945, Part I: 1900–1919," *Amerasia Journal* 4, no. 1 (1977): 76.

war front, and undertook relief work among Koreans devastated by war and famine. The relief society was headed by Maria Hwang, the woman who had rebuked her husband with the words, "I shall become a wonderful woman!" and her daughter, Hai-Won Kim, was elected the first president of the Korean Women's Patriotic Society of California in 1919. Two years later, the society charted a new course for women. Korean independence, it declared, should be accompanied by women's liberation. "Sisters! Stop dreaming in a family which is actually an invisible prison," exhorted the society's publication. "Stand up and unshackle our next generations from [traditional] constraints. Our utmost tasks are to free ourselves of bondage, to build our wealth, to enlist as soldiers, and to obtain an education. If we are prepared, there will be no discrimination against us women in political participation or legal activities. . . . Recently, magazines have spoken about women's liberation. We should educate ourselves so that we can gain equality with men (in the independence movement) and be second to no one in responding to our national duty."[33]

The Asian American civil rights movement mainly sought to ensure and expand the guarantees of equal protection under the Fourteenth Amendment. A landmark case in the application of equal protection was *Yick Wo v. Hopkins*, decided by the U.S. Supreme Court in 1886. Between 1873 and 1884, the San Francisco board of supervisors enacted fourteen "laundry ordinances" that employed neutral language for licensing and regulating laundries in the city but were meant for and applied directly to Chinese-owned businesses. Associate Justice Stanley Matthews, speaking for a unanimous court, declared that although the laws appeared neutral, their administration discriminated against the Chinese minority and thus violated the equal protection clause of the Fourteenth Amendment. *Yick Wo*, by subjecting to scrutiny the intent and application of the law in determining discrimination, became

33 Eun Sik Yang, "Korean Women of America: From Subordination to Partnership, 1903–1930," *Amerasia Journal* 11, no. 2 (1984): 12–18, 20.

one of the most cited decisions in considerations of equal protection under the Constitution.[34]

Perhaps more basic than the application of equal protection was the movement's struggle for inclusion within the category of citizen, when the state was just as determined to preserve America for, in the words of Benjamin Franklin, "the lovely White." Asians, as we have noted, were "aliens ineligible to citizenship" and as such could not become naturalized citizens, most of them, until 1952. In 1879, because of a suit filed by Ah Kow Ho, the U.S. Supreme Court ruled that equal protection applied to noncitizen as well as to citizen.[35] But even their birthright of citizenship was questioned and threatened. In 1895, Kim Ark Wong, an American citizen by birth, was refused entry into the United States on the grounds that he was not a citizen, having been born to parents who were "aliens ineligible to citizenship." Wong petitioned the U.S. Supreme Court, which ruled in 1898 that the Fourteenth Amendment provided that everyone born within America was a citizen, and although the amendment was designed to establish the citizenship of free blacks, "all persons" were included within its guarantee.[36]

Of course, Asians were not always excluded from membership in the American community. Their persistence and the coming of the second generation, citizens by birth, led to the "second-generation problem," that is, the assimilation, or Americanization, of those "new Americans."[37] Because Asians made up such a large proportion of Hawaii's people during the 1920s and

34 Charles J. McClain and Laurene Wu McClain, "The Chinese Contribution to the Development of American Law," in Chan, *Entry Denied*, pp. 14–15.

35 Ibid., pp. 10–12.

36 Ibid., pp. 20–21.

37 See, e.g., Edward K. Strong, *The Second-Generation Japanese Problem* (Stanford: Stanford University Press, 1934); and William Carlson Smith, *The Second Generation Oriental in America* (Honolulu: Institute of Pacific Relations, 1927); and idem, *Americans in Process: A Study of Our Citizens of Oriental Ancestry* (Ann Arbor, Mich.: Edwards Brothers, 1937).

1930s, the eradication of Asian tendencies and the promotion of European values were a pressing concern for the territory's rulers. Toward those ends, Americanizers sought to control or eliminate Japanese-language schools, reduce the influence of Buddhism and the ethnic press, and install an educational system that would mold "dependable, patriotic, and worthy citizens," according to a 1920 federal survey.[38]

Hawaii's public schools, the report recommended, should direct the masses of children to "find their opportunities either in agriculture itself or in occupations directly related to agricultural enterprises." The elementary school curriculum should stress "the various forms of handwork, manual work, cooking, simple sewing, the making of beds, and the care of the house, the making of school and home gardens, the organizing of pig clubs and poultry clubs," and every high school should train the youth to seek employment opportunities in the sugar and pineapple industries. Among the leading proponents of that brand of vocational education during the 1920s was Hawaii's governor, Wallace Rider Farrington, who directed the territory's superintendent of education that his department "should be friendly to industry and should instruct the children in the dignity of manual labor."[39]

In 1921, with the support of Hawaii's oligarchy, Japanese Christian minister Takie Okumura launched the Educational Campaign, whose goal was "to make the Japanese laborers see the value of labor on the sugar plantation and encourage the young element to follow the footsteps of their parents," according to Okumura's son and co-leader of the campaign, Umetaro. Lest

38 Okihiro, *Cane Fires*, pp. 134–35.

39 Ibid., p. 141. From 1868 to 1893, Samuel Chapman Armstrong founded and headed the Hampton Normal and Agricultural Institute in Virginia to teach African Americans "industrial training" to promote racial order and to train teachers who would instruct blacks to accept a subordinate role in society. Many of Armstrong's racial views were shaped in Hawaii, where he was born and where his father served as a missionary (James D. Anderson, "The Hampton Model of Normal School Industrial Education, 1868–1900," in *New Perspectives on Black Educational History*, ed. Vincent P. Franklin and James D. Anderson [Boston: G. K. Hall, 1978], pp. 61–96).

the emphasis on education among Hawaii's Japanese be misconstrued as a means for upward mobility, University of Hawaii president David Crawford lectured the youth: "Do not count on education to do too much for you, do not take it too seriously. Do not expect a college degree, an A.B. or a Ph.D., to get you ahead unduly in this world."[40]

Meanwhile, the children of the white elite attended the private schools that sent their graduates to Stanford, Harvard, and Yale, and the children of other whites flocked to segregated English standard schools established in 1920. The dual public school system, standard schools for whites and nonstandard schools for Asians, was shown to be unequal in a 1941 survey. Sixth-graders in standard schools achieved a 6.2 grade level in tests administered by the study, whereas sixth-graders in nonstandard schools scored at a 5.4 grade level. The gap widened as the children progressed in school. Ninth-graders in standard schools achieved a 9.4 grade level, while their counterparts in nonstandard schools scored at a 7.6 level, and standard school twelfth-graders scored two full grades above nonstandard students.[41] Separate was unequal, and Americanization meant, in that system of public education, maintenance of the established order, the status quo.

The definition and meanings of citizenship and equal protection were severely tested during World War II, when an international conflict impinged upon domestic relations and when nationality and race, loyalty and patriotism, bubbled to the surface as dross. Despite their birthright of citizenship, Japanese Americans were always Japanese—a race apart—and bore the blood of the hated enemy. A February 1942 *Los Angeles Times* editorial explained: "A viper is nonetheless a viper wherever the egg is hatched—so a Japanese-American, born of Japanese parents—grows up to be a Japanese, not an American."[42] Lieutenant General John L. De Witt, the commander in charge of the Western

40 Okihiro, *Cane Fires*, pp. 133, 144.
41 Ibid., p. 140.
42 Daniels, *Concentration Camps*, p. 62.

Defense Command, subscribed to that view, and in early 1942 he recommended the mass detention of alien and citizen on the grounds that "the Japanese race is an enemy race and while many second and third generation Japanese born on United States soil, possessed of United States citizenship, have become 'American-ized,' the racial strains are undiluted." He put it more succinctly a year later: "A Jap is a Jap."[43] When Attorney General Francis Biddle demurred on the necessity of violating the rights of citizens during a meeting held about two and a half weeks before the issuing of Executive Order 9066, which authorized the mass removal and detention of Japanese, Assistant Secretary of War John McCloy replied: "If it is a question of the safety of the country [and] the Constitution. . . . Why the Constitution is just a scrap of paper to me."[44]

But the Constitution was more than "a scrap of paper" to Japanese Americans, who claimed its guarantee of equal protection, forming the Fair Play Committee at Heart Mountain concentration camp in Wyoming. The group was started by Hawaii-born Kiyoshi Okamoto, who held "open forums" to discuss the racism of camp administrators, the denial of free speech, the substandard wages and living conditions, and the injustice of the entire program of detention. His "Fair Play Committee of One" gained members and soon became the Fair Play Committee, which held meetings and posted bulletins advocating draft resistance after Secretary of War Henry Stimson announced on January 20, 1944, that the *nisei* (second-generation Japanese) would be subject to the draft. "The Fair Play Committee took up the draft issue," explained Frank Emi, a committee member. "We conducted public meetings to discuss all the ramifications of this program. We initially received permits to hold these meetings. But when the administration got wind of the subject of the gatherings, they refused to give us the permits. Still, we kept holding these meetings.

43 Commission on Wartime Relocation, *Personal Justice Denied*, p. 66.
44 Daniels, *Concentration Camps*, pp. 55–56.

Since the draft was of great concern to the internees, the meetings usually attracted a full house."[45]

Members of the committee, numbering about two hundred, debated a formal challenge to the government's action. Those in attendance, recalled Emi, were in complete agreement with the committee's stand, "that drafting nisei from these concentration camps, without restoration of their civil rights and rectification of the tremendous economic losses suffered by them, was not only morally wrong, but legally questionable." They issued their third and final bulletin, knowing that they thereby risked federal prosecution, but declared nonetheless:

We, the Nisei have been complacent and too inarticulate to the unconstitutional acts that we were subjected to. If ever there was a time or cause for decisive action, IT IS NOW!

We, the members of the FPC are not afraid to go to war—we are not afraid to risk our lives for our country. We would gladly sacrifice our lives to protect and uphold the principles and ideals of our country as set forth in the Constitution and the Bill of Rights, for on its inviolability depends the freedom, liberty, justice, and protection of all people including Japanese-American and all other minority groups. But have we been given such freedom, such liberty, such justice, such protection? NO!! Without any hearings, without due process of law as guaranteed by the Constitution and Bill of Rights, without any charges filed against us, without any evidence of wrongdoing on our part, one hundred and ten thousand innocent people were kicked out of their homes, literally uprooted from where they have lived for the greater part of their lives, and herded like dangerous criminals into concentration camps with barb wire fence and military police guarding it, AND THEN, WITHOUT RECTIFICATION OF THE INJUSTICES COMMITTED AGAINST US NOR WITHOUT RESTORATION OF OUR RIGHTS AS GUARANTEED BY THE CONSTITUTION, WE ARE ORDERED TO JOIN THE ARMY THRU *DISCRIMINATORY PROCEDURES* INTO A *SEGREGATED COMBAT UNIT*! Is that the American way? NO! The FPC believes that unless such actions are opposed *NOW*, and steps taken to remedy such

45 Frank Seishi Emi, "Draft Resistance at the Heart Mountain Concentration Camp and the Fair Play Committee," in *Frontiers of Asian American Studies: Writing, Research, and Commentary*, ed. Gail M. Nomura et al. (Pullman: Washington State University Press, 1989), p. 42.

injustices and discriminations, *IMMEDIATELY*, the future of all minorities and the future of this democratic nation is in danger.

Members of the committee thus resolved to refuse to comply with the physical examination and the induction notices to test the constitutionality of their detention.[46]

The camp administrators branded Kiyoshi Okamoto and other committee leaders "disloyal" and transferred them to Tule Lake concentration camp, designated since July 1943 as the site for dissidents and disloyals. They charged the sixty-three draft resisters and seven members of the Fair Play Committee's executive council with draft evasion and conspiracy to violate the law. Federal district judge Blake Kennedy found all sixty-three guilty, sentenced them to three years' imprisonment, and assailed their loyalty: "If they are truly loyal American citizens," he wrote, "they should . . . embrace the opportunity to discharge the duties [of citizenship] by offering themselves in the cause of our National Defense."[47] The seven leaders were likewise found guilty by federal district judge Eugene Rice, who sentenced them to four years at Leavenworth Federal Penitentiary. After the war with Japan had ended, the Tenth Circuit Court of Appeals reversed the convictions of the seven, and on Christmas Eve, 1947, President Harry Truman granted a presidential pardon to all *nisei* draft resisters. Guntaro Kubota, one of the seven, perhaps best summed up the feelings of the draft resisters when he told Frank Emi one day while sitting together in a Leavenworth prison cell: "Emi, I'm really proud to be here with you fellows. If I don't ever do anything else in my life, this will be the proudest thing I ever did because I had a part in your fight for a principle." Remembered Emi, "I will never forget his words. Mr. Kubota passed away at the age of sixty-two."[48]

46 Ibid., pp. 43–44. For a summary of the debate among Japanese Americans in the Heart Mountain camp sparked by the Fair Play Committee's stand, see Daniels, *Concentration Camps*, pp. 124–25.

47 Daniels, *Concentration Camps*, pp. 125–27.

48 Emi, "Draft Resistance," pp. 45–48. During World War I, Chinese who could not become naturalized citizens but who were still subject to the draft contested the Wilson administration's mandate. Writing to the Chinese min-

Excluded, exploited, and said to have no more effect than "cattle on the ranges," Asian American laborers went on strike for equality "irrespective of race, color, creed, nationality, or previous condition of servitude," and they organized workers into unions "without regard to their color or race." Segregated into "nonstandard" and "colored" schools, Asian American students and their parents condemned the practice and, to paraphrase Mary McGladery Tape, found themselves to be more American than those who would deny a child equal education on the basis of race. Their refusal to accept the undemocratic idea of "separate but equal" would result in victory in the 1954 landmark decision *Brown v. Board of Education*, widely remembered as a triumph only for African Americans. The foreign-language school challenge of the 1920s, an act of resistance that taught Asian Americans "to stand up for our rights as guaranteed under the Constitution," presaged the bilingual education suit filed in 1970 by Kinney Kinmon Lau and twelve other Chinese American students on behalf of nearly 3,000 Chinese-speaking students in the San Francisco Unified School District. Four years later, the U.S. Supreme Court rendered its decision of *Lau v. Nichols*, which extended *Brown* and held that "there is no equality of treatment merely by providing students with the same facilities, textbooks, teachers, and curriculum; for students who do not understand English are effectively foreclosed from any meaningful education."[49] And the student-inspired critique of higher education that

ister in Washington, D.C., they declared: "Without any rights, [the Chinese] should not be drafted. . . . The United States declared war on Germany for justice. But why are all kinds of exclusion acts and regulations applied to the Chinese, not to [the people from] other countries? Is it justice?" They concluded: "When not needed, we are cruelly oppressed and treated like meat on somebody's chopping board. When needed, we are forced to toil like oxen and horses. We have responsibilities but no rights. We may be ignorant, but we are not so foolish as to tolerate this" (*China and the West*, December 8, 1917, cited in Yong Chen, "China in America: A Cultural Study of Chinese San Francisco, 1850–1943" [Ph.D. diss., Cornell University, 1993]).

49 L. Ling-Chi Wang, "*Lau v. Nichols*: History of a Struggle for Equal and Quality Education," in *Counterpoint*, ed. Gee, pp. 240–63.

sought a sounder and more inclusive curriculum led to the formal establishment of new programs and fields of inquiry, including ethnic and women's studies.

The Asian American struggle for inclusion within the American community, as migrants and citizens, was principally based upon the guarantee of equal protection under the Fourteenth Amendment. As neither white nor black, Asians were deemed "aliens ineligible to citizenship" and were denied the privileges of life, liberty, and property, exemplified by their exclusion from the white courtroom, restrictions placed upon their choice of spouses and livelihoods, and land laws that limited their access to real property. But Asians sought to escape the restrictive and exploitative bonds by forming labor unions, contesting the intent and application of discriminatory legislation, epitomized by *Yick Wo*, and affirming their birthright of citizenship, as in *Kim Ark Wong*. The antidemocratic concentration camps spawned the democratic demand in 1944 for "fair play," whose leaders endorsed President Abraham Lincoln's reasoning, "If by the mere force of numbers a majority should deprive a minority of any Constitutional right, it might in a moral point of view justify a revolution."[50] And they initiated the 1980s campaign for redress and reparations, which culminated in the Civil Liberties Act of 1988.

The American ideals of independence and national self-determination inspired, in part, the decolonization and feminist movements among Third World peoples both within and without the United States, as exemplified by the Gadar movement and the Korean Women's Patriotic Society of California. The Asian American disposition to test the sincerity of the Declaration of Independence undergirded an Asian American civil rights movement that, among other accomplishments, defined the American identity as inclusive of white, black, and yellow. The Asian American experience, when considered in the light of the "when and where" of its entry into the European consciousness and the recentering of women within its history, extends the borders of the American

50 Emi, "Draft Resistance," p. 53.

identity to a global arena. Although that transnational context
was determined by the course of European expansion and incorporation, Asian and Asian American resistance sought to disman-
tle imperialism at home and abroad, employing the principles and
tools of the colonizers at the margins, but also at the core, in what
writer Salman Rushdie has called the "empire within."[51] The results of the Asian American struggle for nonracialism in the workplace, equality in education, linguistic and cultural rights,
decolonization, and women's liberation are significant contributions toward securing the fundamental freedoms of all
Americans.

Over the course of these six chapters, I have sought to examine
the margins of historical consciousness (when and where I enter),
race (is yellow black or white?), gender (recentering women),
class (family album), and culture (perils of the body and mind).
The view from those sites, those positions, it seems to me, affords
a clearer perspective on the mainstream, its location, ambiguities,
and contradictions. Although situating itself at the core, the mainstream is not the center that embraces and draws the diverse nation together. Although attributing to itself a singleness of
purpose and resolve, the mainstream is neither uniform nor all-
powerful in its imperialism and hegemony. Although casting the
periphery beyond the bounds of civility and religion, the mainstream derives its identity, its integrity, from its representation of
its Other. And despite its authorship of the central tenets of democracy, the mainstream has been silent on the publication of its
creed. In fact, the margin has held the nation together with its expansive reach; the margin has tested and ensured the guarantees
of citizenship; and the margin has been the true defender of American democracy, equality, and liberty. From that vantage, we can
see the margin as mainstream.

51 Salman Rushdie, "The New Empire within Britain," *New Society*, December 9, 1982.

Bibliography

Adams, Brooks. *The Law of Civilization and Decay: An Essay on History.* New York: Macmillan, 1895.

Adamson, Alan H. *Sugar without Slaves: The Political Economy of British Guiana, 1838–1904.* New Haven: Yale University Press, 1972.

Alexander, Adele Logan. *Ambiguous Lives: Free Women of Color in Rural Georgia, 1789–1879.* Fayetteville: University of Arkansas Press, 1991.

Alpers, Edward A. *The East African Slave Trade.* Dar es Salaam: East African Publishing House, 1967.

Anderson, James D. "The Hampton Model of Normal School Industrial Education, 1868–1900." In *New Perspectives on Black Educational History*, edited by Vincent P. Franklin and James D. Anderson. Boston: G. K. Hall, 1978.

Appleby, Joyce. "Recovering America's Historic Diversity: Beyond Exceptionalism." *Journal of American History* 79, no. 2 (September 1992): 419–31.

Aptheker, Herbert. *American Negro Slave Revolts.* New York: International Publishers, 1983.

Arrian's History of the Expedition of Alexander the Great, and Conquest of Persia. Translated by John Rooke. London: W. McDowall, 1813.

Barth, Gunther. *Bitter Strength: A History of the Chinese in the United States, 1850–1870.* Cambridge: Harvard University Press, 1964.

Beard, Charles A. "Introduction." In *The Law of Civilization and Decay: An Essay on History*, by Brooks Adams. New York: Macmillan, 1895.

Beck, Louis. *New York's Chinatown: An Historical Presentation of Its People and Places.* New York: Bohemia Publishers, 1898.

Beechert, Edward D. *Working in Hawaii: A Labor History*. Honolulu: University of Hawaii Press, 1985.

Berthoff, Rowland T. "Southern Attitudes toward Immigration, 1865–1914." *Journal of Southern History* 17, no. 3 (August 1951): 328–60.

Binder, Frederick M. *The Color Problem in Early National America as Viewed by John Adams, Jefferson and Jackson*. The Hague: Mouton, 1968.

Black, Doris. "The Black Chinese." *Sepia*, December 1975, pp. 19–24.

Bloom, Allan. *The Closing of the American Mind*. New York: Simon & Schuster, 1987.

———. "Responses to Fukuyama." *National Interest* 16 (Summer 1989): 19–21.

Breman, Jan. *Taming the Coolie Beast: Plantation Society and the Colonial Order in Southeast Asia*. Delhi: Oxford University Press, 1989.

Caldwell, Dan. "The Negroization of the Chinese Stereotype in California." *Southern California Quarterly* 53 (June 1971): 123–31.

Campbell, Mary B. *The Witness and the Other World: Exotic European Travel Writing, 400–1600*. Ithaca: Cornell University Press, 1988.

Campbell, Persia C. *Chinese Coolie Emigration to Countries within the British Empire*. London: P. S. King & Son, 1923.

Castelli, Elizabeth. "'I Will Make Mary Male': Pieties of the Body and Gender Transformation of Christian Women in Late Antiquity." In *Body Guards: The Cultural Politics of Gender Ambiguity*, edited by Julia Epstein and Kristina Straub. New York: Routledge, 1991.

Caudill, William, and George De Vos. "Achievement, Culture and Personality: The Case of the Japanese Americans." *American Anthropologist* 58 (1956): 1102–26.

Chalfen, Richard. *Turning Leaves: The Photograph Collections of Two Japanese American Families*. Albuquerque: University of New Mexico Press, 1991.

Chan, Sucheng. *Asian Americans: An Interpretive History*. Boston: Twayne Publishers, 1991.

———. "The Exclusion of Chinese Women, 1870–1943." In *Entry Denied: Exclusion and the Chinese Community in America, 1882–1943*, edited by Sucheng Chan. Philadelphia: Temple University Press, 1991.

———. "Introduction." In *Bitter Melon: Stories from the Last Rural Chinese Town in America*, by Jeff Gillenkirk and James Motlow. Seattle: University of Washington Press, 1987.

———. *This Bitter-Sweet Soil: The Chinese in California Agriculture, 1860–1910*. Berkeley and Los Angeles: University of California Press, 1986.

Char, Tin-Yuke, comp. and ed. *The Sandalwood Mountains: Readings and Stories of the Early Chinese in Hawaii*. Honolulu: University Press of Hawaii, 1975.

Chen, Yong. "China in America: A Cultural Study of Chinese San Francisco, 1850–1943." Ph.D. diss., Cornell University, 1993.

Cheng, Lucie. "Free, Indentured, Enslaved: Chinese Prostitutes in Nineteenth-Century America." In *Labor Immigration under Capitalism: Asian Workers in the United States before World War II*, edited by Lucie Cheng and Edna Bonacich. Berkeley and Los Angeles: University of California Press, 1984.

Chien, Vanessa. "Unravelling Popular Spinsterhood in the Canton Delta: Marriage Resistance Re-imagined." B.A. thesis, Amherst College, 1992.

Chin, Frank. *The Chinaman Pacific & Frisco R. R. Co.* Minneapolis: Coffee House Press, 1988.

———. *Donald Duk*. Minneapolis: Coffee House Press, 1991.

Chuman, Frank F. *The Bamboo People: The Law and Japanese-Americans*. Del Mar, Calif.: Publisher's Inc., 1976.

Cohen, Lucy M. *Chinese in the Post–Civil War South: A People without a History*. Baton Rouge: Louisiana State University Press, 1984.

———. "Early Arrivals." *Southern Exposure*, July/August 1984, pp. 24–30.

———. "Entry of Chinese to the Lower South from 1865 to 1879: Policy Dilemmas." *Southern Studies* 17, no. 1 (Spring 1978): 5–37.

Commission on Wartime Relocation and Internment of Civilians. *Personal Justice Denied*. Washington, D.C.: Government Printing Office, 1982.

The Complete Works of William Shakespeare. New York: Walter J. Black, 1937.

Conniff, James C. G. "Our Amazing Chinese Kids." *Coronet* 39 (December 1955): 31–36.

Cordova, Joan May T., and Alexis S. Canillo, eds. *Voices: A Filipino American Oral History*. Stockton: Filipino Oral History Project, 1984.

Crèvecoeur, J. Hector St. John de. *Letters from an American Farmer.* New York: Fox, Duffield & Co., 1904.

Crichton, Michael. *Rising Sun.* New York: Alfred A. Knopf, 1992.

Croll, Elisabeth. *Feminism and Socialism in China.* London: Routledge & Kegan Paul, 1978.

Daniels, Douglas. *Pioneer Urbanites: A Social and Cultural History of Black San Francisco.* Philadelphia: Temple University Press, 1980.

Daniels, Roger. *Asian America: Chinese and Japanese in the United States since 1850.* Seattle: University of Washington Press, 1988.

————. *Concentration Camps: North America, Japanese in the United States and Canada during World War II.* Malabar, Fla.: Robert E. Krieger Publishing, 1981.

————. "Westerners from the East: Oriental Immigrants Reappraised." *Pacific Historical Review* 36 (1966): 373–83.

Davis, David Brion. *Slavery and Human Progress.* New York: Oxford University Press, 1984.

Desai, Neera, and Maithreyi Krishnaraj. *Women and Society in India.* Delhi: Ajanta Publications, 1987.

Dodgeon, Michael H., and Samuel N. C. Lieu, comps. and eds. *The Roman Eastern Frontier and the Persian Wars (AD 226–363): A Documentary History.* London: Routledge, 1991.

Dooner, Pierton W. *Last Days of the Republic.* San Francisco: Alta California Publishing, 1880.

Drinnon, Richard. *Facing West: The Metaphysics of Indian-Hating and Empire-Building.* New York: New American Library, 1980.

duBois, Page. *Centaurs and Amazons: Women and the Pre-history of the Great Chain of Being.* Ann Arbor: University of Michigan Press, 1982.

Du Bois, W. E. B. *The World and Africa, An Inquiry into the Part Which Africa Has Played in World History.* New York: International Publishers, 1965.

Emi, Frank Seishi. "Draft Resistance at the Heart Mountain Concentration Camp and the Fair Play Committee." In *Frontiers of Asian American Studies: Writing, Research, and Commentary,* edited by Gail M. Nomura et al. Pullman: Washington State University Press, 1989.

Espina, Marina E. *Filipinos in Louisiana.* New Orleans: A. F. Laborde & Sons, 1988.

Ethnic Studies Oral History Project and the United Okinawan Association of Hawaii. *Uchinanchu: A History of Okinawans in Hawaii*. Honolulu: Ethnic Studies Program, University of Hawaii, 1981.

Facts about Filipino Immigration into California. State of California, Department of Industrial Relations. Special Bulletin no. 3. San Francisco, 1930.

Fiedler, Leslie A. *The Return of the Vanishing American*. New York: Stein & Day, 1968.

Fiman, Byron G., Jonathan F. Borus, and M. Duncan Stanton. "Black–White and American–Vietnamese Relations among Soldiers in Vietnam." *Journal of Social Issues* 31, no. 4 (1975): 39–48.

Flowers, Montaville. *The Japanese Conquest of American Opinion*. New York: George H. Doran Co., 1917.

Foner, Philip S. "Reverend George Washington Woodbey: Early Twentieth Century California Black Socialist." *Journal of Negro History* 61, no. 2 (April 1976): 149–50.

Fong, Sit Yin. *Tales of Chinatown*. Singapore: Heinemann Asia, 1983.

Francisco, Luzviminda. "The First Vietnam: The Philippine–American War, 1899–1902." In *Letters in Exile: An Introductory Reader on the History of Pilipinos in America*, edited by Jesse Quinsaat. Los Angeles: UCLA Asian American Studies Center, 1976.

Fredrickson, George M. *The Arrogance of Race: Historical Perspectives on Slavery, Racism, and Social Inequality*. Middletown: Wesleyan University Press, 1988.

Freeman, James M. *Hearts of Sorrow: Vietnamese-American Lives*. Stanford: Stanford University Press, 1989.

Freeman, Jo, ed. *Women: A Feminist Perspective*. Palo Alto, Calif.: Mayfield Publishing, 1975.

Freeman-Grenville, G. S. P., ed. *The East African Coast: Select Documents from the First to the Earlier Nineteenth Century*. London: Oxford University Press, 1962.

Fukuyama, Francis. "The End of History?" *National Interest* 16 (Summer 1989): 3–18.

Garrow, David J. *The FBI and Martin Luther King, Jr.* New York: Penguin Books, 1981.

Gatewood, Willard B., Jr. *"Smoked Yankees" and the Struggle for Empire: Letters from Negro Soldiers, 1898–1902*. Urbana: University of Illinois Press, 1971.

Genovese, Eugene D. "Herbert Aptheker's Achievement and Our Responsibility." In *In Resistance: Studies in African, Caribbean, and Afro-American History*, edited by Gary Y. Okihiro. Amherst: University of Massachusetts Press, 1986.

Giddings, Paula. *When and Where I Enter: The Impact of Black Women on Race and Sex in America*. New York: William Morrow, 1984.

Gill, Gerald R. *Meanness Mania: The Changed Mood*. Washington, D.C.: Howard University Press, 1980.

Gillenkirk, Jeff, and James Motlow. *Bitter Melon: Stories from the Last Rural Chinese Town in America*. Seattle: University of Washington Press, 1987.

Glenn, Evelyn Nakano. "The Dialectics of Wage Work: Japanese-American Women and Domestic Service, 1905–1940." In *Labor Immigration under Capitalism: Asian Workers in the United States before World War II*, edited by Lucie Cheng and Edna Bonacich. Berkeley and Los Angeles: University of California Press, 1984.

———. *Issei, Nisei, Warbride: Three Generations of Japanese American Women in Domestic Service*. Philadelphia: Temple University Press, 1986.

Goode, Kenneth G. *California's Black Pioneers: A Brief Historical Survey*. Santa Barbara: McNally & Loftin, 1974.

Grant, Madison. *The Passing of the Great Race; or, the Racial Basis of European History*. New York: Charles Scribner's Sons, 1916.

The Greek Alexander Romance. Translated by Richard Stoneman. London: Penguin Books, 1991.

Green, William A. *British Slave Emancipation: The Sugar Colonies and the Great Experiment, 1830–1865*. London: Oxford University Press, 1976.

Handlin, Joanna F. "Lu K'un's New Audience: The Influence of Women's Literacy on Sixteenth-Century Thought." In *Women in Chinese Society*, edited by Margery Wolf and Roxane Witke. Stanford: Stanford University Press, 1975.

Harris, Joseph E. *The African Presence in Asia: Consequences of the East African Slave Trade*. Evanston: Northwestern University Press, 1971.

Hart, Henry H. *Marco Polo: Venetian Adventurer*. Norman: University of Oklahoma Press, 1967.

Hellwig, David J. "Afro-American Reactions to the Japanese and the

Anti-Japanese Movement, 1906–1924." *Phylon* 38, no. 1 (March 1977): 93–104.

———. "Black Reactions to Chinese Immigration and the Anti-Chinese Movement: 1850–1910." *Amerasia Journal* 6, no. 2 (1979): 25–44.

Higham, John. *Send These to Me: Jews and Other Immigrants in Urban America*. New York: Atheneum, 1975.

Hill, Robert A., ed. *The Marcus Garvey and Universal Negro Improvement Association Papers*. 7 vols. to date. Berkeley and Los Angeles: University of California Press, 1983–90.

Hippocrates. Translated by W. H. S. Jones. Cambridge: Harvard University Press, 1923.

Hom, Marlon Kau. "Some Cantonese Folksongs on the American Experience." *Western Folklore* 42, no. 2 (April 1983): 126–39.

———. *Songs of Gold Mountain: Cantonese Rhymes from San Francisco Chinatown*. Berkeley and Los Angeles: University of California Press, 1987.

Hoover, Dwight W. *The Red and the Black*. Chicago: Rand McNally, 1976.

Hosokawa, Bill. *Nisei: The Quiet Americans*. New York: William Morrow, 1969.

Ichihashi, Yamato. *Japanese in the United States*. Stanford: Stanford University Press, 1932.

Ichioka, Yuji. "*Ameyuki-san*: Japanese Prostitutes in Nineteenth-Century America." *Amerasia Journal* 4, no. 1 (1977): 1–21.

———. *The Issei: The World of the First Generation Japanese Immigrants, 1885–1924*. New York: Free Press, 1988.

Ito, Kazuo. *Issei: A History of Japanese Immigrants in North America*, translated by Shinichiro Nakamura and Jean S. Gerard. Seattle: Japanese Community Service, 1973.

Iwata, Masakazu. "Japanese Immigrants in California Agriculture." *Agricultural History* 36, no. 1 (January 1962): 25–37.

Jane, Cecil, ed. and trans. *The Four Voyages of Columbus*. New York: Dover Publications, 1988.

Jayawardena, Kumari. *Feminism and Nationalism in the Third World*. London: Zed Books, 1986.

Jensen, Joan M. *Passage from India: Asian Indian Immigrants in North America*. New Haven: Yale University Press, 1988.

Jordan, Winthrop. *White over Black*. Chapel Hill: University of North Carolina Press, 1968.

Katz, William Loren. *The Black West*. Seattle: Open Hand Publishing, 1987.

Kelly-Gadol, Joan. "The Social Relation of the Sexes: Methodological Implications of Women's History." *Signs* 1, no. 4 (1976): 809–23.

Kim, Elaine H. "War Story." In *Making Waves: An Anthology of Writings by and about Asian American Women*, edited by Asian Women United of California. Boston: Beacon Press, 1989.

Kim, Yung-Chung, ed. and trans. *Women of Korea: A History from Ancient Times to 1945*. Seoul, Korea: Ewha Woman's University Press, 1976.

Kingston, Maxine Hong. *China Men*. New York: Ballantine Books, 1977.

———. *The Woman Warrior: Memoirs of a Girlhood among Ghosts*. New York: Alfred A. Knopf, 1975.

Kluger, Richard. *Simple Justice: The History of* Brown v. Board of Education *and Black America's Struggle for Equality*. New York: Vintage Books, 1975.

Knight, Franklin W. *Slave Society in Cuba during the Nineteenth Century*. Madison: University of Wisconsin Press, 1970.

Kochiyama, Yuri. "Because Movement Work Is Contagious." *Gidra*, 1990, pp. 6, 10.

Kotkin, Joel. *Tribes: How Race, Religion and Identity Determine Success in the New Global Economy*. New York: Random House, 1992.

LaFeber, Walter. *The New Empire: An Interpretation of American Expansion, 1860–1898*. Ithaca: Cornell University Press, 1963.

Lai, Him Mark, Genny Lim, and Judy Yung. *Island: Poetry and History of Chinese Immigrants on Angel Island, 1910–1940*. Seattle: University of Washington Press, 1991.

Lapp, Rudolph M. *Blacks in Gold Rush California*. New Haven: Yale University Press, 1977.

Laurence, K. O. *Immigration into the West Indies in the 19th Century*. Mona, West Indies: Caribbean Universities Press, 1971.

Lea, Homer. *The Valor of Ignorance*. New York: Harper & Brothers, 1909.

Lee, Joann Faung Jean, ed. *Asian American Experiences in the United States: Oral Histories of First to Fourth Generation Americans from China, the Philippines, Japan, India, the Pacific Islands,*

Vietnam and Cambodia. Jefferson, N.C.: McFarland & Co., 1991.

Lee, Mary Paik. *Quiet Odyssey: A Pioneer Korean Woman in America*, edited by Sucheng Chan. Seattle: University of Washington Press, 1990.

Lee, Yan Phou. "The Chinese Must Stay." *North American Review* 148, no. 389 (April 1889): 476–83.

Leonard, Karen. "Marriage and Family Life among Early Asian Indian Immigrants." In *From India to America: A Brief History of Immigration; Problems of Discrimination; Admission and Assimilation*, edited by S. Chandrasekhar. La Jolla: Population Review Publications, 1982.

Lerner, Gerda. "Placing Women in History: Definitions and Challenges." *Feminist Studies* 3, no. 1/2 (Fall 1975): 5–14.

Loewen, James W. *The Mississippi Chinese: Between Black and White.* Cambridge: Harvard University Press, 1971.

The Log of Christopher Columbus. Translated by Robert H. Fuson. Camden, Maine: International Marine Publishing, 1987.

Loraux, Nicole. "Herakles: The Super-male and the Feminine." In *Before Sexuality: The Construction of Erotic Experience in the Ancient Greek World*, edited by David M. Halperin, John J. Winkler, and Froma I. Zeitlin. Princeton: Princeton University Press, 1990.

Lovejoy, Arthur O. *The Great Chain of Being: A Study of the History of an Idea.* Cambridge: Harvard University Press, 1936.

Low, Victor. *The Unimpressible Race: A Century of Educational Struggle by the Chinese in San Francisco.* San Francisco: East/West Publishing Co., 1982.

Lowe, Lisa. *Critical Terrains: French and British Orientalisms.* Ithaca: Cornell University Press, 1991.

Lukes, Timothy J., and Gary Y. Okihiro. *Japanese Legacy: Farming and Community Life in California's Santa Clara Valley.* Cupertino: California History Center, 1985.

Lydon, Sandy. *Chinese Gold: The Chinese in the Monterey Bay Region.* Capitola, Calif.: Capitola Book Co., 1985.

Lyu, Kingsley K. "Korean Nationalist Activities in Hawaii and the Continental United States, 1900–1945, Part I: 1900–1919." *Amerasia Journal* 4, no. 1 (1977): 23–90.

McClain, Charles J., and Laurene Wu McClain. "The Chinese Contribution to the Development of American Law." In *Entry Denied: Exclusion and the Chinese Community in America, 1882–1943*, edited by Sucheng Chan. Philadelphia: Temple University Press, 1991.

McCunn, Ruthanne Lum. *Chinese American Portraits: Personal Histories, 1828–1988*. San Francisco: Chronicle Books, 1988.

Mahabir, Noor Kumar. *The Still Cry: Personal Accounts of East Indians in Trinidad and Tobago during Indentureship (1845–1917)*. Tacarigua, Trinidad: Calaloux Publications, 1985.

Mannoni, O. *Prospero and Caliban: The Psychology of Colonization*. Translated by Pamela Powesland. London: Methuen, 1956.

Manson, Marsden. *The Yellow Peril in Action: A Possible Chapter in History*. San Francisco: n.p., 1907.

Masumoto, David Mas. *Country Voices: The Oral History of a Japanese American Family Farm Community*. Del Rey, Calif.: Inaka Countryside Publications, 1987.

Mathew, Gervase. "The East African Coast until the Coming of the Portuguese." In *History of East Africa*, edited by Roland Oliver and Gervase Mathew, vol. 1. London: Oxford University Press, 1963.

Mazumdar, Sucheta. "General Introduction: A Woman-Centered Perspective on Asian American History." In *Making Waves: An Anthology of Writings by and about Asian American Women*, edited by Asian Women United of California. Boston: Beacon Press, 1989.

Mei, June. "Socioeconomic Origins of Emigration: Guangdong to California, 1850 to 1882." In *Labor Immigration under Capitalism: Asian Workers in the United States before World War II*, edited by Lucie Cheng and Edna Bonacich. Berkeley and Los Angeles: University of California Press, 1984.

Meier, Matt S., and Feliciano Rivera, eds. *Readings on La Raza: The Twentieth Century*. New York: Hill & Wang, 1974.

Melville, Herman. *The Confidence-Man: His Masquerade*. Edited by Elizabeth S. Foster. New York: Hendricks House, 1954.

Memmi, Albert. *The Colonizer and the Colonized*. Boston: Beacon Press, 1967.

Miller, Christopher. *Blank Darkness: Africanist Discourse in French*. Chicago: University of Chicago Press, 1985.

Miller, Kelly. *The Everlasting Stain*. Washington, D.C.: Associated Publishers, 1924.

Miller, Stuart Creighton. *The Unwelcome Immigrant: The American Image of the Chinese, 1785–1882*. Berkeley and Los Angeles: University of California Press, 1969.

Misawa, Steven, ed. *Beginnings: Japanese Americans in San Jose*. San Jose: Japanese American Community Senior Service, 1981.

Morgan, David. *The Mongols*. London: Basil Blackwell, 1986.

Mosse, George L. *Toward the Final Solution: A History of European Racism*. New York: Howard Fertig, 1978.

Murase, Mike. "Ethnic Studies and Higher Education for Asian Americans." In *Counterpoint: Perspectives on Asian America*, edited by Emma Gee. Los Angeles: UCLA Asian American Studies Center, 1976.

Myrdal, Gunnar. *An American Dilemma: The Negro Problem and Modern Democracy*. New York: Harper & Brothers, 1944.

Nash, Gary B. *Red, White, and Black: The Peoples of Early America*. Englewood Cliffs, N.J.: Prentice-Hall, 1974.

Nee, Victor G., and Brett de Bary Nee. *Longtime Californ': A Documentary Study of an American Chinatown*. Boston: Houghton Mifflin, 1974.

O'Brien, Kenneth B., Jr. "Education, Americanization and the Supreme Court: The 1920s." *American Quarterly* 13, no. 2 (Summer 1961): 161–71.

Odo, Franklin S., and Harry Minoru Urata. "Hole Hole Bushi: Songs of Hawaii's Japanese Immigrants." *Mana* (Hawaii ed.) 6, no. 1 (1981): 69–75.

Ogawa, Dennis M. *From Japs to Japanese: The Evolution of Japanese-American Stereotypes*. Berkeley: McCutchan Publishing, 1971.

Okihiro, Gary Y. *Cane Fires: The Anti-Japanese Movement in Hawaii, 1865–1945*. Philadelphia: Temple University Press, 1991.

Omi, Michael, and Howard Winant. *Racial Formation in the United States: From the 1960s to the 1980s*. New York: Routledge & Kegan Paul, 1986.

Ono, Kazuko. *Chinese Women in a Century of Revolution, 1850–1950*. Edited by Joshua A. Fogel. Stanford: Stanford University Press, 1989.

Osajima, Keith. "Asian Americans as the Model Minority: An Analysis of the Popular Press Image in the 1960s and 1980s." In *Reflections on Shattered Windows: Promises and Prospects for Asian American Studies*, edited by Gary Y. Okihiro et al. Pullman: Washington State University Press, 1988.

Painter, Nell Irvin. *Standing at Armageddon: The United States, 1877–1919*. New York: W. W. Norton, 1987.

Park, Robert E. "Introduction." In *The Japanese Invasion: A Study in the Psychology of Inter-racial Contacts*, by Jesse Frederick Steiner. Chicago: A. C. McClurg & Co., 1917.

Pearce, Roy Harvey. *Savagism and Civilization: A Study of the Indian and the American Mind*. Baltimore: Johns Hopkins University Press, 1965.

Peffer, George Anthony. "From under the Sojourner's Shadow: A Historiographical Study of Chinese Female Immigration to America, 1852–1882." *Journal of American Ethnic History* 2, no. 3 (Spring 1992): 41–67.

The Politics of Aristotle. Translated by Benjamin Jowett. Oxford: Clarendon Press, 1885.

Posadas, Barbara M. "The Hierarchy of Color and Psychological Adjustment in an Industrial Environment: Filipinos, the Pullman Company, and the Brotherhood of Sleeping Car Porters." *Labor History* 23, no. 3 (1982): 349–73.

Pozzetta, George E. "Foreigners in Florida: A Study of Immigration Promotion, 1865–1910." *Florida Historical Quarterly* 53, no. 2 (October 1974): 164–80.

Rankin, Mary Backus. "The Emergence of Women at the End of the Ch'ing: The Case of Ch'iu Chin." In *Women in Chinese Society*, edited by Margery Wolf and Roxane Witke. Stanford: Stanford University Press, 1975.

Reich, Robert B. "Is Japan Really out to Get Us?" *New York Times Book Review*, February 9, 1992.

Roark, James L. *Masters without Slaves: Southern Planters in the Civil War and Reconstruction*. New York: W. W. Norton, 1977.

Ross, Robert. *Cape of Torments: Slavery and Resistance in South Africa*. London: Routledge & Kegan Paul, 1983.

Rubin, Arnold. *Black Nanban: Africans in Japan during the Sixteenth Century*. Bloomington: African Studies Program, Indiana University, 1974.

Rushdie, Salman. "The New Empire within Britain." *New Society*, December 9, 1982.

Said, Edward W. *Orientalism*. New York: Random House, 1978.

Sandmeyer, Elmer Clarence. *The Anti-Chinese Movement in California*. Urbana: University of Illinois Press, 1973.

Sarasohn, Eileen Sunada, ed. *The Issei: Portrait of a Pioneer*. Palo Alto: Pacific Books, 1983.

Saxton, Alexander. *The Indispensable Enemy: Labor and the Anti-Chinese Movement in California*. Berkeley and Los Angeles: University of California Press, 1971.

———. *The Rise and Fall of the White Republic: Class Politics and Mass Culture in Nineteenth Century America*. London: Verso, 1990.

Schlesinger, Arthur M. *The Disuniting of America*. Knoxville, Tenn.: Whittle Direct Books, 1991.

Schuster, Nancy. "Changing the Female Body: Wise Women and the Bodhisattva Career in Some *Maharatnakutasutras*." *Journal of the International Association of Buddhist Studies* 4, no. 1 (1981): 24–69.

Schwendinger, Robert J. *Ocean of Bitter Dreams: Maritime Relations between China and the United States, 1850–1915*. Tucson: Westernlore Press, 1988.

Scott, Joanna C. *Indochina's Refugees: Oral Histories from Laos, Cambodia and Vietnam*. Jefferson, N.C.: McFarland & Co., 1989.

Scott, Rebecca J. *Slave Emancipation in Cuba: The Transition to Free Labor, 1860–1899*. Princeton: Princeton University Press, 1985.

Shafer, Michael D., ed. *The Legacy: The Vietnam War in the American Imagination*. Boston: Beacon Press, 1990.

Shankman, Arnold. *Ambivalent Friends: Afro-Americans View the Immigrant*. Westport, Conn.: Greenwood Press, 1982.

———. "'Asiatic Ogre' or 'Desirable Citizen'? The Image of Japanese Americans in the Afro-American Press, 1867–1933." *Pacific Historical Review* 46, no. 4 (November 1977): 567–87.

———. "Black on Yellow: Afro-Americans View Chinese-Americans." *Phylon* 39, no. 1 (Spring 1978): 1–17.

Singh, Jane. "The Gadar Party: Political Expression in an Immigrant Community." *South Asia Bulletin* 2, no. 1 (Spring 1982): 29–38.

Smith, William Carlson. *Americans in Process: A Study of Our Citizens of Oriental Ancestry*. Ann Arbor, Mich.: Edwards Brothers, 1937.

———. *The Second Generation Oriental in America*. Honolulu: Institute of Pacific Relations, 1927.

Spoehr, Luther W. "Sambo and the Heathen Chinee: Californians' Racial Stereotypes in the Late 1870s." *Pacific Historical Review* 42, no. 2 (May 1973): 185–204.

Steiner, Jesse Frederick. *The Japanese Invasion: A Study in the Psychology of Inter-racial Contacts.* Chicago: A. C. McClurg & Co., 1917.

Stevenson, Robert Louis. *Across the Plains, with Other Memories and Essays.* New York: Charles Scribner's Sons, 1900.

Stewart, Watt. *Chinese Bondage in Peru.* Durham: Duke University Press, 1951.

Stockard, Janice E. *Daughters of the Canton Delta: Marriage Patterns and Economic Strategies in South China, 1860–1930.* Stanford: Stanford University Press, 1989.

Stoddard, Lothrop. *Racial Realities in Europe.* New York: Charles Scribner's Sons, 1924.

———. *The Rising Tide of Color against White World-Supremacy.* New York: Charles Scribner's Sons, 1920.

Strong, Edward K. *The Second-Generation Japanese Problem.* Stanford: Stanford University Press, 1934.

Sunoo, Harold Hakwon, and Sonia Shinn Sunoo. "The Heritage of the First Korean Women Immigrants in the United States: 1903–1924." *Korean Christian Scholars Journal* 2 (Spring 1977): 142–71.

Sutton, J. E. G. *The East African Coast: An Historical and Archaeological Review.* Dar es Salaam: East African Publishing House, 1966.

Takaki, Ronald T. *Iron Cages: Race and Culture in Nineteenth-Century America.* New York: Alfred A. Knopf, 1979.

———. *Pau Hana: Plantation Life and Labor in Hawaii, 1835–1920.* Honolulu: University of Hawaii Press, 1983.

———. *Strangers from a Different Shore: A History of Asian Americans.* Boston: Little, Brown & Co., 1989.

Tateishi, John. *And Justice for All: An Oral History of the Japanese American Detention Camps.* New York: Random House, 1984.

tenBroek, Jacobus, Edward N. Barnhart, and Floyd W. Matson. *Prejudice, War and the Constitution: Causes and Consequences of the Evacuation of the Japanese Americans in World War II.* Berkeley and Los Angeles: University of California Press, 1954.

Thaker, Suvarna. "The Quality of Life of Asian Indian Women in the Motel Industry." *South Asia Bulletin* 2, no. 1 (Spring 1982): 68–73.

Thompson, Richard Austin. *The Yellow Peril, 1890–1924.* New York: Arno Press, 1978.

Tinker, Hugh. *A New System of Slavery: The Export of Indian La-*

bour Overseas, 1830–1920. London: Oxford University Press, 1974.

———. *South Asia: A Short History*. Honolulu: University of Hawaii Press, 1990.

Topley, Marjorie. "Marriage Resistance in Rural Kwangtung." In *Women in Chinese Society*, edited by Margery Wolf and Roxane Witke. Stanford: Stanford University Press, 1975.

The Travels of Marco Polo the Venetian. London: J. M. Dent, 1908.

The Travels of Sir John Mandeville. London: Macmillan, 1900.

Trotman, David Vincent. *Crime in Trinidad: Conflict and Control in a Plantation Society, 1838–1900*. Knoxville: University of Tennessee Press, 1986.

Tsai, Shih-shan H. "American Involvement in the Coolie Trade." *American Studies* 6, nos. 3 and 4 (December 1976): 47–66.

———. *The Chinese Experience in America*. Bloomington: Indiana University Press, 1986.

Tyrrell, W. Blake. *Amazons: A Study in Athenian Mythmaking*. Baltimore: Johns Hopkins University Press, 1984.

Umemoto, Karen. "'On Strike!' San Francisco State College Strike, 1968–69: The Role of Asian American Students." *Amerasia Journal* 15, no. 1 (1989): 3–41.

U.S. Congress. Senate. *Report of the Joint Special Committee to Investigate Chinese Immigration*. 44th Cong., 2d sess., 1877.

———. *Some Reasons for Chinese Exclusion*. 57th Cong., 1st sess., 1902. Document no. 137.

Vallangca, Roberto V. *Pinoy: The First Wave*. San Francisco: Strawberry Hill Press, 1977.

Wang, L. Ling-Chi. "*Lau v. Nichols*: History of a Struggle for Equal and Quality Education." In *Counterpoint: Perspectives on Asian America*, edited by Emma Gee. Los Angeles: UCLA Asian American Studies Center, 1976.

Washburn, Wilcomb E. "Columbus: On and off the Reservation." *National Review*, October 5, 1992, pp. 55–58.

Watson, R. L. *The Slave Question: Liberty and Property in South Africa*. Hanover: University Press of New England, 1990.

Weller, Judith Ann. *The East Indian Indenture in Trinidad*. Rio Piedras, P.R.: Institute of Caribbean Studies, University of Puerto Rico, 1968.

Winkler, John J. *The Constraints of Desire: The Anthropology of Sex and Gender in Ancient Greece*. New York: Routledge, 1990.

Wollenberg, Charles M. *All Deliberate Speed: Segregation and Exclusion in California Schools, 1855–1975*. Berkeley and Los Angeles: University of California Press, 1976.

Wong, Kevin Scott. "Encountering the Other: Chinese Immigration and Its Impact on Chinese and American Worldviews, 1875–1905." Ph.D. diss., University of Michigan, 1992.

Wong, Shawn. *Homebase*. New York: Plume, 1979.

Woo, Merle. "Letter to Ma." In *This Bridge Called My Back: Writings by Radical Women of Color*, edited by Cherríe Moraga and Gloria Anzaldúa. New York: Kitchen Table, Women of Color Press, 1983.

Wood, Peter H. *Black Majority: Negroes in Colonial South Carolina from 1670 through the Stono Rebellion*. New York: Alfred A. Knopf, 1975.

Wu, Cheng-Tsu, ed. *"Chink!" A Documentary History of Anti-Chinese Prejudice in America*. New York: World Publishing, 1972.

Wu, William F. *The Yellow Peril: Chinese Americans in American Fiction, 1850–1940*. Hamden, Conn.: Archon Books, 1982.

Yang, Eun Sik. "Korean Women of America: From Subordination to Partnership, 1903–1930." *Amerasia Journal* 11, no. 2 (1984): 1–28.

Yen, Ching-Hwang. *Coolies and Mandarins: China's Protection of Overseas Chinese during the Late Ch'ing Period (1851–1911)*. Singapore: Singapore University Press, 1985.

Yim, Sun Bin. "Korean Immigrant Women in Early Twentieth-Century America." In *Making Waves: An Anthology of Writings by and about Asian American Women*, edited by Asian Women United of California. Boston: Beacon Press, 1989.

Young, Robert. *White Mythologies: Writing History and the West*. London: Routledge, 1990.

Yu, Connie Young. "The World of Our Grandmothers." In *Making Waves: An Anthology of Writings by and about Asian American Women*, edited by Asian Women United of California. Boston: Beacon Press, 1989.

Yu, Renqiu. "Little Heard Voices: The Chinese Hand Laundry Alliance and the *China Daily News'* Appeal for Repeal of the Chinese Exclusion Act in 1943." In *Chinese America: History and Perspectives, 1990*, edited by Marlon K. Hom et al. San Francisco: Chinese Historical Society of America, 1990.

———. *To Save China, To Save Ourselves: The Chinese Hand Laundry*

Alliance of New York. Philadelphia: Temple University Press, 1992.

Yung, Judy. *Chinese Women of America: A Pictorial History*. Seattle: University of Washington Press, 1986.

————. "The Social Awakening of Chinese American Women as Reported in *Chung Sai Yat Po*, 1900–1911." In *Unequal Sisters: A Multicultural Reader in U.S. Women's History*, edited by Ellen Carol DuBois and Vicki L. Ruiz. New York: Routledge, 1990.

Yung, Wing. *My Life in China and America*. New York: Henry Holt, 1909.

Index

Adamnan, 11
Adams, Brooks, 130–31
Aeschylus, 11n
affirmative action, xiv
Africa: as habitat of monsters, 10;
    trade with Asia, 35–37
African Americans, x, xi, 29, 31–63,
    124–28, 129, 136, 140, 146, 147,
    150, 155, 159, 167, 168n, 173,
    174, 175; and conflicts with
    Asians, 31–32; racialisms of, xv,
    31, 54–55; significance of, ix, 155;
    as slaves, 4n, 21, 34, 44, 47, 48,
    49, 52, 124–27, 135; and solidar-
    ity with Asians, 30, 34–63, 90; as
    wage laborers, 45, 47; women, 3n,
    7, 39, 53, 55, 59
Africans, 6, 20, 21, 22, 24, 34–35,
    37; as the Other, 11n, 37, 48, 50,
    62; as slaves, 36–37, 39, 40, 41n,
    42, 43, 46, 47, 61; and slave trade,
    36–38, 45
Alexander the Great, 9, 10, 12, 13,
    26, 27
All India Women's Conference, 82
Almoravids, 37
Amazons, 13, 14. See also Asian
    women
Ambar, Malik, 36–37
American Federation of Labor, 54,
    158
American Indians, xi, 6, 16, 17, 20,
    21, 22–23, 24, 26, 28, 29, 33, 49,
    50, 51–52, 62, 109, 120–24, 146,
    150; significance of, ix

Americanization. See assimilation
An, Ch'ang ho, 165
Angel Island, 3, 4, 5, 66, 103
anti-Asianism, xii, xiii, 20, 48, 62, 89,
    108, 109–10, 115, 137, 151, 152,
    156, 164, 174. See also exclusion;
    racism
antimiscegenation. See miscegenation
Appleby, Joyce, 148
Appo, Quimbo, 145–46
apprenticeships, 39, 40
Aptheker, Herbert, 126
Arculf, Bishop, 11
Aristotle, 8–9, 11
Armstrong, Samuel Chapman, 168n
Arrian, 9, 11, 12
Asia, xii, 129–30; as habitat of mon-
    sters, 10, 11, 15, 17; representa-
    tions of, x, 8, 10, 11, 14, 15, 16,
    17, 19, 24, 68, 138
Asian Americans, xi, xii, xiii, xiv, xvi,
    xvii, 49, 59, 60, 68, 93–117,
    140–41, 151, 154; as cheap labor,
    45, 52, 54, 124, 140–41; as
    middlemen, xi; racialisms of, xv,
    54; significance of, ix–x, 156,
    173–75; and solidarity with Afri-
    cans, 34–63; women, 64–65, 66,
    67–68, 74–77, 78–80, 83–92. See
    also Asian Indian Americans;
    Chinese Americans; Filipino
    Americans; Japanese Americans;
    Korean Americans; migrant labor;
    model minority; picture brides;
    South Asian Americans; Southeast

Asian Americans; Vietnamese
  Americans
Asian American studies, xiv, xv, 93,
  116; exceptionalism of, xiv. *See
  also* ethnic studies
Asian Indian Americans, 39, 103–4,
  156, 164–65; women, 67, 105,
  115
Asian Indians, 9, 12, 16, 18, 19, 34,
  35, 36–37, 39, 127, 164–65;
  indentures, 39–41; women, 12,
  81–82, 103–4, 113, 115
Asians, 6, 22–23, 141–42; as cheap
  labor, 29, 34, 37, 45, 52, 130,
  131, 139; feminization of, 8, 9, 16,
  17, 120, 142; as oppressors, xv; as
  the Other, x, xiii, 9, 10, 11, 18, 19,
  26, 37, 48, 50, 52, 62, 138, 140,
  175; sexuality of, 11; as slaves, 8,
  9, 21,34, 38, 39
—men, 95–96; feminization of, 12,
  26, 142, 143, 144, 145
—women, 64–65, 68–74, 77–78, 79–
  83, 85, 92, 95, 97, 98, 144; feminization of, 11; masculinization of,
  10, 12, 144; sexuality of, 12, 14,
  15, 81, 144. *See also* Amazons;
  Asian Indians; Chinese; feminism;
  Filipinos; footbinding; Japanese;
  Korean women; nationalism; prostitutes; South Asians; Southeast
  Asians; Third World; Vietnamese
assimilation, xiv, xv, 5, 34, 61, 92,
  110–11, 134, 149, 167–69

Baba, Kozaburo, 158
bachelor society, xii, 67, 68, 91
Ballay, John, 39
Barnsley, Godfrey, 44
Batholdi, Frederic Auguste, 5
Beard, Charles A., 130
Beck, Louis, 145
Biddle, Francis, 170
Biggers, Earl Derr, 143–45
biracials, xii, xiv, 53, 53n, 59, 145
blackface minstrel shows, 50
blacks. *See* African Americans;
  Africans
Black Student Union, 163

Bloom, Allan, 60n
body: Asian, 8, 26, 143–44, 175;
  constructions of, xiv; emotions
  and, 12; European, 8, 146, 147,
  175
Bradford, William, 121–22
Brerewood, Edward, 22
Brotherhood of Sleeping Car Porters,
  54
Brown v. Board of Education, 58, 173
Bruce, Blanche K., 48
Buck, Pearl, 146
Buffon, Georges, 23
Bureau of Investigation. *See* Federal
  Bureau of Investigation
Burwell, William M., 45
Bush, George, xiv, 150
Byrd, William, 124

Caliban. *See Tempest, The*
Campbell, Mary B., 10, 11
Cape Coloured, 39
Caudill, William, 32–33
Chalfen, Richard, 94
Chan, Charlie, 143–45
Chan, Sucheng, 86
Chang, Chao, 43
Chen, Lilac, 99
Cheng, Lucie, 77
Chicanos, 88, 90, 123n, 158
Chin, Frank, 152
Chinese, 15, 37, 119; coolies, 38, 40n,
  41–44, 45, 46, 47, 48, 131; representations of, 20, 24, 25, 26, 70,
  118–19, 142–45; trade, 35, 36;
  women, 15, 64–65, 68–74, 77–
  78, 80–81, 85, 97, 99, 144–45
Chinese Americans, xiv, 50, 52–53,
  58, 59, 88, 99–100, 108–9, 111–
  13, 114–15, 131–32, 140, 141,
  142, 143–46, 147, 166–67, 172n,
  173, 174; exclusion of, 4, 49–50,
  50–51, 132, 151, 152, 156, 157,
  158–60, 162, 172n; immigration
  of, 7, 103; as laborers, 4, 44–48,
  62, 109, 131, 135, 152–53; naturalization of, 7; women, 64, 67,
  77–78, 85, 99, 111, 112–13, 114–
  15, 152. *See also* Angel Island

*Island: Poetry and History of Chinese
Immigrants on Angel Island, 1910–1940*
Him Mark Lai, Genny Lim, and Judy Yung

*Japanese American Ethnicity:
The Persistence of Community*
Stephen S. Fugita and David J. O'Brien

*Japanese Americans: From Relocation to Redress,
Revised Edition.* Edited by Roger Daniels,
Sandra C. Taylor, and Harry H. L. Kitano

*Los Angeles—Struggles toward Multiethnic Community:
Asian American, African American, and Latino Perspectives*
Edited by Edward T. Chang and Russell C. Leong

Nisei Daughter. Monica Sone

No-No Boy. John Okada

*Personal Justice Denied: Report of the Commission
on Wartime Relocation and Internment of Civilians.*
Foreword by Tetsuden Kashima

Picture Bride. Yoshiko Uchida

Quiet Odyssey: A Pioneer Korean Woman in America
Mary Paik Lee. Edited with an Introduction by Sucheng Chan

Scent of Apples: A Collection of Stories
Bienvenido N. Santos

Sushi and Sourdough: A Novel
Tooru J. Kanazawa

Whispered Silences: Japanese Americans and World War II
Essay by Gary Y. Okihiro. Photographs by Joan Myers

*Years of Infamy: The Untold Story of America's
Concentration Camps.* Michi Nishiura Weglyn

Yokohama, California. Toshio Mori